CONRAD AND THEORY

Edited by

Andrew Gibson and Robert Hampson

Amsterdam - Atlanta, GA 1998

THE CONRADIAN

Series Editor:
Allan Simmons

∞ The paper on which this book is printed meets the requirements of "ISO 9706:1994, Information and documentation - Paper for documents - Requirements for permanence".

ISBN: 90-420-0369-3
©Editions Rodopi B.V., Amsterdam - Atlanta, GA 1998
Printed in The Netherlands

INTRODUCTION

ROBERT HAMPSON

This collection of essays was originally conceived as the third in a series of volumes in which current Conradian critical activity was brought into dialogue with new developments in contemporary critical practice. In *Conrad and Gender*, Andrew Michael Roberts assembled various readings of Conrad's work that drew on current critical and theoretical engagements with gender.[1] The essays in that volume ranged over gender and genre, gender and colonialism, and constructions and representations of masculinity. The second volume in the series, *The Conradian* 21.1, was dedicated to `The Sociology of Texts'.[2] It was designed as a response to developments in bibliography, as exemplified in the work of Donald F. MacKenzie and Jerome J. McGann.[3] The essays in that volume addressed the `network of people, materials and events' which produces literary works and explored how writing and reading practices are shaped by the context (indeed, the various contexts) of publication.[4]

In editing the present volume, however, we were also conscious of Gail Fincham and Myrtle Hooper's *Joseph Conrad: Under Postcolonial Eyes*, which brought together a number of

---

[1] Andrew Michael Roberts (ed.), *Conrad and Gender* (Amsterdam/ Atlanta, GA: Rodopi, 1993).

[2] *The Conradian*, 21.1 (Spring 1996).

[3] See, for example, Donald F. MacKenzie, *Bibliography and the Sociology of Texts* (London: British Library, 1985) and Jerome J. McGann, *The Beauty of Inflections: Literary Investigations in Historical Method and Theory* (Oxford: Clarendon Press, 1985).

[4] *The Beauty of Inflections*, p. 80.

essays considering Conrad from the perspective of postcolonialism.[5] As a result, we have tried to avoid gender, the new bibliography and postcolonialism to engage with other areas of contemporary theoretical exploration. This volume was designed to stage an encounter between Conrad and theory — or rather, to see what kinds of encounter between Conrad and theory were taking place in the late nineties. It was not conceived of as subjecting Conradian texts to various theoretical approaches, but rather as an exploration of the relevance to Conrad studies of some of the kinds of theoretical work that is currently taking place, where one of the issues might be the direction in which theory itself might be moving.

From the outset, we opted for a generous rather than a narrow sense of theory. Accordingly, the essays in the volume range from the philosophical (Sandra Dodson's engagement with Kant) to the Lacanian (the essays by Carola Kaplan and Josiane Paccaud-Huguet); from the philosophy of language (Anthony Fothergill) to ethics (Andrzej Gąsiorek and Andrew Gibson); from Bakhtin (Gail Fincham) and Benjamin (Anthony Fothergill) to postmodernism (Andrew Roberts). But certain themes recur: in particular, the contributors to this volume are much concerned with the idea of a `sovereign power', as in Marlow's meditation on `the doubt of the sovereign power enthroned in a fixed standard of conduct' (*Lord Jim*, p. 50). For Sandra Dodson, the `sovereign power' is Kant's transcendental moral Law. For Gail Fincham, on the other hand, it is a mystification which Marlow resorts to in order to legitimate imperial power in a social and racial elite, while denying the politics of class and race. For Andrzej Gąsiorek, the `sovereign power' is the ontological warranty for a code of conduct, whose absence means that the code is contingent and arbitrary; for Andrew Gibson, it is the transcendental sanction with which a significant ethics can have nothing to do. Finally, in Andrew Roberts's essay, it is `the doubt of the sovereign power' that, while trying to affirm

[5]   Gail Fincham and Myrtle Hooper (eds), *Joseph Conrad: Under Postcolonial Eyes* (Rondebosch: Cape Town University Press, 1997).

an absolute value, also enacts the opposition between particular values and the ethical imperative to continue evaluating — indeed, the inescapability of evaluation. This is merely one example, both of the concerns that bind these essays together, and the diversity of the contributors' approaches to those concerns.

In *Joseph Conrad and the Fictions of Skepticism*, Mark Wollaeger began by characterising the `dialogue of opposing attitudes' in Conrad's fiction in terms of `the primacy of perception in the empirical tradition' and `the visionary response to the epistemological limitations of that tradition'.[6] He suggested that Conrad's scepticism arose from rigorous empiricism, but that Conrad was also drawn to `the stance of the Romantic seer who yearns to achieve knowledge beyond the horizons of empiricism' (p. xiv). Sandra Dodson re-asserts Conrad's affinities with Romantic and pre-Romantic philosophy. But in her formulation of the politics of the sublime, Conrad is not a Romantic visionary. Dodson rather derives from the sceptical aesthetics of the sublime a conservative politics in which morality and political practice are divorced: the aesthetics of the sublime produces a spectatorial rather than a visionary politics. Her reading of *Nostromo* thus introduces a concern with aesthetics, ethics and politics that repeats itself through these essays.

Anthony Fothergill's essay on `The Politics of Utterance' attends to interpolations, speech-situations and non-verbal signs in *Under Western Eyes* to demonstrate the grounding of signs in social reality. Gail Fincham's analysis of double-voiced discourse in *Lord Jim* develops this foregrounding of the social and historical context of utterances. Her essay emphasises the imperialist ideology implicit in Marlow's narration, the ideology concealed and denied in Marlow's project of ethical recuperation, and demonstrates how the ethical issues of the officer class that dominate Marlow's narrative are inserted by the novel into a political context marked by race, class, and trade. These questions of ethics and politics are addressed

---

[6] Mark A. Wollaeger, *Joseph Conrad and the Fictions of Skepticism* (Stanford: Stanford University Press, 1990), xiv.

again, in very different ways, in the essays by Andrzej Gąsiorek and Andrew Gibson. Gąsiorek takes off from the liberal humanist debate of the seventies, within which moral critics detected the ethical imperatives underpinning political criticism, whilst political critics rejected moral criticism as dehistoricizing, decontextualizing and occluding ideology. As a way of breaking the deadlock, Gąsiorek offers a dialogue between ethics and politics by showing the intertwining of ethical and political discourses in *Lord Jim*. His essay also extends the kind of attention to questions of class, race, and gender in *Lord Jim* that is evident in Fincham's essay. While Gąsiorek's account of ethics and politics is inflected through postcolonialism, Gibson's account of *Heart of Darkness* deploys a post-modern, post-Levinasian, non-foundational ethics. Since the ethical relation for Levinas is the encounter with the Other, this involves a challenge to the cognitive and ontological assumptions according to which a traditional ethics has proceeded. Gibson's essay shifts the focus from ethics and representation to ethics and unrepresentability, and offers a reading of *Heart of Darkness* in terms of the play of totalizing or Kurtzian discourse against another discourse (Marlow's) that is haunted by the thought of an irreducible alterity.

Carola Kaplan's essay provides an account of the disruptive effect of the Real on the symbolic order by examining human relationships, the regulation of time, and the mapping of space in *The Secret Agent*. She focusses on *The Secret Agent* as a `domestic drama', showing how the public sphere collapses into the private, and the private sphere, in turn, implodes. In a very different and highly suggestive use of Lacan, Josiane Paccaud-Huguet reads *The Shadow-Line* as an oblique exploration of the death-drive through attention to intertextual relations with Shakespeare, Coleridge and Baudelaire and through a focus on symbolic castration, the paternal metaphor and *jouissance*. She produces a Lacanian revisioning of `delayed decoding' as the realization and negation of fantasy, the almost simultaneous release and withdrawal of repressed material. In the final essay in the volume, again, Andrew Michael Roberts's concern with the theory of value is also a concern with the relations of the aesthetic, the ethical and the political. Through a critique of

Steven Connor's *Theory and Cultural Value* and Fredric Jameson's *The Political Unconscious*, Roberts returns to the ethico-political deadlock described by Gąsiorek. By setting Connor against Jameson, however, and by using one to interrogate the other, Roberts ultimately argues for a shift from binary thought to multiple forms of value in accounts of Conrad, a shift which his essay not only advocates but exemplifies.[7]

The essays in this volume, then, are intended to demonstrate the usefulness of recent and current developments in philosophy and literary and critical theory in shedding new light on a range of Conrad's works. They recognize and address contemporary debates about Conrad's ethics, politics and aesthetics, and, in particular, the relationship between all three. But they also set out to shift some of the terms in which such debates have previously been couched. In other words, they raise questions for Conrad criticism. Above all, perhaps, they raise some of the questions that theory precisely exists to raise: questions, not only of the limits of the power of established critical vocabularies, but of premises, values, even modes of constructing Conrad that such vocabularies cannot help but bring with them.

---

[7] Steven Connor, *Theory and Cultural Value* (Oxford: Blackwell, 1992) and Fredric Jameson, *The Political Unconscious: Narrative as Socially Symbolic Act* (London: Methuen, 1981).

CONRAD AND THE POLITICS OF THE SUBLIME

SANDRA DODSON

The term `sublime,' in its Romantic sense, typically evokes the spectre of the eighteenth-century sage of Königsberg, Immanuel Kant. At first sight the pre-Romantic German philosopher and Conrad, the writer of early modernist English fiction, seem an incongruous pair, and not only because of the centuries which separate them and the different idioms in which they wrote. Kant lectured at the University of Königsberg, and, though he gave courses not only in philosophy, but also in physical geography for forty years, notoriously never travelled further than forty miles from his native town. It would be hard to think of a less likely secret sharer than Conrad, the sage of the seas turned writer, whose intimate knowledge of colonial `outposts of progress' led him to speak scornfully of `armchair' explorers like Kant. Moreover, while Conrad alludes to Nietzsche and Schopenhauer in his letters and essays, there is no conclusive evidence that he was familiar with Kantian aesthetics and philosophy.

Yet if Conrad's pessimism about human nature, particularly the human will to power, and his recognition of the discursive, interpretative nature of reason and truth closely recall Schopenhauer and Nietzsche, his moral stoicism and the sublime, solipsistic cast of his aesthetics and politics situate him firmly in the tradition of Kant. Indeed, without denying that Conrad is indebted in significant ways to Schopenhauer and Nietzsche, I believe that his work reveals a far more striking affinity with Romantic and pre-Romantic philosophy, notably that of Kant, than with the philosophy of the later nineteenth century. Forgetting for a while their superficial differences, Conrad and Kant share a profoundly Romantic preoccupation, not only with the relation between Man and Nature, but with crucially related questions of ethics, epistemology, and politics. From a contemporary critical vantage point one could say that for both writers the ideology of Nature is inseparable from the nature of Ideology, the complex topographies of human morality, thought and history. Moreover for both, whether overtly or covertly, the aesthetic discourses of the sublime and the beautiful are deeply implicated in these broader philosophical themes, and for both the aesthetics of the sublime take precedence over the beautiful, leaving us stranded in a dark, discomfiting world, drained of immanent meaning and value. Finally, as I will demonstrate, though Conrad's corrosive irony results in a more radically pessimistic view of human nature and history than Kant's, his didactic preoccupation with the question of `how to be' signifies a deep nostalgia for Kant's transcendental moral Law, the `sovereign power' which salvages the Kantian sublime from its abyssal depths and redeems Kant's tragic politics.

While these assertions may be irksome to critics who recognise the validity of literary-philosophical comparisons only where there is evidence of a direct influence, it is my belief that strictly empirical studies all too often lead into critical cul-de-sacs or peter out because of a paucity of reliable evidence. Moreover the idea of a connection between Conrad and Kant is not as outlandish or conceited as it may at first seem. Conrad himself remarks that, at his public school in Austrian Cracow, `historical studies were naturally tinted with Germanism',[1] while Eloise Knapp Hay suggests that Conrad's childhood exposure to German historiography had a

---

[1] Conrad, letter to George T. Keating, 14 December 1922, in G. Jean-Aubry (ed.) *Joseph Conrad: Life and Letters II* (Garden City, New York: Doubleday, 1927), hereafter *LL II*; p. 289.

significant influence on his political fiction.[2] We know, too, that Conrad had read the works of Thomas Carlyle, whose late Romantic prose poem, *Sartor Resartus*, was steeped in German Romantic philosophy, and in the discourse of the sublime in particular. Given the influence of Schopenhauer and Nietzsche on Conrad, it is also worth noting that Kant was the philosophical forefather of Schopenhauer, whose idea of an unfathomable, malevolent Will, a pessimistic travesty of the Kantian *Ding-an-sich*, can in turn be traced in Nietzsche's ideas of the will to power and the death of God.

Thus far I have omitted what would seem the most plausible route of Kantian `influence' on Conrad, namely, the culture of Polish Romanticism. Primarily as a result of the Austro-Prussian occupation of a large part of Poland after the first partition in 1772, late eighteenth- and early nineteenth-century Polish culture was permeated by German literature and philosophy, and, as numerous critical studies have shown, Polish Romantic playwrights and poets like Adam Mickiewicz, Juliusz Słowacki and Zygmunt Krasiński had an important influence on Conrad's work and temperament.[3] Given that Kant, whose philosophy played a significant part in the broader tradition of European Romanticism, was himself Prussian, and since, moreover, Polish Romanticism retained much of the

[2] Eloise Knapp Hay writes: `Conrad was deprecating in his references to these German historians, but their tracks are evident in his political fiction'. Eloise Knapp Hay, *The Political Novels of Joseph Conrad* (Chicago: University of Chicago Press, 1963), hereafter Hay, *PN*; p. 20.

[3] See, for example, Adam Gillon, *The Eternal Solitary: A Study of Joseph Conrad* (New York: Bookman Associates, 1960), pp. 89-98; Zdzisław Najder, *Joseph Conrad: A Chronicle*, tr. Halina Carroll (London: Oxford University Press, 1964); Czesław Miłosz, `Joseph Conrad in Polish Eyes', *Atlantic Monthly*, 200.5 (1957), pp. 219-28; and Andrzej Busza, `Conrad's Polish Literary Background and some Illustrations of the Influence of Polish Literature on his Work', *Antemurale*, 10 (Rome and London: Institutum Historicum Polonicum/Societas Polonica Scientarium et Litterarium in Exteris, 1966), pp. 109-255.

ethos of the European Enlightenment,[4] one would expect Kantian philosophy to have made a deep impression on Polish Romantic culture. Yet what emerges is a very different scenario. For specific ideological reasons, which I shall explore shortly, the Prussian philosopher was invariably marginalised in favour of high Romantic German writers like Hegel, Goethe and Schiller. Although the latter's early work, particularly his essay `On the Sublime', reproduces many of Kant's central ideas, Schiller's Kantian writings appear to have had less influence in Poland than his later, resolutely idealist poetry, plays, and aesthetics. If, from an empirical point of view, the Königsberger's subordinate status in Polish Romanticism seems a drawback for the present study, I believe that, paradoxical as it may seem, the Polish suppression of the Kantian sublime is of crucial importance in relation to Conrad's politics and aesthetics. In

[4] Initially I surmised that, although Kant was not fully assimilated into the Polish literary-philosophical tradition, the idea of the sublime may nevertheless have entered Polish culture via other works of the European Enlightenment. Miłosz mentions that the seventeenth-century French critic, Boileau, whose translation of Longinus's *Peri Hypsous* was largely responsible for popularising the idea of rhetorical sublimity in England and Europe, was widely read and translated by Enlightenment writers and critics in Poland. See Czesław Miłosz, *The History of Polish Literature* (Berkeley: University of California Press, 1969), hereafter Miłosz, *HPL*; p. 158, p. 181. Moreover, *The Monitor* magazine, founded in 1765, was closely modelled upon the London *Spectator*, which throughout the 1760s published criticism indebted to Burke's philosophy of the sublime in *A Philosophical Enquiry into the Origin of Our Ideas of the Sublime and Beautiful*. See Miłosz, p. 162. However, in a recent letter to me, Dr. Tadeusz Rachwal comments that, despite a tendency toward sublime obscurity and excess in much Polish literature, the sublime never took firm root as an aesthetic concept in Poland. To corroborate this he points out that, although Longinus's rhetorical treatise on the sublime was finally translated into Polish in the nineteenth century, `the word used as an equivalent (*gornosc*) was not a happy one'. Dr. Tadeusz Sławek similarly remarks in recent correspondence that, although I am right in my intuition regarding the dark, alienated, anti-Hegelian side of Polish Romanticism, this was never formally articulated as an aesthetics of sublimity in Polish literary-philosophical discourse.

the discussion that follows I will show that his uncanny ability to speak the unspeakable, to articulate the sublime `heart of darkness', not only of Polish culture, but of human nature and history, has a profoundly Kantian resonance.

Conrad's father, Apollo Korzeniowski, a political activist, translator and late Romantic playwright, was an ardent reader of Mickiewicz, and at an early age Conrad was introduced to works such as *Forefathers' Eve*, *Konrad Wallenrod*, *Grażyna* and *Pan Tadeusz*. In a famous interview with Marian Dąbrowski Conrad recalls:

> English critics — and after all I am an English writer — whenever they speak of me they add that there is in me something incomprehensible, inconceivable, elusive. Only you can grasp this elusiveness, and comprehend what is incomprehensible. *That is Polishness*. Polishness which I took from Mickiewicz and Słowacki. My father read *Pan Tadeusz* aloud to me and made me read it aloud. Not just once or twice. I used to prefer *Konrad Wallenrod*, *Grażyna*. Later I liked Słowacki better. You know why Słowacki? *Il est l'âme de toute la Pologne, lui*.[5]

If this `incomprehensible, inconceivable, elusive' thing in Conrad's writing is the true signature of his Polishness, it is also, unmistakeably, the signature of the Kantian sublime. Indeed, Conrad's suggestion that English critics lack an aesthetic framework within which to make sense of his elusiveness and, dialectically, `comprehend what is incomprehensible' amounts to a reflection on his own belatedly romantic sublimity, for the definitive feature of the negative Kantian sublime (as opposed to the Wordsworthian egotistical or positive sublime) is the ambiguous collapse and restoration of meaning in the face of the ungraspable, the indistinct,

---

[5] Marian Dąbrowski, `An Interview with J. Conrad', in Zdzisław Najder (ed.), *Conrad Under Familial Eyes*, tr. Halina Carroll-Najder (Cambridge: Cambridge University Press, 1983), p. 199.

the obscure.[6] While the immanentist aesthetics of the beautiful bring the reassuring promise of an harmonious unity between self and other, mind and world, the sublime brings a painful recognition of the illusory nature of this identification. In the pre-Romantic work of Kant the sublime is articulated as a definitively modern aesthetics of alienation from Nature, and resonates thus through the literary-philosophical culture of European Romanticism.

In the aesthetic sphere of the Romantic sublime, meaning seems no longer centripetal and sensuous, but abstract and centrifugal, or, in Thomas Weiskel's terms, `negative, dialectical, a movement between two states, an indeterminate relation' (*RS*, p. 43). Weiskel provides a literary-historical context for the sublime as a disruption of meaning and sensuous experience, a breakdown of the unity which had underpinned and sustained the aesthetic, as well as moral and political, ideology of the Enlightenment:

> [I]n the history of literary consciousness the sublime revives as God withdraws from an immediate participation in the experience of men. The secondary or problematic sublime is pervaded by the nostalgia and uncertainty of minds involuntarily secular — minds whose primary experience is shaped by their knowledge and perception of secondary causes. (pp. 3-4)

Accordingly, Weiskel suggests, the secular, alienated mode of the sublime is incompatible with the idealist's faith in the meaning or efficacy of political praxis. In contrast with the `revolutionary program of beauty', he argues, the detached, spectatorial stance of the sublime is invariably `missing in the aesthetics of activists and idealists....'[7] Weiskel has little more to say on the negative political

---

[6] See Thomas Weiskel, `The Ethos of Alienation: Two Versions of Transcendence', *The Romantic Sublime: Studies in the Structure and Psychology of Transcendence* (Baltimore: Johns Hopkins University Press, 1986), hereafter Weiskel, *RS*; pp. 34-62.

[7] *RS*, p. 46. Weiskel elaborates that `the sublime, lacking a ground in external reality, comes into play precisely insofar as man cannot attain the totality; the intensity of the sublime experience is a direct function of the

(continued...)

implications of the sublime. Yet his idea of a stillborn politics is particularly apt in the context of Polish Romanticism, where the sphere of the aesthetic is ridden with the contradiction between a fervent ethos of revolutionary nationalism on the one hand and a tragic reality of revolutionary failure on the other. The disastrous outcome of three successive nationalist uprisings in occupied Poland led to a pervasive, culturally-specific sense of God's withdrawal from the human world, and seemed an outrageous betrayal of the popular messianic idea of Poland's historical destiny.[8] Indeed, it is interesting in this context that the Messianist poet-philosopher, Mickiewicz, criticises not only Słowacki's de-idealised politics, but also his early poetry, which he describes as technically impressive, but empty, like `a church without God inside'.[9]

Tensions between a providential or messianic philosophy of history and an inadmissible scepticism about its political efficacy are

[7] (...continued)
impossibility of realising (in any way) the idea of humanity (or any supersensible idea' (p. 45).

[8] The politics of Polish nationalism determined the almost obsessive prominence of questions of national identity, moral duty and political destiny in the literature, philosophy and historiography of the period. The dominant philosophy of Hegelian idealism reinforced the ideology of Polish Messianism, fervently promulgated by the philosophers August Cieszkowski and Bronisław Trentowski, by the political mystics Hoene Wronski, Andrzej Towiański and his poetic disciple, Adam Mickiewicz, and later by Apollo Korzeniowski. According to the messianic myth the people of Poland were the national incarnation of Christ, the martyr among the nations of Europe, destined to rise up and overthrow foreign domination on the `third day', the prophesied occasion of the third nationalist rebellion. The failure of the 1863 uprising, upon which activists like Apollo Korzeniowski had staked their hopes, led to widespread disillusionment with the doctrine of Messianism, and reinforced a conservative counter-current in Polish political philosophy. See Andrzej Walicki, *Philosophy and Romantic Nationalism: The Case of Poland* (Oxford: Clarendon Press, 1982), H. G. Schenk, *The Mind of the European Romantics* (London: Constable, 1966), pp. 187-194, and the introduction to Harold B. Segel's *Polish Romantic Drama: Three Plays in English Translation* (Ithaca: Cornell University Press, 1977).

[9] Adam Mickiewicz, in Miłosz, *HPL*, p. 233.

evident not only in the political philosophy, but also in the literature of the period. Słowacki is an interesting case in point. Although, in theory, the younger poet and polemicist advocated social revolution as the only viable means to achieve Polish liberation, he remained sceptical of Romantic Messianism, and unceremoniously rejected the notion of `committed art'. Subversive themes of political betrayal, defeat and disengagement in his work served as a deliberate counter to Mickiewicz's idealistic nationalism and the messianic idea of the `providential man'. In the verse-drama *Kordian* (written in ironic response to Mickiewicz's *Forefathers' Eve III*) the Warsaw insurgents emerge, despite their revolutionary *élan*, as a politically unsophisticated mob betrayed by incompetent leaders, while in lieu of the providential Romantic hero, we find a protagonist whose moral scruples and neurotic self-consciousness fatally undermine his ability to act. After an abortive attempt to assassinate the Czar, Kordian is committed to an insane asylum and condemned to death. Subjected to the same uncompromising irony, the conflictual stances of revolutionary activism and an historically entrenched moral conservatism fail to provide political solutions. Significantly, Słowacki's propensity for political satire coincides with formal strategies of narrative fragmentation, obfuscation and self-irony, producing what Claude Backvis describes as `amazing literary cocktails'.[10] The incongruous medley of genres and historical epochs in *Balladyna*, for example, produces a bathetic, mock-heroic effect reminiscent of Pope's *Dunciad*, in which linguistic decorum is similarly violated, and words and meanings threaten to spin apart entirely. Another apt comparison is Carlyle's *Sartor Resartus*, in which the `Clothes-philosopher' Teufelsdröckh's colossal work, `Die Kleider, Ihr Werden und Werken' is similarly described as a `mad banquet, wherein all courses had been confounded'.[11] It is fitting that Słowacki's aesthetics have therefore been designated sublimely `centrifugal' rather than `centripetal', a tendency demonstrated not only in the ironic bathos of *Balladyna*,

---

[10]   Claude Backvis, in Miłosz, *HPL*, p. 233.
[11]   Thomas Carlyle, *Sartor Resartus* (London: Dent, 1908), Book I, Chapter V, p. 25.

but in an obfuscatory, allegorical style which, in Miłosz's words, `dissolves every object into a...fluid maze of images and sonorities' and frequently leads to `nearly automatic writing'.[12] Słowacki's work anticipates not only the sublime obscurity of Nietzsche and the later French Symbolists, as Miłosz suggests, but the characteristic elusiveness, indeterminacy and narrative discontinuity of Conrad's fiction, which Ian Watt similarly defines as `centrifugal' rather than `centripetal'.[13] Indeed, from this perspective we are able to appreciate more fully Conrad's preference for Słowacki's often sublime, or, conversely, bathetic, art, over Mickiewicz's more consistent political and aesthetic idealism. Throughout Conrad's work we witness the same ambivalent assertion and interrogation of the immanentist or `"ideal" value of things, events and people',[14] the same coincidence of a de-idealised politics with a sublimely obfuscatory poetics. At this point, therefore, I leave the literary-historical context of Conrad and Polish Romanticism, to explore in depth his relation to the poetics and politics of the Kantian sublime.

The consolatory aesthetics of the beautiful and the bleak, stoical discourse of the sublime are the foundations upon which both Kant and Conrad's political philosophies rest, and this means that a discussion of the politics of the sublime cannot proceed without a

---

[12] Miłosz, *HPL*, pp. 242-243. Słowacki's `automatic writing' sounds uncannily like the postmodern textual sublime. I am reminded here of Fredric Jameson's remarks on Conrad in *The Political Unconscious*: `A case could be made for reading Conrad not as an early modernist, but rather as an anticipation of that later and quite different thing we have come to call variously textuality, *écriture*, post-modernism, or schizophrenic writing. Certainly the first half of *Lord Jim* is one of the most breathtaking exercises in nonstop textual production that literature has to show, a self-generating sequence of sentences for which narrative and narrator are mere pretexts, the realisation of a mechanism of well-nigh random free association....' Fredric Jameson, *The Political Unconscious: Narrative as a Socially Symbolic Act* (London: Methuen, 1981), hereafter Jameson, *PU*; p. 219.

[13] See Ian Watt, *Conrad in the Nineteenth Century* (London: Chatto, 1980), hereafter Watt, *CNC*; p. 180.

[14] Conrad, letter to Sir Sidney Colvin, 18 March 1917, in *LL II*, p. 185.

closer examination of Kant's aesthetics.[15] From the vantage point of the beautiful, Kant asserts, Nature is an orderly arrangement of things, clearly visible and intimately knowable, seen as if perpetually in the light of day. `Der Tag ist schön',[16] he writes. Here everything is what it seems, for reading the world and seeing the world amount to the same thing: meaning is coherently embodied in the beautiful, symmetrical forms of Nature, and we need only read Nature's signs to take our moral and epistemological bearings in the world. Nature seems exquisitely adapted to the contours of the human mind, uniquely designed to suit our needs. And from the idea of a beautifully contained (and reassuringly containable) natural world, we are naturally led to faith in a beneficent Creator and to a charitable view of our fellow beings. The beautiful is therefore a kind of theodicy, a source of hope and consolation. Nature is made over in our own image, and we can rest reassured that the world is, after all, a place we can call home.

But there is no doubt that Kant regards the beautiful as a form of symbolic mystification, in which immanent meaning is artificially and retrospectively attributed to a vast, unknowable and wholly indifferent world, the shadowy realm of the *Ding-an-sich* or `thing-in-itself'. In the sublime, by contrast, we are forced to acknowledge the incongruity between Nature and our humanising projections, are reminded that we construct our meanings alone in the world and have no recourse to a moral or semantic ground outside ourselves. For Kant, like Schiller — and Conrad — after him, human beings are therefore unhappy, self-conscious artists, who must stoically

---

[15] William Booth demonstrates brilliantly how the premises of the sublime and beautiful pervade Kant's political thinking in *Interpreting the World: Kant's Philosophy of History and Politics* (London: University of Toronto Press, 1986), hereafter Booth, *IW*; Booth's analysis is particularly illuminating in the context of Polish Romanticism, where the sphere of the aesthetic is everywhere overshadowed by a predominant interest in political and moral matters.

[16] Immanuel Kant, *Observations on the Feeling of the Beautiful and Sublime*, tr. J.T. Goldthwait (Berkeley: University of California Press, 1960), hereafter Kant, *BS*; p. 47.

forge meanings out of a scattered, incoherent reality. From the sublime standpoint Nature shows a shocking irregularity and contingency in its workings, appearing dark, immense, formless, violent, a realm of blind chance rather than Providential necessity. Any aspect of Nature which suggests Ideas of Infinity or excessive power is for Kant sublime, and he refers specifically to violent storms, volcanoes, hurricanes, darkness, objects devoid of form, the Milky Way and the ocean as a boundless expanse or a restless, threatening abyss. If natural beauty relies on an ideology of vision and legibility, form and limitation, the sublime is an aesthetics of darkness, formlessness and indeterminacy: `*Die Nacht ist erhaben*' (Kant, *BS*, p. 47). While the beautiful provides us with a guiding narrative thread, the consolation of Providential design or metaphysical teleology, in the abyssal formlessness of the sublime no design or Designer is evident, and we are denied the consolation of a world made in our own image, a `speaking face of Nature'[17] which would tell us a reassuring tale and restore our moral and psychic bearings. Instead we are reminded of our dwarfish insignificance in relation to a Nature that exceeds and defeats comprehension, that can be read and re-read, but never known/seen. For Kant, this is tantamount to the threat of self-annihilation: `The point of excess for the imagination...is like an abyss in which it fears to lose itself', he writes in *The Critique of Judgement*. Later in the *Critique*, remarking on the fact that, from the sublime point of view, Nature fails to reward moral worth, so that the just suffer equally with the evil, he writes, `And so it will continue to be until one wide grave engulfs them all — just and unjust, there is no distinction in the grave — and hurls them back into the abyss of the

---

[17] The expression is Wordsworth's in Book 5 of *The Prelude*. See Paul de Man's remarks on Wordsworth and Kant in `Phenomenality and Materiality in Kant', Gary Shapiro and Alan Sica (eds.) *Hermeneutics: Questions and Prospects* (Amherst: University of Massachusetts Press, 1984), pp. 134-136. See also his comment on Kant's `"mirror" of the sea', (p. 136), which has an uncanny relevance to Conrad's work of the same title.

aimless chaos of matter from which they were taken....'[18]

In the face of this, however, moral duty is for Kant, as for Schiller, all the more imperative. The `unmistakable and ineffaceable idea of morality' remains, he concludes, even `when nothing any longer meets the eye of sense'.[19] If the sublime violates teleological purposiveness in Nature, by the same ingenious, but perhaps disingenuous, stroke it reveals a different kind of purposiveness, a moral purposiveness in the subject. The terror of incomprehension therefore gives way to a pleasurable intuition of the sublimity of the moral Law within us, a law which lifts us above the dominion of nature and `evidences a faculty of mind transcending every standard of sense' (*CJ*, p. 98). Yet if this should fail, he writes, `nothingness (immorality) with gaping throat, would drink the whole kingdom of (moral) beings like a drop of water'.[20] It is not difficult to detect echoes of this warning in the famous words of Nietzsche's madman in *The Gay Science*:

[18] Kant, *The Critique of Judgement*, tr. James Creed Meredith (Oxford: Clarendon, 1992), hereafter Kant, *CJ*; p. 107, p. 121. Cf Schiller: `Then away with falsely construed forbearance and vapidly effeminate taste which cast a veil over the solemn face of necessity and, in order to curry favour with the senses, *counterfeit* a harmony between good fortune and good behaviour of which not a trace is to be found in the actual world. Let us stand face to face with the evil fatality.' Friedrich Schiller, `On the Sublime', in *Naive and Sentimental Poetry and On the Sublime: Two Essays*, tr. Julius A. Elias (New York, 1966), hereafter Schiller, *OS*; p. 209.

[19] Kant, *CJ*, p. 127. Cf Schiller, *OS*, pp. 207-208.

[20] Kant, *The Doctrine of Virtue*, tr. Mary J. Gregor (Philadelphia: University of Pennsylvania Press, 1971), hereafter Kant, *DV*; p. 448. The moral Law is always already threatened in Kant by the possibility of engulfment and defeat. In the *Critique of Judgement* he writes: `[W]ithout the development of moral ideas, that which, thanks to preparatory culture, we call sublime, merely strikes the untutored man as terrifying. He will see in the evidences which the ravages of nature give of her dominion, and in the vast scale of her might, compared with which his own is diminished to insignificance, only the misery, peril and distress that would compass the man who was thrown to its mercy' (*CJ*, p. 115).

`Where has God gone?' he cried. `I shall tell you! *We have killed him*, — you and I! We are all his murderers! But how have we done this? How were we able to drink up the sea? Who gave us the sponge to wipe away the entire horizon? What did we do when we unchained this earth from its sun? Whither is it moving now? Whither are we moving now? Away from all suns? Are we not perpetually falling? Backward, sideward, forward, in all directions? Is there any up or down left? Are we not straying as through an infinite nothing?[21]

Against this background I would like to turn to Conrad, and to suggest that Kant's speculation on the potential subversion of the sovereign power of moral Ideas anticipates not only the Nietzschean death of God, but the definitively secular mode of the Conradian sublime. In Conrad the redemptive intervention of a transcendent morality never comes, except in ironic, demystified form. Consider these famously pessimistic remarks in *A Personal Record* and in his letters to Cunninghame Graham, in which an uneasy, late Victorian sense of the contingency of consciousness and morality (the legacy of Darwin and Nietzsche) is assimilated into a discourse of de-idealised sublimity:

What makes mankind tragic is not that they are the victims of nature, it is that they are conscious of it.... We can't return to nature, since we can't change our place in it.... There is no morality, no knowledge and no hope; there is only the consciousness of ourselves which drives us about a world that whether seen in a convex or a concave mirror is always but a vain and floating appearance.

Of course reason is hateful — but why? Because it demonstrates (to those who have the courage) that we, living, are out of life — utterly out of it.... Life knows us not and we do not know life — we don't know even our own thoughts. Half the words we use have no meaning whatever and of the other half each man understands each word after the fashion of his own folly and conceit. Faith is a myth and beliefs shift like mists on the shore....

[21] Friedrich Nietzsche, *The Gay Science*, tr. Walter Kaufmann (New York: Random House, 1974), hereafter Nietzsche, *GS*; p. 125.

Would you seriously wish to tell...a man: `Know thyself.' Understand that thou art nothing, less than a shadow, more insignificant than a drop of water in the ocean, more fleeting than the illusion of a dream. Would you?

The ethical view of the universe involves us at last in so many cruel and absurd contradictions, where the last vestiges of faith, hope, charity, and even of reason itself, seem ready to perish, that I have come to suspect that the aim of creation cannot be ethical at all. I would fondly believe that its object is purely spectacular: a spectacle for awe, love, adoration or hate....[22]

If Conrad in *A Personal Record* finally sounds a note of optimism, arguing that `[t]hose visions, delicious or poignant, are a moral end in themselves', that the appointed task of the writer is to bear testimony to `the haunting terror, the infinite passion...the supreme law and the abiding mystery of the sublime spectacle" (*PR*, p. 92), this is the beleaguered optimism of someone who has no recourse to moral absolutes. Conrad's `supreme law' is only a tenuous, secular remnant of the sovereign power of the Kantian moral Law, painfully aware of its arbitrary, de-idealised status. Moreover Conrad's attitude here represents something more like stoicism than the optimism one associates with Nietzsche's celebration of the end of ethics, the transvaluation of all values. As further testimony to his Kantian temperament, Conrad remains incapable of the yea-saying with which the Nietzschean Overman celebrates his new-found freedom from the moral Law in a universe devoid of anthropomorphic `afterworlds and false divinities'.[23] This is particularly evident in Conrad's fiction, where the solace of an objective moral ground is consistently denied, and Nature, far from

[22] Conrad, letters to Cunninghame Graham, 31 January 1898, 14 January 1898, 14 December 1897, in C.T. Watts (ed.) *Joseph Conrad's Letters to Cunninghame Graham* (Cambridge: Cambridge University Press, 1969), hereafter Conrad, *LCG*; pp. 70-71, p. 65, p. 54; *CL*II, p.30, pp.16-17, *CL*I, p.423. The final quotation is from *PR*, p. 92.
[23] Friedrich Nietzsche, *The Will to Power*, tr. Walter Kaufmann and R. J. Hollingdale (New York: Vintage Books, 1967), p. 13.

being compliant and communicative, is everywhere dark, mute, and indecipherable, everywhere a sign of moral and semantic absence. In *Heart of Darkness*, for example, the sinister backdrop of the jungle is `immense', `impenetrable to human thought', `pitiless to human weakness', profoundly subversive of the luminosity and readability of the beautiful (*HD*, p. 136, p. 127). Moreover, as in Kant, the image of the abyss in Conrad repeatedly conveys a sense of the world experienced as absence, aporia, signification without significance: `A brooding gloom lay over this vast and monotonous landscape; the light fell on it as if into an abyss' (*LJ*, p. 264), he writes in *Lord Jim*.

In a self-reflexive, post-Kantian move, the topos of sublime, abyssal landscapes in Conrad is always already a simulacrum of the emptiness underlying all discursive, ideological constructs. Conrad's descriptions of a shadowy, illegible, non-signifying Nature in works like *The Nigger of the `Narcissus'*, *Heart of Darkness* and *Lord Jim* invariably coincide with an obsesssive preoccupation with the failure of language to signify truths or, in the famous words of the 1897 Preface to *The Nigger of the `Narcissus'*, `to make you *see*' (*NN*, p. xlii). Everywhere the visual and the verbal, the ungraspable sublimity of Nature and the sublime indeterminacy of the sign, are conflated, so that, quite contrary to the promises of the Preface (perhaps an unwieldy attempt by Conrad to insert himself into an English aesthetic tradition?),[24] we are precluded from seeing and

---

[24] I would argue that David Thorburn in *Conrad's Romanticism* (New Haven: Yale University Press, 1974), pp. 149-152, and Ian Watt in *CNC*, pp. 78-81, erroneously take Conrad's Preface at face value, and detect significant affinities between Conrad's aesthetic claims and those of Wordsworth in his Preface to *Lyrical Ballads*. Avoiding the problematical relation between the visionary aspects of Wordsworth's aesthetics and Conrad's secularised theory of artistic vision, neither Watt nor Thorburn sees any disjunction between the Prefaces. Michael Jones, in *Conrad's Heroism: A Paradise Lost* (Ann Arbor, Michigan: UMI Research Press, 1985), more appositely compares Wordsworth's Preface to Conrad's primarily to illustrate `the historical displacement...and the despiritualization of...romanticism in Conrad's fiction" (p. xviii). He argues: `For all its questing after the Beautiful and the True,

(continued...)

knowing by an obscurity which is as pervasively rhetorical as it is thematic. The reader's sensation of visual, semantic, and, above all, moral failure, therefore has to do not only with the de-idealised sublimity of Conrad's land- and sea-scapes, but with the secular sublimity of language as an opaque, interpretative construct. Consistently we encounter Marlow and frame-narrators like him, thwarted by the difficulties of representation, baffled before an epistemological abyss which denies any possibility of narrative rendering and moral and semantic closure. As Marlow says of Kurtz: `He was just a word for me. I did not see the man in the name any more than you do. Do you see him? Do you see the story? Do you see anything?'(*HD*, p. 82).

Again, however, if Conrad's recognition of the linguistic, interpretative predicament in which we find ourselves has Nietzschean, or even, one might say, de Manian, overtones, it lacks the celebratory confidence with which Nietzsche's Overman is able to assert:

> In what a marvellous and new and at the same time terrible and ironic relationship with the totality of existence do I feel myself to stand with my knowledge!...I have suddenly awoken in the midst of this dream, but only to the consciousness that I am dreaming and that I *have* to go on dreaming in order not to be destroyed: as the sleepwalker has to go on dreaming in order not to fall .... [A]mong all these dreamers, I, too, the `man of knowledge', dance my dance.... (*GS*, p. 206)

If Nietzsche's Overman sleepwalks joyously on a tightrope of human metaphors, for Conrad an ironic consciousness of the dream, or even a momentary glimpse of the abyss, tends to be fatal, as the deaths of Decoud and Kurtz testify. Moreover, while it would be true to say that the philosopher-narrator Marlow agrees to live the lie of language in a gesture of Nietzschean forgetfulness, to `lie

[24] (...continued)
the romanticism of the Preface in the Wordsworthian sense of that term rests upon a foundation of outdated clichés and platitudes rescued from a century of progressive skepticism' (p. 36).

according to a fixed convention...in a style binding for all',[25] his negative knowledge coincides with a deep nostalgia for moral and semantic authority, the sovereign truth behind the inconclusive flux of discursive interpretations. More importantly in this context, if Nietzsche regards the will to ignorance as a partial means of avoiding the malady of historical knowledge (`the antidotes to the historical are called — *the unhistorical and the superhistorical....* By the word `the unhistorical' I denote the art and the strength of being able to *forget* and enclose oneself in a limited *horizon*'),[26] for Conrad, the problem of human history is not so easily erased. In the historical/political sphere the deflated idealism of the Conradian sublime, or what amounts to a contradictory condemnation of Nietzschean forgetfulness and an acknowledgement of the tragic futility of historical action, leads to a serious ideological impasse. What is at stake is not only the Grand Narrative of human history, but, by extension, the form of the historical novel itself.

Nietzsche was not the first to challenge the authority of historical knowledge. Kant before him had subjected the teleological assumptions of philosophical history to a radical critique under the aegis of the sublime `Ideas of human justice,' and it is therefore to Kant's philosophy of history and politics that I now turn. As I will demonstrate, a reading of Conrad's politics proves enormously profitable in the light of a post-Kantian articulation of the beautiful and the sublime with a mystified history on the one hand and a demystified politics on the other. If Conrad's aesthetics take us to the `threshold of the invisible', his politics likewise lead us `beyond the pale' into a space which defies representation. Far from being a politics of destiny, a utopian politics of vision, this is a politics of blindness and obfuscation, an unrepresentable politics, in short, a politics of the sublime.

As William Booth demonstrates brilliantly in his *Interpreting the*

[25] Nietzsche quoted in the translator's preface to Jacques Derrida, *Of Grammatology*, tr. Gayatri Chakravorty Spivak (Baltimore: Johns Hopkins University Press, 1976), p. xxxi.

[26] Nietzsche, *On the Advantage and Disadvantage of History for Life*, tr. Peter Preuss (Indianapolis: Hackett Publishing Company, 1980), p. 62.

World: Kant's Philosophy of History and Politics, Kant's theory of philosophical history is deeply imbued with the ideological presuppositions of the beautiful. Just as the beautiful forms of Nature assume attributes of identity and purposiveness, reciprocity and design, so, from the philosophical historian's stance, the course of human history is a teleological movement, each moment of which symbolises, contains within itself, the *telos* of Destiny. While philosophical history provides what Kant describes as a `consoling view of the future', a `sweet dream' of progress,[27] in which even war and the bloody facts of history seem providential, the politics of the sublime coincide with a deeply pessimistic, non-teleological view. For Kant, as for Schiller, Schopenhauer and Nietzsche after him, the ahistorical perspective coincides with a view of history as wholly chaotic, contingent and amoral, devoid of any guiding teleological thread which would justify the atrocities of war and revolution in the name of world-historical progress (what Adorno refers to sceptically as Hegel's `world-historic derring-do').[28] Yet, unlike Nietzsche, for whom the end of history signifies the emergence of an exhilarating, amoral `eternal recurrence',[29] in Kant the transcendent Infinity of the moral Reason finally redeems both the misguided optimism of philosophical history and the secular negativity of the sublime point of view. Indeed, while the consolatory aesthetics of the beautiful typically coincide with a fanatical, visionary politics, the negative, sceptical aesthetics of the sublime lead to a conservative political perspective, in which the idea of morality `precludes all positive presentation' and therefore remains aloof from political praxis. For this reason Kant resists the

[27] Kant, `On the Old Saw: That May Be Right in Theory But It Won't Work in Practice', and `An Old Question Raised Again: Is the Human Race Constantly Progressing?', in Booth, *IW*, p. 107.

[28] Theodor Adorno, *Negative Dialectics*, transl. E. B. Ashton (London: Routledge, 1990), p. 13.

[29] Nietzsche, *Thus Spoke Zarathustra*, tr. R.J. Hollingdale (Harmondsworth: Penguin, 1969), Part 3, `The Convalescent', p. 237. In the same section Zarathustra announces, joyously, `My abyss *speaks*, I have turned my ultimate depth into the light' (p. 233).

visionary tradition in Romantic philosophy:

> This pure, elevating, merely negative presentation of morality involves...no fear of *fanaticism*, which is a *delusion* that would *will some VISION beyond all the bounds of sensibility*; i.e. would dream according to principles (rational raving).... For the *inscrutability of the idea of freedom* precludes all positive presentation. If enthusiasm is comparable to *delirium*, fanaticism may be compared to *mania*. Of these the latter is least of all compatible with the sublime, for it is *profoundly* ridiculous. (*CJ*, p. 128)

It is worth recalling that, although Conrad has no redeeming faith in the authority of the moral Law, such fanaticism is for him equally untenable. In *A Personal Record* he writes:

> I have not been revolutionary in my writings. The revolutionary spirit is mighty convenient in this, that it frees one from all scruples as regards ideas. Its hard, absolute optimism is repulsive to my mind by the menace of fanaticism and intolerance it contains. No doubt one should smile at these things; but, imperfect Esthete, I am no better Philosopher. All claim to special righteousness awakens in me that scorn and anger from which a philosophical mind should be free.... (*PR*, pp. xxi-xxii)

In this regard Conrad is much closer to Kant than he is to Rousseau, about whom he disparagingly remarks in the same text: `[Rousseau] was an artless moralist, as is clearly demonstrated by his anniversaries being celebrated with marked emphasis by the heirs of the French Revolution, which was not a political movement at all, but a great outburst of morality' (*PR*, p. 95). Remarks like these reverberate with Kantian echoes. Indeed, while Conrad's conservative politics have often been discussed in relation to Edmund Burke, it is worth noting that, while Burke's anti-revolutionary *Reflections on the Revolution in France* marks a rejection of the dangerous excesses of the sublime and an endorsement of the order and sociability of the beautiful, for Conrad and Kant it is all too often the beautiful which incites a dangerously fanatical politics in the first place.[30] The example of Burke's anti-revolutionism allows for an important *caveat*, namely, that I am not seeking to identify Conrad with Kant on the general grounds of their political conservatism. The crucial point is that, in Conrad and in Kant, a *sublime* aesthetics becomes virtually coterminous with a detached, spectatorial politics.

Kant expresses the view that while the French Revolution appears to the philosophical historian as a beautiful `historical sign' revealing the unfolding teleological progress of the race, the same events, from the stance of the `Ideas of Justice', fill the soul only with `horror'. The philosophical historian's `wishful participation' in the `game of great revolutions' is therefore, in sublime terms, dangerously deluded.[31] The future, from this perspective, looks to be a senseless and violent repetition of the past or, worse still, a further decline. In his story of the innkeeper's sign in `Perpetual Peace', Kant satirises the visionary dreamers, the philosophical millenarians, who, oblivious of history's bloody reproach, arouse great hopes by speaking of beautiful cities to come. The sign depicts, not the usual cluster of grapes or kegs, but the gloomy

[30] Recognising that the dark, asocial, potentially anarchic qualities of the sublime could, inadvertently, serve to promote a revolutionary ethos which might in turn destroy the hegemony of the middle class, Burke, in *Reflections on the Revolution in France* (1790), deliberately sets out to counteract his aesthetic endorsement of sublimity in the *Enquiry*. See Tom Furniss, *Edmund Burke's Aesthetic Ideology: Language, Gender and Political Economy in Revolution* (Cambridge: Cambridge University Press, 1993).

[31] Kant, in `An Old Question Raised Again' and *The Metaphysical Elements of Justice*, in Booth, *IW*, pp. 121-122. For the conservative Kant, war and revolution by definition subvert legality, and therefore cannot be justified within a legalistic framework of political Right. Crucially, then, the politics of the sublime amount to a wholesale rejection of political praxis, because the latter is predicated on a beautiful, visionary ideology which turns words into deeds, belief into action, reading into seeing. Cf Conrad in `Autocracy and War', *Notes on Life and Letters*: `There can be no evolution out of a grave. Another word of less scientific sound has been very much pronounced of late in connection with Russia's future, a word of more vague import, a word of dread as much as of hope - Revolution' (*NLL*, p. 99).

scene of a graveyard, above which appears the anomalous title, `Perpetual Peace'. In `Autocracy and War' Conrad expresses a similarly subversive, pessimistic view: `[I]t must be confessed that the architectural aspect of the universal city remains as yet inconceivable — that the very ground for its erection has not been cleared of the jungle' (*NLL*, p. 107).

There are other marked affinities between Conrad and Kant. From the sublime point of view, society seems constantly threatened from within by the innate human capacity for evil and unbridled egotism. While the philosophical historian sees the antagonistic basis of society, or what Kant calls the principle of `unsociable sociability',[32] as an invigorating source of strife necessary to the advancement of culture, the same thing looks like a precariously contained anarchy from the perspective of the sublime. `One cannot suppress a certain indignation', Kant writes, when one looks at human affairs. Here on the great `world stage' what do we see but childish vanity, evil and destructiveness: `Falsehood, ingratitude, injustice, the childishness of the purposes regarded by ourselves as important...in the pursuit of which men inflict upon one another all imaginable evils, are so contradictory to the idea of what men might be...that, in order that we may not hate them we withdraw from all contact with them'.[33]

Conrad's famously pessimistic remarks on human nature in his essays and letters sound a similar note: `To him whose indignation is qualified by a measure of hope and affection, the efforts of mankind to work its own salvation present a sight of alarming comicality', he writes in `Autocracy and War', for the `intellectual stage of mankind [is] as yet in its infancy' (*NLL*, p. 108). And in a letter to Cunninghame Graham: `We can't return to nature, since we can't change our place in it. Our refuge is in stupidity, in drunken[n]ess of all kinds, in lies, in beliefs, in murder, thieving, reforming — in negation, in contempt — each man according to the

---

[32] Kant, `Idea for a Universal History from a Cosmopolitan Point of View,' in Booth, *IW*, p. 104.

[33] Kant, `Idea for a Universal History', and *The Critique of Judgement*, in Booth, *IW*, pp. 99-100.

promptings of his particular devil'.[34] Moreover his decidedly un-English view of democracy as a `lovely phantom', and his conviction that human society has its origins less in fraternity than in the conflicts of human egoism, has a striking affinity, not only with Hobbes, but with the `unsociable sociability' of Kant's tragic politics: `L'homme est un animal méchant. Sa méchanceté doit être organisée.... La société est essentielment criminelle — ou elle n'existerait pas.... C'est comme une forêt ou personne ne connait la route'.[35] Like Kant, Conrad therefore lays a heavier onus on organised society than on man, in whom he has little faith, yet this tense equilibrium of community and anarchy is a precarious one indeed: `C'est un egoisme rational et féroce que j'exerce envers moi même. Je me repose la-dedans. Puis la pensée revient. La vie recommence, les regrets, les souvenirs et un desespoir plus sombre que la nuit' (*LCG*, p. 117; *CL*II, p. 160). Again, this recalls Kant:

> The principle of mutual love admonishes men constantly to *come nearer* to each other; that of the respect which they owe each other, to keep themselves at a *distance* from one another. And should one of these great moral forces fail, `then nothingness (immorality) with gaping throat, would drink the whole kingdom of moral beings like a drop of water. (*DV*, p. 448)

But perhaps Conrad's most striking affinity with a Kantian politics of sublimity lies in the contradictory combination of satiric, spectatorial detachment and moral dignity which he assumes in the face of `the vast panorama of anarchy and futility'[36] which is human history:

> The earth is a temple where there is going on a mystery play childish and poignant, ridiculous and awful enough, in all conscience. Once

[34] Conrad, letter to Cunninghame Graham, 31 January 1898, in *LCG*, p. 71, *CL*II, p. 30.
[35] Conrad, letter to Cunninghame Graham, 8 February 1899, *LCG*, p. 117, *CL*II, p. 159.
[36] T.S. Eliot, `Ulysses, Order, Myth', in *Selected Prose* (London: Faber, 1975), p. 102.

in I've tried to behave decently. I have not degraded the quasi-religious sentiment by tears and groans; and if I have been amused or indignant I've neither grinned nor gnashed my teeth. In other words I've tried to write with dignity, not out of regard for myself but for the sake of the spectacle, the play with an obscure beginning and an unfathomable *dénouement*.[37]

Kant, too, conjures the picture of a stagnant, Sisyphean history in which action threatens to become farce, but argues that respect (*Achtung*) for the human race requires that we avert our eyes from this undignified drama and concentrate instead on humanity's moral worth. Indeed, Kant cannot countenance the notion of a never-ending play that will go on in the same way *ad infinitum*. In his essay, `On the Old Saw', he writes: `To watch this tragedy for a while may perhaps be touching and instructive, but eventually the curtain has to fall. For in the long run the tragedy becomes a farce, and though the actors, fools that they are, do not tire of it, the spectator will'.[38] For both Kant and Conrad this sublime spectacle accordingly leaves us, in Kant's words, with the moral problem of what `one must be in order to be a man'. (Note here the echoes of Stein in *Lord Jim*, on the question of `how to be'.)[39] In Kant's

---

[37] Conrad, letter to Arthur Symons, 29 August 1908, *LL* II, pp. 83-84, *CL*IV, pp. 113-114.

[38] Kant, `On the Old Saw', hereafter Kant, *OOS*, in Booth, *IW*, p. 100. Cf Schopenhauer's more intense pessimism: `[O]ur life must contain all the woes of tragedy, and yet we cannot even assert the dignity of tragic characters, but, in the broad detail of life, are inevitably the foolish characters of a comedy'. Arthur Schopenhauer, *The World as Will and Representation*, tr. E.F.J. Payne (New York: Dover, 1969), Vol. 1, p. 322. Cf Vol. 2, p. 357: `[N]o-one has the remotest idea why the tragi-comedy exists, for it has no spectators, and the actors themselves undergo endless worry with little and merely negative enjoyment'.

[39] Kant, *OOS*, p. 124. Cf Stein in *Lord Jim*: `"One thing alone can us from being ourselves cure!" ... There was a pause. "Yes," said I, "strictly speaking, the question is not how to get cured, but how to live." He approved with his head, a little sadly as it seemed. "*Ja! Ja!*... That is the question...." He went on nodding sympathetically.... "How to be! *Ach*! How to be"' (pp. 212-213).

philosophy the politics of the sublime need not disqualify historical progress altogether, for, he argues, if we abide by the moral law (now in the form of civic Duty and political Justice) we can hope, if not for a millenial path towards Utopia, at least for a trajectory from worse to better.[40] Conrad, however, like Nietzsche, has less faith in the moral end of human history, as the pessimistic politics of his `largest canvas', *Nostromo*, demonstrate most powerfully.

The theatrical image of life as a tragic farce, in which humankind, mystified by tales of Utopia, persists in the always already foredoomed, Sisyphean labour of rolling the boulder of history uphill, is an apt representation of the futile, repetitive nature of history in *Nostromo*. Decoud's detached, ironical remarks on Costaguanan politics, in this context, have a familiar ring:

> `Imagine an atmosphere of opéra-bouffe in which all the comic business of stage statesmen, brigands, etc. etc., all their farcical stealing, intriguing, and stabbing is done in dead earnest. It is screamingly funny, the blood flows all the time, and the actors believe themselves to be influencing the fate of the universe. Of course, government in general, any government anywhere, is a thing of exquisite comicality to a discerning mind; but really we Spanish-Americans do overstep the bounds. No man of ordinary intelligence can take part in the intrigues of *une farce macabre*'. (*N*, p. 152)

Throughout *Nostromo*, theatrical imagery like this conveys a sense of the self-deluded nature of revolutionary praxis, the misconception that political action can bring about a desired transformation of human existence. Thus, as Jim Reilly remarks, in *Nostromo* we are constantly offered dramatic settings for political `action' which fails to materialise. It is as if `the stage is set for an absent epic action...which fails to turn up or which swept off long ago'.[41] Or, as Kiernan Ryan puts it: `The novel delivers no sense of developing action emerging through the vital interplay of the characters with

[40] Kant, *OOS*, in Booth, *IW*, p. 112.
[41] Jim Reilly, *Shadowtime: History and Representation in Hardy, Conrad and George Eliot* (London: Routledge: 1993), p. 157.

each other and their world. Quite the reverse. The narration does not flow, it coils and eddies through a configuration of still centres, congealed *settings for action* which, if recounted at all, is not fully narrated from the "inside"'.[42] The opening description of Sulaco, for example, suggests an amphitheatre awaiting a performance: `Sulaco had found an inviolable sanctuary ... in the solemn hush of the deep Golfo Placido as if within an enormous semi-circular and unroofed temple open to the ocean, with its walls of lofty mountains hung with the mourning draperies of cloud' (*N*, p. 3). When, finally, some pages later, there are signs of revolutionary action to reassure us that this is, after all, a political novel, we are granted only a fleeting, surrealistic impression. The events of the Monterist rebellion are at once depicted and dematerialised by the sublime indifference of the mountain backdrop:

> Horsemen galloped towards each other, wheeled round together, separated at speed. Giorgio saw one fall, rider and horse disappearing as if they had galloped into a chasm, and the movements of the animated scene were like the passages of a violent game played upon the plain by dwarfs mounted and on foot, yelling with tiny throats, under the mountain that seemed a colossal embodiment of silence. (*N*, pp. 26-27)

The mountain's `colossal embodiment of silence' augments the `solemn hush of the Golfo Placido', that enormous `blind spot' or `vanishing point' around which the narrative rotates; a shadowy correlative of the novel's obfuscatory, dislocatory politics. Together these natural settings, suggestive of overwhelming stasis, undermine all empty propagandist discourses of historical progress, bring home the sublime irrelevance of human action to a dark, amoral,

---

[42] Kiernan Ryan, `Revolution and Repression in Conrad's *Nostromo*', in Douglas Jefferson and Graham Martin (eds.), *The Uses of Fiction: Essays on the Modern Novel in Honour of Arnold Kettle* (Milton Keynes: Open University Press, 1982), p. 167. Cf also Edward Said on the `denial of a beginning intention' in *Nostromo*, in *Beginnings: Intention and Method* (New York: Basic Books, 1975), pp. 100-137.

recalcitrantly indifferent Nature:

> At night the body of clouds advancing higher up the sky smothers the whole quiet gulf below with an impenetrable darkness, in which the sound of the falling showers can be heard beginning and ceasing abruptly — now here, now there.... Sky, land and sea disappear together out of the world when the Placido — as the saying is — goes to sleep under its black poncho. The few stars left below the seaward frown of the vault shine feebly as into the mouth of a black cavern. In its vastness your ship floats unseen under your feet, her sails flutter invisible above your head. The eye of God Himself — they add with grim profanity — could not find out what work a man's hand is doing in there; and you would be free to call the devil to your aid with impunity if even his malice were not defeated by such a blind darkness. (*N*, pp. 6-7)

The sublime image of the Golfo Placido also, significantly, serves to underscore the irony of Monygham's belief that Nostromo (of whose moral degradation we are already aware) has proved his moral and physical tenacity by surviving the sinking of the lighter:

> Having had to encounter single-handed during his period of eclipse many physical dangers, [Monygham] was well aware of the most dangerous element common to them all: of the crushing, paralyzing sense of human littleness, which is what really defeats a man struggling with natural forces, alone, far from the eyes of his fellows. He was eminently fit to appreciate the mental image he made for himself of the Capataz, after hours of tension and anxiety, precipitated suddenly into an abyss of waters and darkness, without earth or sky, and confronting it not only with an undismayed mind, but with sensible success....
> `It must have been terribly dark!'
> `It was the worst darkness of the Golfo,' the Capataz asserted, briefly. (*N*, p. 433)

Decoud's suicide on the Golfo Placido, where he sinks `without a trace, swallowed up in the immense indifference of things', (*N*, p. 501) makes this moment all the more ironic. For Decoud's death is one of the most sombre and tragic moments in Conrad's `long dialogue with the darkness'.[43] Driven to despair by days of silence and solitude, the sensible world shatters into a schizophrenic `succession of incomprehensible images' (*N*, p. 498), while the silence assumes the impossible shape of a dark thin string, a schizophrenic parody of historical linearity, vibrating with `senseless phrases, always the same but utterly incomprehensible, about Nostromo, Antonia, Barrios, and proclamations mingled into an ironical and senseless buzzing' (*N*, p. 499).

Interestingly, Schiller, in his version of the sublime, takes the Kantian theme of moral alienation to an extreme which culminates in an act of moral suicide: here man has `no other means of withstanding the power of nature than to anticipate her, and by a free renunciation of all sensuous interest to kill himself morally before some physical force does it'. Moreover, for Schiller, `confusion' is the pre-eminent occasion of the sublime, and by `confusion' he means not merely `the spiritual disorder of a natural landscape' but also `the uncertain anarchy of the moral world', including the amoral chaos of human history in which all best things are confused to ill: `Should one approach history with great expectations of illumination and knowledge — how very disappointed one is!' (*OS*, pp. 208, 204, 205, 207).

Decoud, we recall, has `the first moral sentiment of his manhood' (*N*, p. 498) in the days preceding his death, and, indeed, one could argue that, in a devastating irony, his suicide is the most profound and decisive moral gesture he makes. Yet, in a typically Schillerian conflation, Decoud's moral self-immolation is also a political suicide, a deliberate renunciation of the nightmare of history in which he finds himself. The play on the French *découdre* (to unpick or unstitch) reinforces the association of the sceptical journalist's fate with the suicidal unravelling of the beautiful `guiding-thread' of history, and recalls a similar tendency in

[43]   J. Hillis Miller, *Poets of Reality: Six Twentieth Century Writers* (Cambridge, Mass.: The Belknap Press of Harvard University Press, 1965), p. 39.

Carlyle's disillusioned `Clothes-philosopher', Teufelsdröckh.[44] The historical theme is sustained in the description of his distorted perceptions as he prepares for death. In the moments of schizophrenic depersonalisation which precede the fatal shot, we are given an impossible `rendering' of history seen no longer as a humanised, teleological narrative, but as the ruin of representation: a sublime concatenation of `senseless phrases, always the same but utterly incomprehensible' (*N*, p. 499). Indeed, if Decoud is finally `swallowed up in the immense indifference of things' (*N*, p. 501), this is an indifference not only of Nature, but of the sublime spectacle of human history, and the discourse in which it is constructed.[45] The self-reflexive interplay between the sublimity of Nature and ideology is made similarly explicit in Decoud's earlier, premonitory loss of consciousness during an attempted act of historical representation. Struggling to depict the disparate events of the Monterist Revolution in a letter to his sister, he blacks out inexplicably: `With the writing of the last line there came upon Decoud a moment of sudden and complete oblivion. He swayed over the table as if struck by a bullet' (*N*, p. 249). In Fredric Jameson's post-modernist terms, it is as if the discourse itself `suddenly yawns and discloses at its heart a void which is at one with the temporary extinction of the subject'.[46]

The representational task of the liberal historian, Don José Avellanos, who has close political links with the benign Dictator of

[44] I am indebted to Keith Carabine for this point.

[45] It is surely no mere coincidence that Decoud's `moral' act of self-annihilation finds a political parallel in Conrad's `Autocracy and War'. For Holy Russia, `Le Néant', Conrad writes, `the only conceivable self-reform is — suicide' (*NLL*, p. 101).

[46] Fredric Jameson, *PU*, p. 260. Throughout Conrad's fiction sublime moments of alienation and self-loss are signalled by experiences of amnesia, delirium, dizziness, falling and sudden sleep or loss of consciousness. Moreover, in keeping with his preoccupation with discursivity, or what one could legitimately describe as his modern, Nietzschean sublimity, these moments are frequently associated with scenes of reading and/or writing. Cf Viola's death at the end of *Nostromo*, as the literal extreme of Jameson's sublime `extinction of the subject'.

Costaguana and doctor of philosophy, Don Vincente Ribiera, is similarly doomed to failure. When the Monterists seize the print offices in Sulaco, the newly-printed sheets of his *magnum opus* on the history of Costaguana, *Fifty Years of Misrule* are used as ammunition, `fired out as wads for trabucos loaded with handfuls of type' (*N*, p. 235), while discarded pages blow about in random gusts of wind through the deserted streets. This image becomes a self-reflexive mirror image, at a thematic level, of Conrad's formal strategies of narrative dislocation in the novel, which similarly disrupt order and intelligibility and violate expectations of a beautiful, sequential rendering of historical events. Eloise Knapp Hay remarks on the way in which the fragmentary narrative of Part 1 in particular obscures and confuses the novel's historical plot. Challenging Jocelyn Baines's view that these chronological involutions convey `the simultaneity of visual experience which a painting offers', she argues, employing the vocabulary of the sublime, that the technique in fact has `the reverse effect to that of ordinary painting, since [it] break[s] all the pictures...into fragments' and thereby contributes to *Nostromo*'s `dramatic impenetrability', and `"hollow" reverberation'. She concludes that `[i]t would be just as true to say that abstractionist painters are endeavouring to approach the *concatenation* (as opposed to simultaneity) of disconnected visual effects achieved by Conrad in *Nostromo*'.[47]

Against this backdrop, Mitchell's pompous discourse on the providential course of Sulacan history, his romantic conception of Sulaco's future as the `Treasure-House of the World', stands out as a travesty of the philosophical historian's beautifully framed, teleological narratives, which fail to account for the forces of blind chance. `[U]tterly in the dark, and imagining himself to be in the thick of things"(*N*, p. 112), he recalls the *Sprecher* in post-Renaissance depictions of historical events, the authority figure who engages the viewer with a direct gaze and, pointing to the battle

---

[47] Hay, *PN*, p. 176. Cf Jean-François Lyotard on the sublime and abstract painting in `The Sublime and the Avant-Garde', in Andrew Benjamin (ed.), *The Lyotard Reader* (Oxford: Basil Blackwell, 1989), p. 204.

scene depicted on the canvas, seems to announce `I was there. I am your witness and moral guarantor':

> Almost every event out of the usual daily course `marked an epoch'...or else was `history'; unless with his pomposity struggling with a discomfited droop of his rubicund...face,...he would mutter — `Ah, that! That, sir, was a mistake'. (*N*, pp. 112-113)

Like the accountant in *Heart of Darkness*, with his `faint blush' and beautifully immaculate appearance, the affable Mitchell at once personifies and caricatures the `sweet dream' of colonial history and its corollary, capitalist enlightenment. Proudly displaying his golden chronometer, marking historical time, his enthusiastic commentary goes on `relentless, like a law of Nature' (*N*, p. 481),[48] while his trapped victims listen `like a tired child to a fairy tale' (*N*, p. 487). Significantly, among the litany of those who have `made history' in Mitchell's starry eyes are Nostromo, whose heroic ride to Cayta `would make a most exciting book' (*N*, p. 482), and Don José Avellanos, whose political efforts are romantically commemorated on a plaque in the cathedral as a `lifelong struggle for Right and Justice at the dawn of the New Era' (*N*, p. 477).[49]

   This picturesque view of things, which erroneously conflates political and imaginative vision, reading and seeing, words and deeds, is associated not only with the optimistic narrative of the

[48] In his essay, `An Old Question Raised Again', Kant similarly describes the way in which philosophical historians view the French Revolution as part of the natural growth of history, or, in Kant's words, as `the evolution of a constitution in accordance with *natural law*' (in Booth, *IW*, p. 122).

[49] The capitalist financier Holroyd takes Mitchell's picturesque, providential ideology to a megalomaniacal extreme: `Time itself has got to wait on the greatest country in the whole of God's Universe. We shall be giving the word for everything: industry, trade, law, journalism, art, politics, and religion, from Cape Horn clear over to Smith's Sound, and beyond, too, if anything worth taking hold of turns up at the North Pole. And then we shall have the leisure to take in hand the outlying islands and continents of the earth. We shall run the world's business whether the world likes it or not. The world can't help it — and neither can we, I guess' (*N*, p. 77).

self-appointed historian, Mitchell, but to a greater or lesser degree with all the novel's characters, for all display some form of visionary fanaticism, typically associated with a surfeit of reading. Pedrito Montero's grandiose political schemes, for example, have their origins in his reading of French light literature of an historical kind: `His ability to read did nothing for him but fill his head with absurd visions.... A long course of reading historical works, light and gossipy in tone, carried out in garrets of Parisian hotels, sprawling on an untidy bed, to the neglect of his duties, menial or otherwise, had affected the manners of Pedro Montero' (*N*, p. 387, pp. 403-404). However the picturesque, fairy-tale view of things is associated most obviously with those seductive aesthetic representatives of the barren capitalist ideology of `material interests', the Incorruptible Capataz de Cargadores and Emilia Gould, the `good fairy' (*N*, p. 520) of Sulaco, who believes in the preservation of `simple and picturesque things' (*N*, p. 120). While Emilia Gould observes her husband's growing ideological abstraction with dread, she responds imaginatively and sympathetically to Nostromo, whose `sensuous and picturesque' identity gives him an equally seductive power within the People.[50]

Yet there remains no doubt of the superficiality of the ideology of the beautiful, and its myths of sensuous immanence, as the implosion of Nostromo's identity testifies. The `abyss left by the collapse of his vanity' leaves him `as ready to become the prey of any belief, superstition, or desire as a child' (*N*, p. 417). Like T.S. Eliot's hollow men, Nostromo, Our Man, is at once everyman and no-man, everything and nothing, the debased symbol of an ideology whose immanent meaning has drained away and betrayed an ugly gap. `"Ah, yes! True. I am nothing"', he says to Monygham, who replies, `"Not at all. You are everything"' (*N*, p. 457). Nostromo's

[50] Cf Decoud on Gould's sentimentalism: `I think he can be drawn into it, like all idealists, when he once sees a sentimental basis for his action." (*N*, p. 216). This, of course, is what initially draws the sentimental Emilia to Charles Gould. *Lord Jim* and *Heart of Darkness* similarly take as their starting point the dangerous mystifications of the idealistic Romantic imagination (Jim, Kurtz).

birth into moral and self-awareness is therefore, ironically, synonymous with the failure of moral immanence, although, picturesque to the last, he succumbs in turn to the seductive power of the silver and the clichéd rhetoric of romantic fantasy: `He had kept the treasure for purposes of revenge; but now he cared nothing for it. He cared only for [Giselle]. He would put her beauty in a palace on a hill crowned with olive trees — a white palace above a blue sea. He would keep her there like a jewel in a casket. He would get land for her — her own land fertile with vines and corn — to set her little feet upon' (*N*, p. 541).

Emilia Gould's profound vision of the emptiness underlying the ideals by which she has justified her husband's pursuit of wealth, by contrast denies her the solace of picturesque dreams:

> An immense desolation, the dread of her own continued life, descended upon the first lady of Sulaco. With a prophetic vision she saw herself surviving alone the degradation of her young ideal of life, of love, of work — all alone in the Treasure House of the World. The profound, blind, suffering expression of a painful dream settled on her face with its closed eyes. In the indistinct voice of an unlucky sleeper, lying passive in the grip of a merciless nightmare, she stammered out aimlessly the words —
> `Material interests.' (*N*, p. 522)

If Mrs Gould herself succumbs to a pessimistic, sublime vision of human nature and history, where are we to take our moral bearings in *Nostromo*? The answer is hard to find. The most plausible alternative to her beleaguered sentimental philosophy is the Christian/ Garibaldean ethics of duty represented by Viola and his dark-haired, dutiful daughter, Linda. Yet the novel ends ambiguously, suggesting that even the Garibaldino's moral, and, by implication, political, faith has been eroded. The dying man, his days of revolutionary activism long past, seems to encounter the same blind spot of ideology which undermines Emilia Gould's hold on life. Taking up his Bible and the silver-mounted spectacles she has given to him, he can no longer see beyond the print he reads:

38

'Where are you going?' he asked.
'To the light,' she answered, turning round to look at him balefully.
'The light! Si — duty.'
Very upright, white-haired, leonine, heroic in his absorbed quietness, he felt in the pocket of his red shirt for the spectacles given him by Dona Emilia. He put them on. After a long period of immobility he opened the book, and from on high looked through the glasses at the small print in double columns. A rigid, stern expression settled upon his features with a slight frown, as if in response to some gloomy thought or unpleasant sensation.... [H]e swayed forward, gently, gradually, till his snow-white head rested upon the open pages. A wooden clock ticked methodically on the white-washed wall, and growing slowly cold the Garibaldino lay alone, rugged, undecayed, like an old oak uprooted by a treacherous gust of wind (*N*, p. 565).

SIGNS, INTERPOLATIONS, MEANINGS: CONRAD AND THE POLITICS OF UTTERANCE

ANTHONY FOTHERGILL

For a train of thought is never false. The falsehood lies deep in the necessities of existence, in secret fears and half-formed ambitions, in the secret confidence combined with a secret mistrust of ourselves in the love of hope and the dread of uncertain days. (*UWE*, pp. 33-34)

In Act 2 of *Twelfth Night* Malvolio, steward to Olivia, reads the `obscure epistle' specially written and planted by the servant Maria to dupe him into thinking that he is loved by Olivia, with whom he is secretly enamoured. Literally interpolating meaning into the many gaps in the writing, Malvolio enacts the impossibility and necessity of interpretation:

> *Malvolio*: `M.O.A.I. doth sway my life.' Nay, but first let me see, let me see, let me see.... `I may command where I adore.' Why, she may command me. I serve her; she is my lady. Why, this is evident to any formal capacity. There is no obstruction in this. And the end; what should that alphabetical position portend? If I could make that resemble something in me! Softly, `M.O.A.I.'.... `M. — Malvolio! M. — Why, that begins my name.'[1]

The rest of the play works out the near-fatal hazards of such interpolation. It seems to warn against interpretation, against jumping to meaning in the gaps constituted by another's utterance.

---

[1] William Shakespeare, *Twelfth Night, or, What You Will*, ed. M.M. Mahood (Harmondsworth: Penguin, 1968), 2.5.103-16.

Yet as the opening epigraph from *Under Western Eyes* seems to claim, not only is such interpretation, such wilful belief, inescapable; it is also, somehow, never false. I want to look at some crucial moments in Conrad's writing which exemplify and test this contradiction. The very `jump' in the epigraph figures the contradiction linguistically: `A train of thought is never false. The falsehood ...' This figuring suggests that we will be needing to deal with the contradiction at the narrative level, in examining the ways characters read — and, perhaps more importantly, mis-read — one another to reveal profound truths about themselves.

In a desperate and yet comically absurd moment early in *Under Western Eyes*, the revolutionary assassin Haldin, having burst in upon Razumov, confesses to him that it is he who has `removed' the Minister-President, Mr. de P—. This utterance shatters Razumov's very being:

> Razumov kept down a cry of dismay. The sentiment of his life being utterly ruined by this contact with such a crime expressed itself quaintly by a sort of half-derisive mental exclamation, `There goes my silver medal!' (*UWE*, p. 16)

It is a surreal response to Haldin's words — a bizarre, logic-defying association of contexts and meanings. What does the imagined loss of a not-yet-possessed silver medal have to do with Haldin's assassination of Mr. de P—? No doubt as readers we tend to do what the narrator of Razumov's diaries (the teacher of languages) does: we quickly pass over the obscure moment. Yet the teacher of languages gets increasingly irritated at any subsequent mention of the silver medal. When much later on he alludes to Razumov's confession to Natalia, he dismisses as irrelevant to *his* narrative some pages which contain `even one more allusion to the silver medal' (*UWE*, p. 357). Perhaps this registers his own jealous partiality in what claims to be an unemotional narrative. In claiming to dismiss the medal, he mentions it yet again, as an oyster coats an irritating grain of sand with another pearly layer.

I would like to argue here that the whole of the rest of *Under Western Eyes* can be seen as the working out of the implications of Razumov's half-suppressed exclamation. Beneath its apparent and almost derisory arbitrariness, there lies a political and psychological intuition (I would like to call it `experiential logic') which marks and precisely expresses the crucial turning point in the novel. Note I do not say it was Haldin's *entering* the room that turns the narrative; it is rather the way that his utterance gets internalized and interpreted by Razumov that has that effect. The action of interpreting forces Razumov to construct a hitherto unimagined new life-narrative. It forces him to construe his subjectivity differently, and the sign of the necessity to do so is the surreal exclamation with its embedded political insight. Just as the prospect of the silver medal had functioned as a metonym for a successful academic life, so its proleptic loss demands a revised narrative. We must ask what investment the novel allows Razumov to make in the medal, and hence what meaning the novel allows Razumov to attach to *losing* it.

Let us return to Razumov's exclamation. The logic of his leap of thought is clearly not of the formal, arbitrary sort founded in syllogism. But it is not a false train of thought, for all that. It has the logic borne of and re-producing his experience of himself. Razumov's sense of legitimacy (both legally and existentially) is bound up in his self-definition: `I am he who is working for the silver medal'. His dubious paternity, the sharply-felt absence of family, his precarious anchoring in the world of social relations, his very subjectivity — all are articulated in the metonymic utterance. Who will the Razumov become who intuits that he has lost the medal? What is the cost and what is the gain of such a loss? Haldin's utterance is understood by Razumov as forcing him to alter the narrative of the life he had been legitimizing and through which he was legitimized. The medal had emblematized the politics of the earlier story he had been telling himself: `I have no parentage but Mother Russia; the label "Razumov" will be converted into a real name when I become a professor'. The rupturing of *that* story engenders a new one, a new version of his subjectivity. The rest of the novel plays out the implications of the form that the new story takes.

By `political' I do not mean explicit programmatic policy and articulated ideas. Razumov's attempts at working out a formal politics are short-lived, though they have an afterlife of sorts in the self-serving misinterpretation of the autocratic Government, in the shape of Councillor Mikulin (*UWE*, p. 99). I am using the word in a less specific and more potent sense, which is how I see it functioning in Conrad's mode of political thought. By `political' I mean an awareness of the self's engagement with a specific social reality: the political is at once the personal and social function of behaviour, including the subjective awareness of one's being placed within and behaving in terms of an economically, historically, and materially specific world of interpersonal relations. According to this view, the subjectivity of each person is not a fixed and stable entity that reacts to and within the world. Rather, subjectivity is in a constant process of construction through one's engagement with the world. `Individual' being is articulated through the discourses and institutions of community. Insofar as it is self-conscious, we may speak of `personal choice' or `need' at the level of individual behavior; we might speak of (personal) `moral choice', or a `choice of nightmares' (as Marlow puts it, of his siding with Kurtz). At less conscious levels, where psychic needs are more obviously determining, `choice' would be an inappropriate word: then we might speak of the need for self-justification, for `legitimation,' for instance; or for mutual recognition, respect or indeed love. As soon as these `choices' or `needs' enter the social arena of interpersonal relations, they become proto-political.

Thus, when the teacher of languages quickly by-passes reference to Razumov's desire for the silver medal as merely `the psychological side' (*UWE*, p. 357) of his dilemma, the teacher is attempting to separate off the mental from the social, the personal from the political. This compartmentalizing is symptomatic of *his* sense of the solitary. He ignores the fact of the social construction of subjectivity, our sense of who we are, and how and under what pressures we act within the world. In the massive undertaking of interpolation and interpretation which the teacher's `editing' of Razumov's fragmentary and sporadic diaries represents, we have a prime example of the way his own `necessities of existence' condition his `reading' (literal and metaphorical) of the `text' (literal and metaphorical) which is Razumov. His personal and cultural isolation in Geneva, his hardly articulated affection for Natalia, his anxieties over his age and bachelorhood, his complacent assertion of his western liberalism over Russian autocracy and its revolutionary opponents — all of this `personal' matter conspires to condition the interpolations he makes. The `psychological side' is one formulation he uses to contain potentially disruptive material. Though as an academic he could hardly admit it, the `falsehoods' which his `necessities of existence' require place him quite close to Winnie Verloc, when she acknowledges that it `did not stand looking into very much' (*SA*, p. 241).

His `falsehood' — though insofar as it is a necessity it is not `false' — is not one shared by Conrad. The teacher's separation of the `psychological' from the more broadly political imposes categories and asserts a division of being that Conrad's own work consistently defies. It is not just in *Under Western Eyes* that Conrad explores the intersection of the almost solipsistically personal and the political. Just as Razumov's first thought concerning political assassination is ludicrously but metonymically linked with winning a medal, so, in other works, Conrad presents politically-charged moments as occurring, for the protagonist, in an almost incidental manner. Such apparently casual moments lead the protagonist to potent psychological (and sometimes also political) re-evaluations.

The site of this new understanding is an unpremeditated situation, a seemingly arbitrary occurrence, that engages the character at a deep psychological level. The very arbitrariness of the occurrence, such as Haldin's bursting in upon Razumov, shocks and disrupts the habitually expected. This itself constitutes a gap, one of those `unexpected solutions of continuity, sudden holes in space and time', as Conrad calls it in *The Secret Agent* (*SA*, p. 85). The protagonist must, by interpretation or projection, fill the gap, somehow mastering, that is, making personally coherent sense of, the new, brutally real. In two such incidents in *Heart of Darkness*, to which I now want to turn, Conrad represents Marlow responding to sudden and partially understood encounters (`partially' in both senses). The absence of a fully informed and coherent context for these encounters requires from Marlow an engaged reading of a limited body of signs. Like Malvolio's filling-in of the missing letters, Marlow, too, reveals in his interpolations a level of psychic anxiety. The narratives he reads into the gaps of information have profound but clear moral and political implications. His reading of the first incident highlights Marlow's deep and guilty ambivalence about the Company's colonial enterprises in Africa. This sense of complicity, I would argue, colours his interpretation of the subsequent incident, his siding with Kurtz as his `choice of nightmare'.

Ian Watt's term `delayed decoding'[2] can be used to describe how Marlow's sudden meeting with the chain-gang at the Company's chief station presents him with a series of dislocated impressions which he has to organize into some sort of narrative frame. He does so by recalling his earlier memory of the French destroyer, off the west coast of Africa, futilely shooting shells at similar `enemies' and `criminals'. But Marlow's personal and political commiseration with the slave labourers is abruptly interrupted, and implicitly questioned, by the chain-gang's overseer in the way he regards Marlow:

Behind this raw matter one of the reclaimed, the product of the new forces at work, strolled despondently, carrying a rifle by its middle. He had a uniform jacket with one button off, and seeing a white man on the path, hoisted his weapon to his shoulder with alacrity. This was simple

[2] Ian Watt, *Conrad in the Nineteenth Century* (Berkeley: University of California Press, 1979), pp. 175-79.

prudence, white men being so much alike at a distance that he could not tell who I might be. He was speedily reassured, and with a large, white, rascally grin, and a glance at his charge, seemed to take me into partnership in his exalted trust. After all, I also was a part of the great cause of these high and just proceedings. (*HD*, pp. 64-65)

Determined by the `necessities of [his] existence', the overseer makes a quick, necessarily self-interested, interpolative reading of the scant information Marlow's physical appearance offers him — and falsely deduces that he is simply `a part of the great cause'. But how false *is* this reading? In his own swift reciprocal reading of the guard's look, Marlow experiences himself politically as yet another white man complicit in the brutal scramble for Africa. That is, in his interpolative interpretation of the overseer's obsequious gestures, Marlow feels himself placed in a political narrative he would rather deny. As a `semi-colonial', he is, but is not fully, a part of these `just proceedings': his critical sarcasm is a measure of his distance from the great cause.[3] Naturally, as his psychological `necessities of existence' require him to do, he turns away — but only to find himself in the grove of death, confronted by shades of his wavering complicity in the form of the material, albeit skeletal, detritus of the colonial enterprise (*HD*, p. 66).

The way Marlow (one of the `white men') is regarded by the overseer situates him as a perpetrator of the cruelty he has witnessed. However ironic he may be about the colonial enterprise, Marlow reads the overseer's look and gestures as signs implicating him in it. He has been construed by the overseer as just another one of the pilgrims. Understandably he turns away to avoid the discomfort of the look and its political force. He has read the signs, in this case the visual utterance of body-language and eyes, and has understood the power relation of white over black. At an intuitive rather than a fully articulated level, Marlow's own subjectivity is

---

[3] For a fuller account of the `semi-colonial' argument, see my *Heart of Darkness* (Milton Keynes: Open University Press, 1989), pp. 37-58.

produced and recognized in this moment's turning.

Another such moment of interpolation — again involving a literal and powerful turn — occurs later in the novella. It, too, places Marlow firmly in socio-political relation to his fellow-travellers. I am thinking of Marlow at the Central Station, when aboard his beached steamboat he overhears a disrupted conversation between the Central Station manager and his uncle. The gaps in the half-heard conversation force Marlow to infer a story about Kurtz. Out of utterances not intended for nor directed towards him, Marlow construes an alternative story, or rather image, for Kurtz. For the first time, Marlow says, he `seemed to see Kurtz' (*HD*, p. 90). Precisely by virtue of the disjointed talk, Marlow is made into an active, imaginative, interpolating and partial hearer/reader. It is then, around the trope of `turning away', that he can create a figure for Kurtz. Whether this image is false or not (for he does not even hear the name `Kurtz' mentioned, such is his `necessity'), Marlow subsequently holds to it. He goes from being bored and irritated by all the Company talk of Kurtz to figuring Kurtz imaginatively, `seeing' him turning away from the Central Station and returning upstream. Only at this point does Marlow engage with Kurtz. Only now, that is, after hearing and interpreting broken utterances and forcing them into a narrative is Marlow's own desire to find Kurtz existentially motivated. His `train of thought' — which comes eventually to smack of a sort of falsity, but which remains *self*-confirming for Marlow — follows this line: `Perhaps he [Kurtz] was just simply a fine fellow who stuck to his work for its own sake' (*HD*, p. 90). Seeing himself in Kurtz, Marlow reads Kurtz's `turn' as a renunciation of the Company's economic and political interests. Readerly interpolation has at least empowered Marlow to make his own choice of nightmare.

Let us return to *Under Western Eyes* to recall two parallel occasions, when utterance and interpolation conjoin to provoke a new narrative turn. Both of these occasions are political in the broadest sense: they heavily determine Razumov's socio-political actions. In a novel so self-consciously treating the uses and abuses of language, it is not surprising that both occasions crucially relocate acts of utterance within a specifically experienced socio/political reality. But again, regarded from the viewpoint of narrative action, both moments seem secondary and trivial, indeed slight enough to permit our overlooking them.

The first is the meeting of Natalia Haldin, saint-like sister of the (by this time dead but) heroic Victor Haldin, with Tekla, Peter Ivanovitch's exploited secretary. Natalia is ostensibly on her way to the Château Borel to take up the leading revolutionary Peter Ivanovitch's invitation of a meeting with him and Madame de S—, the aristocratic benefactor of the revolutionary exiles in Geneva. Significantly, that meeting does not occur. More importantly, it is displaced by an alternative narrative event of crucial importance to Natalia. Tekla talks to Natalia of her four months nursing a revolutionist lithographer whose story shadows that of both Victor Haldin and, proleptically, Razumov. He had been arrested and tortured by the Russian government, had confessed information, and had then been flung out sick and dying from a government prison to pass the last days of his life in a miserable den of a place:

> As Miss Haldin looked at her inquisitively she began to describe the emaciated face of the man, his fleshless limbs, his destitution.... And [she] seemed to see for the first time, a name and a face upon the body of that suffering people whose hard fate had been the subject of so many conversations, between her and her brother, in the garden of their country house. (*UWE*, p. 152)

What had remained disassociated in Natalia's experience — the language of revolution uttered by her brother with its abstract knowledge of political and social suffering, and the real world of actual lives in their making and unmaking — is now unwittingly and suddenly linked for her through Tekla's utterance. Natalia interpolates herself into a narrative and thereby creates for herself a new, re-visionary narrative; she is now able to invest the earlier talks with her brother with political meaning. For the first time, she can ground his rhetoric in her own life, but through another's story, through another's utterance. Crucially, both Tekla's and Natalia's stories are stories centring on an absence (the revolutionist lithographer and Victor), on a gap that must be filled. Theirs are stories of pain and loss and of the pain of loss. It is a coming to new terms with loss that binds them.

Significantly enough, Tekla's story actually represents a middle term in a process of narrative transmission or tradition. Her *own* political awareness had been born of another narrative: the story-telling of an old apple-woman, the `old friend and teacher', who eventually introduced her to the revolutionary:

> She had a kind wrinkled face, and the most friendly voice imaginable. One day, casually, we began to talk about a child, a ragged little girl we had seen begging from men in the streets at dusk; and from one thing to another my eyes began to open gradually to the horrors from which innocent people are made to suffer in this world, only in order that governments might exist. (*UWE*, pp. 149-150)

Such narratives constitute moments of moral and political enlightenment for Natalia and Tekla, which redefine their relations to their own social realities. Certainly, in Natalia's case, her mother perceives her as changed, as having stronger convictions, even if the context for that perception causes the mother nervously and selfishly to read Natalia's change as a sort of leaving.

Natalia's understanding and interpolating herself into Tekla's narrative can be described as `experience' in a sense used by Walter Benjamin. In his essay on Leskov's `The Storyteller' and in `On Some Motifs in Baudelaire', Benjamin has described the social role of the story-teller and listener, and the function of memory.[4] He distinguishes between two notions of experience in the essay on

[4] See Walter Benjamin, `The Storyteller' (1936) and `On Some Motifs in Baudelaire' (1939), in *Illuminations*, ed. Hannah Arendt, tr. Harry Zohn (London: Fontana, 1973), hereafter *I*; pp. 83-109, pp. 157-202.

Baudelaire: *Erfahrung*, the fully internalised on-going accumulation and assimilation of life-events, rich in associations, which can be further transmitted through narrative as wisdom or counsel; and *Erlebnis*, which refers to the merely factual occurrence of momentary, as opposed to memorable, incidents. Whereas *Erlebnis* can be recorded and recalled as discrete facts, *Erfahrung* survives in memory impressions that lend coherence and continuity to earlier experiences. Benjamin insists that *this* experience is `a matter of tradition', a joining in `collective existence as well as private life': `It is less the product of facts firmly anchored in memory than of a convergence in memory of accumulated and frequently unconscious data' *(I*, p. 159). Furthermore, this work of remembrance, this abiding revivified experience, involves, according to Benjamin in `A Berlin Chronicle', `the capacity for endless interpolations into what has been'.[5] Crucially, the chain of narrativity joining the apple-woman, Tekla, Natalia and ultimately Razumov (through his conversations with the latter) relies on the immediacy, the physical presence of storyteller and listener, which confirms authenticity and permits the active interpolation of narrative by listener. While it is true that Razumov is not strictly the recipient of a tale, it is Natalia's physical being and her confidence in (which does not mean the truth of) what she says, which allows him to break out of his solipsistic isolation into a new (confessional) sense of self.

This grounding in the subjectively experienced real, which parallels the experiences of Tekla and Natalia, occurs later when Razumov writes of his meeting with Natalia. It records an occasion when the *voice* is redeemed. As the teacher of languages puts it, describing the diary entry, Razumov after some pages of incoherent writing —

[5] Benjamin, `A Berlin Chronicle' (1932), in *One-Way Street and Other Writings*, tr. E. Jephcott and K. Shorter (London: New Left Books, 1979), pp. 293-346, p. 305.

begins to address directly the reader he has in his mind, trying to express in broken sentences, full of wonder and awe, the sovereign (he uses that very word) power of her person over his imagination, in which lay the dormant seed of her brother's words.

`...The most trustful eyes in the world — your brother said of you when he was as well as a dead man already. And when you stood there before me with your hand extended, I remembered the very sound of his voice, and I looked into your eyes — and that was enough. I knew that something had happened, but I did not know then what....' (*UWE*, p. 358)

In his *Joseph Conrad: Narrative Technique and Ideological Commitment*, Jeremy Hawthorn has shrewdly alerted us to Conrad's predominant concern with the expressive language of the body, particularly of the eyes and hands, as an alternative medium of signification in a world where the written and spoken word has become so unreliable.[6] I fully agree with his concentration on the presence of the physical body in Conrad's work. Nonetheless, an insistent physicality does not make the problem of interpretation disappear, for bodily utterances and gestures must also be mediated to have meaning. Though the significance of the touch of a hand or the look of an eye appears to be self-evident, gestures are readable only insofar as they are part of a system of signification, which itself is at least partially conventional and culturally determined. As such, they can be misinterpreted.

As we remember, Razumov's plight — his betrayal of Victor Haldin and his complicity with Councillor Mikulin and the autocratic government — has been generated by a misinterpretation of body language: Haldin misreads Razumov's silence and physical reticence as the literal embodiment of a metaphor for *Englishness*, the 'stiff upper lip'. Apart from the rich Conradian humour in Haldin's misrecognition of Razumov as English, at the very moment he wants to conceive of himself as quintessentially Russian, there

---

[6] See Jeremy Hawthorn, *Joseph Conrad: Narrative Technique and Ideological Commitment* (London: Edward Arnold, 1990), pp. 236-259.

is in this misreading something of the recurrent threat of solipsistic isolation which Conrad constantly explores. Victor's `train of thought,' which figures Razumov as a sympathetic if less active participant in the student revolutionary movement, is an act of wilful interpolation satisfying Victor's own `necessities of existence':

> `Kirylo Sidorovitch,' said [Victor Haldin]...`we are not perhaps in exactly the same camp. Your judgement is more philosophical. You are a man of few words, but I haven't met anybody who dared to doubt the generosity of your sentiments. There is a solidity about your character which cannot exist without courage.... Your reserve has always fascinated me....' (*UWE*, p. 15)

When Haldin lobs the metaphorically explosive confession of his assassination of Mr. de P— into the conversation, he wilfully interpolates the gap represented by Razumov's stunned silence (`There goes my medal') as unspoken support. Readers of Conrad's novel are constantly teased by the names of certain characters, such as Mr. de P— and Madame de S—, which insist upon and frustrate interpretive closure. While in an eighteenth- or nineteenth-century novel this may merely be a conventional claim to realism, in Conrad's novel, it calls attention to the presence of absences. Even the typographical conventions of the page insist that we as readers participate in Haldin's experience of a gap:

> Haldin continued after waiting a while —
> `You say nothing, Kirylo Sidorovitch! I understand your silence. To be sure, I cannot expect you with your frigid English manner to embrace me. But never mind your manners. You have enough heart to have heard the sound of weeping and gnashing of teeth this man raised in the land.' (*UWE*, p. 16)

The narrative Haldin composes for Razumov around his silence is as self-defined as Razumov's response to him. Language in any of its forms, including physical gesture, requires interpolation and interpretation, which can therefore always be wrong. Though, as Conrad says, they are never false.

Implicit in my argument so far (the example of Haldin's misreading notwithstanding) is a view about signification which contests some prevailing theoretical assumptions about language and its relation to the world which the fictional teacher of languages seems to endorse. This is a linguistic model of semiosis and reality which he shares with the post-structuralists. The dilemma may be posed in the form of an image, a scenario, which is provoked by my reading of the opening pages of *Under Western Eyes*. I imagine a street, call it the Rue de Carouge, near the University in Geneva. It is 1907 or thereabouts. Two somewhat *distrait*, otherworldly figures, wandering down the same street, are muttering to themselves. Clearly they are both academics. The first is heard to say, `Words, as is well known, are the great foes of reality.... To a teacher of languages there comes a time when the world is but a place of many words and man appears a mere talking animal not much more wonderful than a parrot' (*UWE*, p. 3). The other figure, in his oblivion almost bumping into the first, suggests to the air that `the bond between the signifier and the signified is arbitrary.... Every means of expression used in society...is based on convention'.[7]

Both the fictional and the real teacher of language, the narrator of the novel I am reading and Ferdinand de Saussure, share a scepticism about the assumptions too readily made by naive users of language, that there is any automatic natural link between the linguistic sign and the object in the world. Indeed latter-day followers of Saussure, particularly influenced by the version of his theories perpetuated by French post-structuralist thinking, have radically extended and perhaps simplified his quite complex definitions. For example, Saussure acknowledges that `the word

---

[7] Ferdinand de Saussure, *Course in General Linguistics*, ed. Charles Bally and Albert Sechehaye, tr. Wade Baskin (London: Fontana Collins, 1974), p. 68.

"symbol" has been used to designate the linguistic sign, or ... the signifier' (id.). He admits that the symbol

> is never wholly arbitrary; it is not empty, for there is the rudiment of a natural bond between the signifier and the signified. The symbol of justice, a pair of scales, could not be replaced by just any other symbol, such as a chariot. (id.)

But, having acknowledged that, Saussure is all the keener to leave symbols out of his arbitrary model of signification. He leaves the way open, therefore, for his commentators to argue that `all meaning in every sphere of human activity consists of closed systems [of signification] wholly independent of the material world'.[8] Thus understood, the process of reading signs is a relatively straightforward matter of decoding hitherto encoded messages into other signs. There is no need to establish any relation between the system of codes and their reference and our being interpreters in an extra-linguistic reality.

Saussure's binary theoretical structure of language (*signifié* and *signifiant*) has been thoroughly dominant in contemporary critical thought. As commonly understood, it has aided and abetted the notion of endlessly deferred meanings, a closed system of signification, which represents a critique of what Derrida calls the `transcendental signified' — the ultimate grounding of acts of signification in a fixed referent or subject in the world. In terms of my argument, what Saussure's model cannot cater for is the speech-situation, the often-contested social space in which the utterance (spoken, written, or gestural) takes place and derives its meaning.

An alternative theory of signs, perhaps less familiar but in my view far richer than Saussure's conceptually bound account, is that

---

[8] David Robey, `Modern Linguistics and the Language of Literature', in David Robey and Ann Jefferson (eds.), *Modern Literary Theory* (London: Batsford, 1982), p. 43.

of C.S. Peirce (1839-1914), the American pragmaticist and philosopher of language, a crucial figure in modern arguments about language, semiosis, and epistemology. I wish to draw attention specifically to a triadic structure inherent in his theory of language and his definition of the sign, which has profound implications for the present argument. Peirce defines the sign thus: `A sign, or representamen, is something which stands to somebody for something in some respect or capacity'. He elaborates the notion of the sign addressing somebody —

> that is, it creates in the mind of that person an equivalent sign, or perhaps a more developed sign. That sign which it creates I call the interpretant of the first sign. The sign stands for something, its object.[9]

Furthermore, crucially, a sign is not merely verbal; it can be gestural or visual; it can function symbolically, but also iconically (as in the relationship of a portrait to a face), and indexically (as in the relationship of smoke to fire, or a paw-print to an animal). Here, the argument for complete arbitrariness breaks down, and there is room for some sort of interpolation of the communally (and not merely conventionally) acknowledged, real world. The brother of that other famous American pragmaticist William James once defined the real as `that which cannot not be true.' The way that Henry James puts it may merely place at one remove a vote of confidence for the arbitrarily-agreed meaning. But it does allow for the acknowledgement, even if only through negation, of an extra-linguistic reality by building into its definition of `the real' a notion of sceptical resistance to that which is too easily accepted as true.

Peirce's relation to a notion such as `the real' is problematic. Like Derrida after him, he acknowledges the play of signifiers; he

---

[9] C. S. Peirce, *Collected Papers* 2, p. 228, cited in Umberto Eco, *The Role of the Reader: Exploration in the Semiotics of Texts* (London: Hutchinson, 1979), p. 180.

agrees that when we use a sign (symbol) like `dog' we do not have automatic and immediate contact with our furry friend. We conceive of alternative interpretants, each a would-be translation of the other: a picture of a dog (icon); a definition of a four-legged carnivorous quadruped; an image of fidelity; a producer of an unpleasant and smelly roadside trace (index). But in any particular language use, while the sign thus partakes in a process of seemingly endless translations or `interpretants', there is for Peirce the notion of a final or `ultimate' interpretant, in what he calls the notion of `habit,' `a tendency towards action' tested against acts in the social world. If I say, `That dog has rabies', there are actual limitations on the play of signifiers insofar as I act, or do not act, on the interpretants through which I conceptualize each of the signs in the statement.

The value of Peirce's model is manifold: he greatly enlarges our notion of the sign — and thus of the utterance — to embrace the non-verbal. As a crucial corollary to this, signs are not purely arbitrary, though they can only function as signs by certain linguistic and communal conventions and with cultural agreement. Thirdly, the sign is not necessarily motivated. That is, a sign may mean without that meaning being intended. This is particularly true of non-linguistic signs, though slips of the tongue would also fall into this category. Thus, we can read as unwitting the grimace in a pained face. The look of a face or other bodily signs are no more *infallibly* readable than are spoken or written words. (Consider Haldin's self-confirming accommodation of Razumov's appearance, his 'stiff upper lip', mentioned above.) But such non-verbal signs may constitute a counter-narrative to the spoken or written; they serve dialogically, that is, to augment or contest other sign systems. Furthermore, Peirce's model asserts the process of someone's interpreting the sign in its relation to an object. The play of meaning thus ends in a grounded interpretation, not as a merely logical decoding or re-encoding of an encoded message. This grounding attaches the sign to the extra-linguistic objects in social reality.

Of course the grounding of signs (whether in linguistic or non-linguistic utterances) in the habitual experience of the addressed person is no guarantee of right interpretation. Peirce shares with Derrida a scepticism about absolute extra-historical meaning. And so would Conrad. We have in *Under Western Eyes* ample evidence of the duplicity of signs; visual or gestural signs are no more reliable or readable than written ones. Conrad is not claiming that the grounding of interpretation is disinterested. If Derrida fairly asked, `What is at stake in the infinite play of meanings ceasing *here*?', Conrad would probably answer, `The (quite probably misconceived) life-interest of the interpreter of the utterance.'

The scepticism of the teacher of languages (and the reader) is profound when alerted to the language practice of Peter Ivanovitch. Through Tekla's excruciating account of taking dictation from him, the conditions of the production of Peter's language are all too clear; the oppressive sexual politics of that sort of utterance, its contradiction of the explicit feminist rhetoric and apparent fluency of the finished result are indisputable. But this insight is achieved precisely because his words are *not* an arbitrary play of meanings. It is because language is also social practice that the disjunction between his discourse and social reality counts. As their interpreter, Tekla takes them as utterances which she grounds politically in her own gendered experience. At the very moment when his language produces one image of the female subject — the woman as natural, amazonian heroine — it also produces a Tekla positioned within a system of labour (an alternative sign system), whose life-habits it dictates.

To return to the Rue de Carouge, I imagine, going in the opposite direction from the two professors of language, two other short and neatly trimmed middle-aged men. The first, his mind on a failed revolution, coolly articulates one politics of utterance: `People always have been and they always will be stupid victims of deceit and self-deception in politics, until they learn to seek out behind every kind of moral, religious, political, social phrase and declaration the interests of this or that class or classes.' But a short way off, apparently taking mental notes of the scene around him, a figure repeats to himself his conviction written ten years earlier: `my task which I am trying to achieve is, by the power of the written word to make you hear, to make you feel — it is, before all, to make you *see*.' So I imagine, on the same street, two professors of language, a Russian revolutionary and a Polish-British novelist.

In their differing ways, the third and fourth bearded gentlemen argue for a dynamics of linguistic behaviour which sees any signifying act, any utterance, as produced by and returning to that social and political ground in which people, users of the language, have their being. Lenin, for it is he, clearly sees the negative function of this dialectic in the way `phrases and declarations' always embody and conceal power interests. Both the agents of discourse and their addressees are regarded as subjects construed through, and therefore subject to, the ideological constraints of these language formations. Conrad, the exiled novelist who, speaking always in a foreign tongue, was probably all the more aware of its local colour, was not unaware of the ideological dangers Lenin perceived. But his preface to *The Nigger of the `Narcissus'* seems to propose the possibility of artistic utterance which does not imprison and victimize but rather liberates user and recipient into vision. Nevertheless, the linguistic work is still a task; its effort does not carry automatic reward; and the relation to the listener/reader is one which borders on the coercive. As he says, he must *make* — not *let* — us see. To make us see through (his) words is Conrad's aesthetic imperative. To ground the complexities of falsity must be part of that imperative. What I would call Conrad's generous humanism led him to recognize that to condemn the false out of hand was too easy; it would not acknowledge the truths lying latent in falsity. The false ways we see and interpolate our experience of the world may belatedly reveal our own real needs.

THE DIALOGISM OF *LORD JIM*

GAIL FINCHAM

Lord Jim is notoriously a novel in two parts. The first half, which describes the apprenticeship and early career of the officer Jim, his desertion of the pilgrim ship *Patna*, and his reactions during and after the subsequent Court of Inquiry, is generally acknowledged to be amongst Conrad's best writing, modulating skilfully between thought and speech in shifting narrative perspectives. The second part begins in Chapter Twenty One with Marlow's question `I don't suppose any of you [have] ever heard of Patusan?' Jim is now released into the dimension of romance; Marlow explains that he `left his earthly failings behind him ... and there was a totally new set of conditions for his imaginative faculty to work upon' (*LJ*, p. 218). Dealing with the explorer-hero in an exotic setting, the language becomes lush, melodramatic, and essentially formulaic, following the conventions of the adventure fiction made familiar by such writers as Rider Haggard, R.L. Stevenson, Rudyard Kipling, Frederick Marryat, and James Fenimore Cooper. Many critics have commented upon the structural rift between the story of the *Patna* and its consequences and the story of Patusan. This transition from high modernism to popular fiction has been seen as symptomatic of a response to capitalist commodification,[1] as a reversion from epistemological crisis to mythic affirmation,[2] and as a failure in

---

[1] Fredric Jameson, *The Political Unconscious* (London: Methuen, 1981), pp. 206-280.

[2] Daphna Erdinast-Vulcan, *Joseph Conrad and the Modern Temper* (Oxford: Clarendon, 1991), pp. 34-47.

sustained creative engagement.[3] In this article I suggest that the novel's narratives, viewed as dialogical strategies, reveal a complementary design in the *Patna* and Patusan halves: they expose the expansionist aggression of imperialism that is concealed within the discourse of romance.

Scott McCracken has recently argued that Conrad constructs a masculinist discourse which reflects Victorian patriarchy.[4] He suggests that Conrad's style in *Lord Jim* is designed to counter the threat posed by new gender alignments in late nineteenth-century social and literary Britain: [it] `preserves a masculine subjectivity as the dominant perspective amid competing subjectivities' (*HACE*, p. 18). Assuming that the speech-act conveyed in the narrative of *Lord Jim* is not significantly different from the narrative speech-act in *Heart of Darkness* (since in both texts the context is `man to man'), McCracken asserts that `other histories, those of women and those of colonized peoples, are excluded by the containment strategy of the modernist text' (p. 25). He concludes that `Textual hegemony is preserved…through Marlow's narration…as a distinct `essence'…. The text defines subject positions as distinct entities, not as historical constructions' (p. 38). I believe that *Lord Jim*'s self-parodic narrative structure makes all such two-dimensional interpretations impossible to sustain. Padmini Mongia is nearer the mark when she contends that *Lord Jim* asks the question of how one can `separate "romantic" urges from imperialist ones' and asserts that `all understanding is finally conceived of in terms of tropes of imperialism'.[5] It is undeniable that the social and historically concrete context in which Lord Jim's characters interact is that of

---

[3] Ian Watt, *Conrad in the Nineteenth Century* (London: Chatto and Windus, 1980), pp. 305-310; and John Batchelor, *The Edwardian Novelists* (London: Duckworth and Co., 1982), pp. 45-46.

[4] Scott McCracken, `A Hard and Absolute Condition of Existence: Reading Masculinity in *Lord Jim*', *The Conradian*, Vol. 17 (1993), pp. 17-38, hereafter McCracken, *HACE*.

[5] Padmini Mongia, `Narrative Strategy and Imperialism in Conrad's *Lord Jim*', *Studies in the Novel*, 24 (1992), pp. 173-86, p. 179.

late nineteenth-century imperialism. But I believe the divergent voices of the novel's narrative structure, its imagery and recurring motifs, can also be interpreted as subverting the ideology of the coloniser/hero, and exposing the narcissism of the masculinist discourse of romance.

I will attempt to demonstrate a difference between Conrad's authorial and narratorial perspectives, starting with the relationship between what Bakhtin calls *addressivity* and *expressivity*. Using Bakhtin's framework of *double-voiced discourse* to show ironic parallels between the *Patna* and Patusan sections of the novel, I will at the same time suggest that for Conrad as for Bakhtin `images of language are inseparable from images of various world-views and from the living beings who are their agents — people who think, talk, and act in a setting that is social and historically concrete'.[6]

Bakhtin and *Lord Jim*

Bakhtin's ideas on dialogicity when applied to Conrad's complex self-reflexive narrative method help to articulate the formal and ideological aspects of *Lord Jim*. For Bakhtin, the novel and the speaking voice cannot be separated: `The fundamental condition, that which makes the novel a novel...is the *speaking person and his discourse*'.[7] This idea is of great interest for a text that is grounded in speaking and listening. And Bakhtin's insistence on the primacy of the *social* — `The word does not exist in a neutral and impersonal language...but rather it exists in other people's mouths, in other people's contexts, serving other people's intentions' (*DN*, p. 294) — bears on a novel whose epigraph reads `It is certain any

[6] Mikhail Bakhtin, `From the Prehistory of Novelistic Discourse', in *The Dialogic Imagination*, ed. Michael Holquist, tr. Caryl Emerson and Michael Holquist (Austin: University of Texas Press, 1981), hereafter Bakhtin, *DI*; p. 49.

[7] Bakhtin, `Discourse in the Novel', hereafter Bakhtin, *DN*, in *DI*, p. 332.

conviction gains infinitely the moment another soul will believe in it'. Self-identity is only achieved in relation to other individuals: `To be means to be for an other, and through the other, for oneself...I cannot become myself without an other; I must find myself in an other...I receive my name from others'.[8] In *Lord Jim*, Marlow and Jim enact self-authoring and self-authorization in whole chapters of confessional dialogue; `Tuan' Jim receives his name from a people culturally and racially removed from himself.

Bakhtin suggests that the meaning of any utterance depends on three factors. These are

> 1) *the common spatial purview* of the interlocutors...2) *the interlocutors' common knowledge and understanding of the situation*, and 3) their *common evaluation of that situation*.

He adds that `on this "jointly seen"..."jointly known"...and "unanimously evaluated"...the utterance *directly depends*'.[9] The idea that the position of the hearer is as important for the meaning of a message as the position of the speaker raises interesting questions for Marlow's narrative in *Lord Jim*, since his auditors are nameless and voiceless. Marlow's function as narrator in *Lord Jim* is not the same as in *Heart of Darkness*, where the frame auditors are clearly identified fictional characters against whom Marlow defines his own subjectivity. Throughout *Heart of Darkness*, Marlow is able to author himself in contradistinction to ideological Others: the complacent frame auditors, the sycophantic `pilgrims', even the Company for which he works. In *Lord Jim*, by contrast, the speech-act is solipsistic rather than `man to man', suggesting perhaps that the discourse of imperialism is inward-looking and

---

[8] Mikhail Bakhtin, *Problems of Dostoevsky's Poetics* , ed. and tr. Caryl Emerson, with an introd. by Wayne C. Booth (Manchester: Manchester University Press, 1984), pp. 287-288.

[9] Bakhtin, `Discourse in Life and Discourse in Art', quoted in Michael Holquist, *Dialogism: Bakhtin and His World* (London and New York: Routledge, 1990), p. 63.

self-referential. In *Lord Jim*, as far as the reader is concerned, Marlow speaks *to himself*. Furthermore, he speaks *about himself*, since his identity as a British merchant seaman abroad is as much at stake as Jim's. His narrative is therefore as much an act of self-reclamation as of rescuing Jim. It is the very *monologic* register of Marlow's situation as narrator that necessitates the *dialogism* of the novel's overall structure.

The novel, Bakhtin writes, `has no canon of its own. It is, by its very nature, not canonic. It is plasticity itself...ever examining itself and subjecting its established forms to review'.[10] If the inclusion of non-canonical material is aesthetically subversive, if it disrupts received views and recombines categories, it must also be ideologically subversive, casting doubt on values inscribed within canonical forms. If the introspective individualism of the *Patna* is yoked with the garish schoolboy romance of Patusan, Conrad is surely implying that the two halves of the novel are informed by the same values. In its `high culture' and its populist modes, *Lord Jim* demonstrates the attraction for imperialist ideology of the pastoral romance, a genre capable of enacting but concealing contradiction. In this interrogation of the idyll, Conrad is thus close to Bakhtin, for whom the novel's central purpose is to `educate man for life in bourgeois society. This educative process is connected with a severing of all previous ties with the idyllic, that is, it has to do with man's *expatriation*'.[11] Novels teach people how to live in the real world by `overturning and demolishing the world view and psychology of the idyll, which prove[s] increasingly inadequate to the new capitalist world' (*FTCN*, p. 234). On such a reading, *Nostromo* shows that in a world of material interests there is no return to the pre-industrial Eden of the Waterfall valley painted by Emilia Gould. Similarly, *Lord Jim* shows that colonial space does not lend itself to the individual regeneration of the imperial

[10] Bakhtin, `Epic and Novel', hereafter Bakhtin, *EN*, in *DI*, p. 39.
[11] Bakhtin, `Forms of Time and Chronotope in the Novel', hereafter Bakhtin, *FTCN*, in *DI*, p. 234.

adventurer.

The frequent use of bathos and parody is only partly accomodated within the narrator's perspective. Throughout *Lord Jim*, the arrangement of the text continually suggests a separate authorial perspective at work which generates a comedy that is compounded by the narrator's ignorance of this perspective. This narrative device is what Bakhtin terms *double-voiced discourse*, which he defines as

> *another's speech in another's language,* serving to express authorial intentions but in a refracted way.... It serves two speakers at the same time and expresses simultaneously two different intentions: the direct intention of the character who is speaking, and the refracted intention of the author. In such discourse there are two voices, two meanings and two expressions. (*DN*, p. 324)

In the next section, I will try to show the gulf between Marlow's limited perspective and the parodic authorial perspective which governs his narrative.

Double-Voiced Discourse

Double-voiced discourse permeates *Lord Jim's* narrative, undermining not only Marlow's perspective but the entire narrative pattern into which his perspective is inserted. Hillis Miller has argued that the novel's repetition of motifs defeats any notion of an originating event.[12] It is equally demonstrable that no protagonist is unambiguously presented. In the first half of the novel, the French Lieutenant, often seen as an embodiment of the virtues of the seaman's code, enunciates gnomic pronouncements like `There is a point — for the best of us — there is somewhere a point when you let go everything (*vous lachez tout*). And you have got to live

---

[12] J. Hillis Miller, *Fiction and Repetition* (Oxford: Basil Blackwell, 1982), hereafter Miller, *FR*; pp. 22-41, pp. 34-35.

with that truth — do you see?' (*LJ*, p. 146). But he modulates from the oracular to the prosaic when he reminisces about his thirty hours on board the *Patna*, deprived of his customary *vin noble*, or at any rate *vin ordinaire*: `I — you know — when it comes to eating without my glass of wine — I am nowhere' (*LJ*, p. 141). The Frenchman's discourse slips between the heroic and the fussy/fastidious, creating a Hercule-Poirot register which sits oddly with his public image and his sentiments about duty and honour. Marlow reproduces his comments at length, with frequent quotations of the original French phrases supplemented by awkward translations (`one has done one's possible'). If Marlow's interest in Jim is also an interest in salvaging an ideal of conduct, then the French Lieutenant — who quietly did what Jim failed to do — is hardly a figure of fun. Yet Marlow reacts with amusement to the Frenchman's account of Jim's dereliction — `And so that poor young man ran away along with the others':

> I don't know what made me smile: it is the only genuine smile of mine I can remember in connection with Jim's affair. But somehow this simple statement of the matter sounded funny in French.... `S'est enfui avec les autres ....' (*LJ*, p. 145)

The French Lieutenant part of the story, peppered as it is with comic fragments (`*Fort intrigués par ce cadavre*'; `*Impossible de comprendre — vous concevez*'; `*en votre qualité de marin*'; `*drôle de trouvaille*'; `*roulé ma bosse*'; `*parbleu*'; `*un dérangement d'estomac*'; `*L'homme est né poltron*') intrudes itself upon the reader's consciousness. Why does Marlow recount this episode so as to emphasise the comic non-equivalence of Gallic and Anglo-Saxon phrases and sentiments? Perhaps because he cannot resist poking fun at his French imperial rival? Does he resent the fact that a foreigner has proved more courageous than `one of us'? For the reader, however, the episode may ring differently, with the joke as much on Marlow's ethnocentrism as on the lieutenant's eccentricity. The notion of heroism is being parodied as well as celebrated. Conrad is questioning not just the self-congratulation of British imperialism but the entire heroic repertoire of the imperial explorer, whatever his nationality. Here Conrad is close to Bakhtin, for whom the notion of identity as self-coincidence cannot exist in the world of the novel:

> Laughter destroyed epic distance; it began to investigate man freely and familiarly, to turn him inside out, expose the disparity between his surface and his center, between his potential and his reality...man ceased to coincide with himself.... (*EN*, p. 35.)

In the French Lieutenant episode, we hear a chain of voices: the Lieutenant's, filtered through Marlow's narration; Marlow's, half-mocking his rival; Conrad's mocking Marlow's nationalism; and finally, Conrad's mocking the pretensions of a macho ideology.

In the second half of the novel, comic non-coincidence is once again foregrounded in the depiction of Stein. Like the French Lieutenant, Stein has morally weighty things to say. In relation to Jim's romantic temperament he speaks of `the Dream' (*LJ*, p. 215) and `the destructive element' (*LJ*, p. 214), yet his real interest is less in human beings than in butterflies:

> `To tell you the truth, Stein,' I said with an effort that surprised me, `I came here to describe a specimen....' `Butterfly?' he asked, with an unbelieving and humorous eagerness. (*LJ*, pp. 211-212)

What Stein really wants is to achieve fame as an entymologist after his death, and to be left alone in life to enjoy his miraculous museum world:

> `To my small native town this my collection I shall bequeath. Something of me. The best.'
> He bent forward in the chair and gazed intently, his chin over the front of the case. I stood at his back. `Marvellous,' he whispered, and seemed to forget my presence. (*LJ*, p. 205)

The reader shares Marlow's amusement at Stein's innocent vanity, his immersion in a miniature insect empire. Yet Conrad creates in the butterfly image a net of ambiguities far deeper than Marlow perceives: beauty; ephemerality; the classificatory instinct of an age steeped in Darwin. Interestingly, Rider Haggard uses the butterfly image to represent the genre of romance itself:

> In the old days such specimens were perhaps more common.... But then their breeding grounds in the dank tropical marshes or the lion haunted forests were less known, and those who devoted themselves to this chase were few in number and supremely qualified for the business. Now travelling is cheap, hundreds handle the net, and all come home with something that is offered for sale under the ancient label. [13]

Stein, like the French lieutenant, is heroic *and* comic. Above all, he is an imperial adventurer; his butterfly collection suggests both the dream world of solipsistic withdrawal and the destructive element of the imperialist-scientist, who conquers, captures, collects and categorises exotic subjects.

I have suggested that Marlow's narrative, communicated after conversations with Jim to nameless, voiceless, disembodied auditors, draws the reader's attention to qualities of self-enclosure and narcissism. Elaborately framed as dialogue, it is in effect monologue. The discourses of the French lieutenant as an imperial adventurer and Stein as an imperial visionary are auto-referential in the same way. Both suppress the political context in which they operate: the French lieutenant, `*fort intrigué par ce cadavre*', is fascinated by the one white man whose corpse he discovers on the *Patna*, never mentioning the hundreds of abandoned Malaysian pilgrims whom he has rescued; and Stein says nothing about the South Sea trading ventures which have made his fortune. It is

[13] H. Rider Haggard, *The Days of My Life: An Autobiography*, ed. C.J. Longman (Longman and Co., 1926), I, p. 95. See David Bunn, `Embodying Africa: Woman and Romance in Colonial Fiction', *English in Africa*, 15 (1988), pp. 1-28, p. 8.

authorial framing and juxtaposing that restores a political dimension to this discourse of the ostensibly ethical and aesthetic.

Double-voicing is striking in those aspects of Marlow's narration which relate to a cryptic colonial space figured by the explorer/hero. Marlow consistently equates the realm of imagination with the menace of unexplored nature. His suspicion of imagination can of course be explained as a defence of the seaman's values of fidelity, solidarity and restraint, which necessitate obedience. It can equally well be seen as the imperialist's fear of engulfment by alien forces he seeks to control. In Patusan, masculine rationality, restraint and order may be overwhelmed by feminine instinct and chaos. So when Stein answers his own question `how to be?' with the advice that one should `follow the dream, and again...follow the dream — and so — *ewig* — *usque ad finem*....', such escape into fantasy strikes Marlow as fascinating but suspect, tainted with the death wish:

> The whisper of his conviction seemed to open before me a vast and uncertain expanse, as of a crepuscular horizon on a plain at dawn — or was it, perchance, at the coming of the night? One had not the courage to decide; but it was a charming and deceptive light, throwing the impalpable poesy of its dimness over pitfalls — over graves. (*LJ*, p. 215)

We hear Marlow's voice and possibly recognise attitudes that derive from his British imperial background. But behind these is surely another voice: Conrad is warning the reader that this vision is limited by fear of the imagination. Marlow `feminises' Jim by associating him with elements of nature, intuition and unreason, whose attendant is death.

Again, Marlow's situation here is quite different from *Heart of Darkness*, where narrative and authorial perspectives are frequently fused. As Hillis Miller points out, the imagery of light and darkness is as significant in *Lord Jim* as it is in *Heart of Darkness* (*FR*, pp. 37-39). But in the latter, an ironic transposition of `civilisation' with `barbarism', carried through imagery patterns mediated by

Marlow's narration, is totally consistent with the authorial perspective. Consider his opening sentence: `And this also ... has been one of the dark places of the earth' (*HD*, p. 48). In *Lord Jim*, by contrast, the narrative perspective is carefully situated in an ideological context that `places' both frame-narrator and protagonist-narrator while allowing authorial detachment.

Marlow's most impassioned rhetoric occurs in the hymn to England which accompanies his recognition that he, unlike Jim, will be going home:

> We return to face our superiors, our kindred, our friends — those whom we obey, and those whom we love; but even they who have neither...have to meet the spirit that dwells within the land, under its sky, in its air, in its valleys, and on its rises, in its fields, in its waters and its trees — a mute friend, judge, and inspirer. (*LJ*, pp. 221-222)

The fervour here is reminiscent of nineteenth-century missionary narratives. Dedications to Mother Church/Mother Country `most often opened with the passage from civilization to the "regions beyond" the crossing of "the great water"'.[14] Like those narratives, Marlow's creates a secular epiphany which conflates personal salvation with nationalism, and blurs the distinction between knightly quest and mercantile imperialism. What is lacking in this jingoistic register are the multiple ironies of *Heart of Darkness*, where the same trope of chivalric exploration is shown to be inseparable from political conquest and material self-enrichment.

To summarise: in *Lord Jim*, Marlow's perspective can be detached from the authorial perspective in which it is enclosed in the following ways. Bathos and parody intrusively enter into Marlow's narrative, but these characteristics are superfluous to — even inimical to — his narrative project of ethical recuperation.

---

[14] Jean and John Comaroff, *Of Revolution and Revelation: Christianity, Colonialism and Consciousness in South Africa* (Chicago and London: University of Chicago Press, 1991), hereafter Comaroff, *RR*; p. 172.

Marlow's fear of imagination, linked with the feminised depiction of the landscape of Patusan, is symptomatic of a larger anxiety on the part of the coloniser-explorer as he confronts the threat of colonial space. Marlow's expressions of patriotic fervour, which divorce the political from the personal in a religiously-inspired rhetoric, is characteristic of the imperial ideology without which his work in the British merchant marine, and his project as narrator in *Lord Jim*, would be compromised. Finally, Conrad's authorial framing of Marlow's narrative exposes political ironies.

As well as making the reader aware of a specific ideological construction, the fluctuating perspectives revealed in the extracts quoted, taken as a whole, illustrate Bakhtin's contention that:

> The author is not to be found in the language of the narrator, not in the normal literary language to which the story opposes itself (although a given story may be closer to a given language) — but rather, the author utilizes now one language, now another, in order to avoid giving himself up wholly to either of them; he makes use of this verbal give-and-take, this dialogue of languages at every point in his work, in order that he himself might remain as it were neutral with regard to language, a third party in a quarrel between two people (although he might be a *biased* third party.) (*DN*, p. 314)

Race, Class and Trade

If Marlow's narrative is concerned with ethical issues facing the officer class, the absent/present authorial voice for which I argued in the last section repeatedly inserts this discourse into a political context. The realities of race, class and trade in the mercantile imperialism of the late nineteenth century are to be inferred from the silences and contradictions of Marlow's narrative. Where Marlow's narrative represses and is therefore symptomatic of this contradiction, the account of the authorial narrator exposes it. He tells us at the very beginning of the novel that Jim, like `[m]any commanders of fine merchant-ships', has a clergyman father `possessed [of] such certain knowledge of the Unknowable as made for the righteousness of people in cottages without disturbing the ease of mind of those whom an unerring Providence enables to live in mansions' (*LJ*, p. 5). God wills social difference, but in his church all are equal; just as on a ship officers and men have unequal status, but are bound together by a service ethic dictated by nationalism.

The first chapter is given to the authorial narrator. Jim's career is sketched from parsonage beginnings to training-ship apprenticeship to service on the *Patna* and `rehabilitation' in Patusan. Much is made of the story's central anomaly: although Jim's `leap' is endlessly reiterated in Marlow's narrative, the thousand-odd Malaysian pilgrims abandoned in that `leap' are never mentioned. The authorial narrator's perspective, *contra* Marlow's perspective, dismisses Jim's early training-ship daydreaming (`he would forget himself, and beforehand live in his mind the sea-life of light literature' [*LJ*, p. 6]) and celebrates with lyrical intensity the mysterious purpose motivating the `[e]ight hundred men and women…with affections and memories…the unconscious pilgrims of an exacting belief' (*LJ*, p. 14-15), who board the ill-fated *Patna* `urged by faith and the hope of paradise' (*LJ*, p. 14).

The Malaysian pilgrims — subject people of another race and culture — play for Marlow as for Jim purely supportive roles, enabling the exploits of the coloniser-explorer. But this is exposed as ethnocentrism at the official Inquiry by the heroism of the Malay helmsmen, who did *not* leap from the stricken ship when the white officers defected. An invisible underpinning of British justice is counterpointed against a visible apparatus of control in the court-room: what emerges most strikingly in the exchanges between the members of the officer class is their inability to distinguish between ethical values and class solidarity. Jim, obsessively re-enacting the events leading to his dereliction, insists that the *Patna* crew `did not belong to the world of heroic adventure', that he `shared the air they breathed, but he was different' (*LJ*, pp. 24-25). His leap into ignominy is represented as a consequence of class betrayal; had his commanding officers been gentlemen, things would surely have been different.

Class loyalty is at the root of Marlow's anger with Jim: `I was aggrieved against him, as though he had cheated me...of a splendid opportunity to keep up the illusion of my beginnings' (*LJ*, p. 131). Class and racial solidarity reinforce each other. Brierly's agitation at the Inquiry centres not on what Jim has done but on the fact that a white officer is publicly on trial amongst inferior races:

> This infernal publicity is too shocking: there he sits while all these confounded natives, serangs, lascars, quartermasters, are giving evidence that's enough to burn a man to ashes with shame. (*LJ*, p. 67)

`Gentleman' Brown's irruption into Jim's Patusan idyll, with his appeal `You have been white once, for all your tall talk of this being your own people' (*LJ*, p. 381) finds a sure target in Jim's latent racism, and Marlow's horror at Brown's atavistic reversion is registered in his description of the murderous attack on Doramin's people:

> It was not a vulgar and treacherous massacre; it was a lesson, a retribution — a demonstration of some obscure and awful attribute of our nature which, I am afraid, is not so very far under the surface as we like to think. (*LJ*, p. 404)

Yet in one of the novel's central ironies, this account of Brown's treachery is enclosed in the same envelope as the letter to the Privileged Reader in which Marlow confidently alludes to `the truth of ideas racially our own, in whose name are established the order, the morality of an ethical progress' (*LJ*, p. 339).

Marlow's narrative contains but `forgets' Brown's genocide because it must re-establish the `saving illusion' of Britain's capacity for fair play as an imperial power, as reflected in all members of her officer class. There are a number of allusions to trade, without which the colonial venture would collapse. Since Marlow's attitude towards the commercial aspects of trading is contemptuous, he, like Jim, rewrites the story of ships, cargoes, goods and markets into the story of exotic adventure. Marlow's narrative figures Patusan as genuinely `primitive' and prelapsarian, `one of the lost, forgotten, unknown places of the earth' (*LJ*, p. 323). But it also reveals that Patusan has been successfully infiltrated by commercial interests for over two centuries:

> You find the name of the country pretty often in collections of old voyages. The seventeenth-century traders went there for pepper, because the passion for pepper seemed to burn like a flame of love in the breast of Dutch and English adventurers about the time of James the First. Where wouldn't they go for pepper? (*LJ*, p. 226)

Although Western incursions into Patusan are pre-industrial, lacking the mines, plantations, docks, warehouses, factories, refineries, railroads, and banks that accompany the development of `material interests', they nevertheless result in a steady supply of commodities for Europe. They also result in frequent violence:

> Of course the quarrels were for trade. This was the primary cause of faction fights, of the sudden outbreaks that would fill this or that part of the settlement with smoke, flame, the noise of shots and shrieks. (*LJ*, p. 256)

Through both halves of the novel Marlow's narrative is torn by such contradictions. He wishes to believe that being `one of us' — belonging to the right race and class — will guarantee the moral rectitude of the `absolute standard' which justifies imperial domination. But, although Jim is `one of us', his potential for heroism is subverted, both on the *Patna* and in Patusan, by a class antagonism which destroys him; `the truth of ideas racially our own' is undermined, not by the power of its own internal contradiction, but by the atavism of a Brown. The colonial frontiers which beckon the romantic have been invaded by the corruption of commerce — yet this world has been made possible by the activities of the merchant marine service, itself underpinned by codes of behaviour, tradition and belief which play down the importance of trade.

Marlow's narrative is driven by two contradictory impulses: to deny the politics of class- and race-difference by stressing the personal and ethical dimensions of the `fellowship of the craft' in which officers and men work together to administer the Empire; but at the same time to locate the `sovereign power' which legitimates Empire in a social and racial elite. Tanner argues that in *Victory* Conrad destabilises the concept of the gentleman because `for Conrad, there simply aren't any fixed and unalterable lines of demarcation — ethnology provides no basis of morality'.[15] In *Lord Jim* the narrative deployment of double-voiced discourse, together with the ironic juxtaposition of the authorial narrator's account with that of the protagonist narrators, similarly interrogates the category `one of us'. This has particular impact in the imperial context: what is brought into question is the legitimacy of colonial authority and by implication the entire epistemology of class and race.

Conclusion

Drawing on Bakhtin, I have attempted to show that Marlow, in narrating Jim's story, simultaneously narrates his own story, that of an imperial explorer in the late nineteenth century. Woven into this story are elements of `heroic, imperious humanism, and of knowledge-as-discovery' (Comaroff, *RR*, p. 15.) Although Marlow's narrative reflects the hegemony and masculinism to which McCracken alludes, these are repeatedly challenged by the dialogism of the novel's alternative discourses. I believe that failure to register and distinguish these competing voices leads to the kind of misreading of the novel diagnosed by Jakob Lothe: `generalisations about the thematic import of *Lord Jim* are often

---

[15] Tony Tanner, `Joseph Conrad and the Last Gentleman', in Colin McCabe (ed.), *Futures for English* (Manchester: Manchester University Press, 1988), pp. 109-42, p. 116.

based on insufficient consideration of the intrinsic variation of its narrative methods'.[16] Conrad's language anticipates contemporary work in cultural studies: Said's adversarial position in relation to dominant culture is foreshadowed in the anti-hegemonic questioning of the novel's double discourse. Conrad's interrogation of the concept of the `gentleman' similarly prefigures Bhabha's contention that in the colonial encounter the discourse of civility becomes incoherent.[17] And Guha's exposure of the epistemic circularity of liberal historiography is precisely the kind of ideological self-enclosure that Marlow's narcissistic narrative reveals.[18]

The explorer-hero's self-authoring and self-authorisation requires several narratologically incompatible but socially supporting contexts: the `real' world of the British merchant marine and of trade and commerce on the one hand, and the fictional or dream-world of heroic self-fulfillment on the other. The two worlds answer the same desire for mastery, the same enabling context of colonial space. Marlow's masculinist discourse, obsessively foregrounding duty, honour and courage as *ethical* imperatives, is undermined by the authorial voice which suggests instead that these values are *cultural*, tied to class, race and history. Bakhtin is particularly valuable in helping us to understand the subtlety of Conrad. Bakhtin draws attention to the social and historical context of all utterances, suggesting that problems of form are also inevitably problems of ideology. On this reading, then, the structural rift that divides the texts of *Lord Jim*, unsatisfactory as it may be, can be seen to reflect and underscore the paradoxical nature of colonialism and the British empire.

[16] Jakob Lothe, *Conrad's Narrative Method* (Oxford: Clarendon Press, 1989), p. 134.

[17] See Homi Bhabha, `Sly Civility', *October,* 34 (1985), pp. 71-80.

[18] See Ranajit Guha, `Dominance Without Hegemony and its Historiography', *Subaltern Studies*, VI (New Delhi: Oxford University Press, 1989), pp. 210-309.

`TO SEASON WITH A PINCH OF ROMANCE': ETHICS AND POLITICS IN *LORD JIM*

ANDRZEJ GĄSIOREK

Wayne Booth begins *The Company We Keep: An Ethics of Fiction* with a chapter titled `Ethical Criticism, a Banned Discipline?'.[1] But if it is true that ethical criticism was sidelined for much of the seventies and eighties, it has made something of a comeback during the last ten years. A whole spate of articles, books, and symposia debating the complex interrelations between literature and moral thought has appeared since Booth's lament.[2] This body of work has

---

[1] Wayne Booth, *The Company We Keep: An Ethics of Fiction* (Berkeley: California University Press, 1988), hereafter Booth, *CWK*.

[2] The bibliography on this topic is already dauntingly large. In addition to Booth, I list here only the major contributions to the debate: S.L. Goldberg, *Agents and Lives: Moral Thinking in Literature* (Cambridge: Cambridge University Press, 1993), hereafter Goldberg, *AL*; A. Phillips Griffiths (ed.), *Philosophy and Literature: Royal Institute of Philosophy Lecture Series: 16* (Cambridge: Cambridge University Press, 1984); Geoffrey Galt Harpham, *Getting it Right: Language, Literature, and Ethics* (Chicago: Chicago University Press, 1992), hereafter Harpham, *GR*; J. Hillis Miller, *The Ethics of Reading* (New York: Columbia University Press, 1987); Adam Zachary Newton, *Narrative Ethics* (Cambridge, Mass.: Harvard University Press, 1995), hereafter Newton, *NE*; Claire Nouvet (ed.), *Literature and the Ethical Question* (New Haven: Yale University Press, 1991); Martha Nussbaum, *Love's Knowledge: Essays on Philosophy and Literature* (Oxford: Oxford University Press, 1992), hereafter Nussbaum, *LK*; Frank Palmer, *Literature and Moral Understanding: A Philosophical Essay on Ethics, Aesthetics, Education, and Culture* (Oxford: Clarendon, 1992), hereafter Palmer, *LMU*;

(continued...)

sought to re-assert the connection between literature and ethics. At its best, it does not treat literature instrumentally, excavating it for detachable moral *aperçus* or guidelines for the conduct of life, but concentrates on the nuanced ways in which literature explores the opacity of the ethical domain. Central to this work is the contention that ethics relies on narrative and that narrative carries an ethical freight.[3] Critics working within this tradition argue that literature is not moral philosophy's handmaiden but is a mode of ethical discourse in its own right, enacting a kind of moral thinking — concrete, particular, and socially specific — that calls into question the abstract approach of most philosophy.[4]

Ethical critics argue that an ostensibly political criticism which rejects ethical discourse as a form of ideological mystification is itself underpinned by ethical imperatives which it either refuses or is unable to disclose.[5] Whereas political critics contemn ethical critics' tendency to universalise human experience and to scant its social and material features, the latter point to political criticism's blindness to its own ethical norms. Both groups see literature as indispensable to their concerns, but neither can see much of value in the other. Geoffrey Galt Harpham suggests that this is because

[2] (...continued)
David Parker, *Ethics, Theory and the Novel* (Cambridge: Cambridge University Press, 1994), hereafter Parker, *ETN*; Jonathan Ree, *Philosophical Tales: An Essay on Philosophy and Literature* (London: Methuen, 1987); Richard Rorty, *Contingency, Irony, and Solidarity* (Cambridge: Cambridge University Press, 1989); *Symposium on Literature and/as Moral Philosophy* in *New Literary History*, 15.1 (1983), pp. 1-208; *Symposium on Morality and Literature* in *Ethics*, 98.2 (January 1988), pp. 223-341; Leona Toker (ed.), *Commitment in Reflection: Essays in Literature and Moral Philosophy* (New York: Garland, 1994).

[3] See Newton, *NE*; p. 8.

[4] See Nussbaum, *LK*, pp. 3-7; Goldberg, *AL*, p. xv, pp. 286-293; Palmer, *LMU*, p. 204, p. 220, p. 244; Newton, *NE*, pp. 7-8; and Parker, *ETN*, p. 38.

[5] For more on this point see Harpham, *GR*, p. 13; Murray Krieger, `In the Wake of Morality: The Thematic Underside of Recent Theory', *New History*, 15.1 (1983), pp. 119-36; and Parker, *ETN*, p. 4.

the distinction between ethics and politics is both easily drawn and easily erased, precisely because each is defined as the repression of the other, as a certain emphasis occurring in a larger field — call it `justice' — that contains both (Galt Harpham, *GR*, p. 31). Ethical critics acknowledge that politics cannot be ignored, but in practice offer analyses of literary works that rarely attend to the socio-political circumstances in which they were produced, the history of their reception, or their ideological function in the present as component parts of a literary canon.[6] Political critics argue that ethical criticism ignores literature's extra-textual determinants, thereby severing it from history, and conceals its embodiment of social contradictions, thereby occluding its (often unwitting) role as a purveyor of ideology. Fredric Jameson claims that `ethical thought projects as permanent features of human "experience," and thus as a kind of "wisdom" about personal life and interpersonal relations, what are in reality the historical and institutional specifics of a determinate type of group solidarity or class cohesion'. His contention that ethics should be transcended `in the direction of the political and the collective' only serves to underline the face-off between these two approaches.[7]

As far as recent ethical criticism is concerned, Jameson's charge can be justified only up to a point, since few of its practitioners elide politics in such a ham-fisted way, and fewer still indulge in promoting bourgeois norms as universal panaceas. David Parker, for example, calls for `a new evaluative discourse — a discourse inclusive enough to recognise that both political criticism and ethical criticism are essential (though neither is sufficient), and open enough to be the site of dialectical interplay between the two' (Parker, *ETN*, p. 194). Wayne Booth, in turn, argues that ethics and

---

[6] For critics who emphasise the close link between ethics and politics without subsequently exploring it, see Booth, *CWK*, p. 12; Parker, *ETN*; p. 5.

[7] Fredric Jameson, *The Political Unconscious* (Ithaca, N.Y.: Cornell University Press, 1981), hereafter Jameson, *PU*; p. 59, p. 60.

politics are inseparable and calls for an ethical criticism that would be `a rough synonym for what many people would call ideological criticism'.[8] But both writers' work actually falls far short of ideological criticism, since it usually focuses on literature's explorations of moral issues in isolation from any political considerations. Even Parker, who holds out the possibility of dialogue between ethics and politics, erects a *cordon sanitaire* between them when he remarks that `there is no last analysis, merely various different sorts of analysis, all of them more or less illuminating, of which ethical analysis is one and political analysis another' (Parker, *ETN*, p. 5).

The problem with most ethical criticism is not that its assumptions are universalist — they frequently are not — but that its reliance on liberal theories of the self produces an atomistic and ahistorical conception of literature. The literary work is treated as a verbal icon that is hermetically sealed off from other socio-cultural practices; analysis of the work then concentrates on the behaviour of its central protagonists, whose fictional dilemmas are presented as refracted analogues of those faced in real life by the reader.[9] Such criticism is relentlessly individualist in focus, in its conception of both literature and ethics. These two issues are closely connected, since a liberal theory of ethics that takes the human agent as its point of focus melds easily with a view of the literary text as a pre-eminent site for the exploration of that agent's most pressing concerns. This individualist bias is particularly noticeable in Martha Nussbaum's influential work. Nussbaum's

---

[8] Booth, *CWK*, p. 12. Newton acknowledges the link between ethics and politics but deliberately sets out to explore the interpenetration of ethics and literature without reference to politics. See Newton, *NE*, pp. 27-29.

[9] Booth writes that `our best narrative friends introduce us to the practice of subtle, sensitive moral inference, the kind that most moral choices in daily life require of us. The reader comes away . . . emulating *that kind* of moral sensitivity - not so much the sensitivity of any one character . . . but, rather, that of the author who insists that I *see* what these people are doing to each other' (*CWK*, p. 287).

point of departure is the belief that `ethics is the search for a specification of the good life for a human being'.[10] Inherent in this pithy definition is a focus on the individual rather than the collective, on what the good life might be for a single agent rather than for a social group. As an Aristotelian, Nussbaum knows that individuals cannot easily be separated from the *polis*, and her reading of literature acknowledges the social constraints placed on fictional characters. But it is still the case that she directs her attention less to the social nature of human life than to the sensitivity with which particular characters try to make sense of, and chart their way through, the moral dimension of their lives. Cora Diamond may be right to claim that literature's capacity to evoke `texture of being' suggests that `moral reflection may be directed not just towards individual human beings but towards forms of social life', but this claim remains largely unexplored in ethical criticism.[11] Literature is cut off from a host of alternative social and political questions. The result is an ahistorical criticism that not only analyses moral issues immanently in terms of their internal treatment by literary texts, thereby effacing these texts' social provenance, but also sees these issues solely in terms of their impact on the individual, thereby ignoring their social aetiology and their ongoing social relevance. Galt Harpham eloquently describes the consequences of such a bias: `The deeply sedimented and traditional practices of everyday life, the longer durations of the events of communal history, the phenomenon of group or mob behavior, the circumstances of a class, social group, race, or religion — all become crushed into the "ethical moment" when an individual confronts a choice and makes a decision' (*GR*, p. 11).

What is missing from ethical criticism is any grasp of the fact that fictional worlds are just as much socially constituted as the

[10] Martha Nussbaum, `Flawed Crystals: James's *The Golden Bowl* and Literature as Moral Philosophy', in *Love's Knowledge*, pp. 125-147, p. 139.
[11] Cora Diamond, `Having a Rough Story About What Moral Philosophy Is', *New Literary History*, 15.1 (1983), pp. 155-69, p. 163.

literary texts in which they are articulated. Such criticism only gestures towards the idea that literary texts are social acts, that they are written at specifiable historical moments and in particular social circumstances. Once the necessary caveats about the relationship between text and context have been put in, the `real' business of criticism turns out to have nothing to do with exploring that relationship in anything but a perfunctory way. How could it be otherwise, if the critic remains in thrall to a text/context paradigm? Insofar as criticism sees the literary `text' as belonging to a `context', it will always construe the `social' as extraneous to the `literary' and will never grasp the multiple ways in which the text is everywhere socially inscribed. As a public act, an intervention in the concerns and debates of its day, the literary text is a cultural practice among other such practices and is socially constituted through and through. To write a criticism that explores the ethical horizons projected in a literary work's fictional world without at the same time exploring how that world and its horizons are bounded by particular — if enormously overdetermined — social forces is to miss just how deeply that work participates in a form of life. The very framework within which a given work articulates its understanding of the ethical domain and its sense of that domain's lacunae and aporias is inextricable from the social form of life in which it was elaborated.[12] The ethics of a literary work, in short, can be treated neither in an individualist nor in a universalist fashion — both the ethics projected by a literary work and the work itself are bounded by inescapable social horizons.

Conrad criticism tends to replicate the dichotomy between ethics

---

[12] As D.Z. Phillips argues, `if we want to appreciate the ways in which moral considerations can be constitutive of a person's perspective, it is important not to think of morality as the agent's guide in choosing between alternative courses of action.... The moral possibilities expressed in his perspective are not self-generated...but are given in the language available to him in his culture'. See his `The Presumption of Theory' in Raimond Gaita (ed.), *Value and Understanding: Essays for Peter Winch* (London: Routledge, 1990), pp. 216-242, p. 222.

and politics. Critics who focus on the moral dimension of Conrad's fiction ignore its political resonances and social concreteness.[13] Political critics, in turn, have read this work in a historicist way, exploring its ideological ramifications. But in their hurry to expose the ahistorical nature of most accounts of Conradian ethics, they tend to reject any serious analysis of ethics, seeing the moral questions that Conrad raises as little more than a rhetorical smokescreen for the political contradictions at the heart of his writing.[14] Michael Sprinker is in my view right to assert that *Lord Jim* is `not just about a universal moral predicament...but about the particular situation of the British imperial administrative class, which was entering its moment of prolonged crisis', but he is wrong to conclude from this that if a universalist reading is rejected then politics must supersede ethics.[15] By so arguing, he ignores the enormously complicated and subtle way in which Conrad weaves

[13] See G.H. Bantock, `The Two "Moralities" of Joseph Conrad', *Essays in Criticism*, 3.2 (April, 1953), pp. 124-42; Christopher Cooper, *Conrad and the Human Dilemma* (New York: Barnes and Noble, 1970); R. A. Gekoski, *Conrad: The Moral World of the Novelist* (London: Elek, 1978); J. Hillis Miller, *Poets Of Reality: Six Twentieth-Century Writers* (Cambridge, Mass.: Harvard University Press, 1966); F.R. Leavis, *The Great Tradition: George Eliot, Henry James, Joseph Conrad* (London: Chatto and Windus, 1948); Newton, *NE*, pp. 73-103; and Ralph Rader, `*Lord Jim* and the Formal Development of the English Novel', in James Phelan (ed.), *Reading Narrative: Form, Ethics, Ideology* (Columbus: Ohio State University Press, 1989), hereafter Phelan, *RN*; pp. 220-235. An interesting attempt to read Conrad in relation to late nineteenth-century utilitarian and associationist psychology is provided in John E. Saveson, *Joseph Conrad: The Making of a Moralist* (Amsterdam: Rodopi, 1972).

[14] See especially Jacques Darras, *Conrad and the West: Signs of Empire*, tr. Anne Luyat and Jacques Darras (London: Macmillan, 1982); Terry Eagleton, *Criticism and Ideology: A Study in Marxist Literary Theory* (London: Verso, 1976), pp. 130-140; Jameson, *PU*; Benita Parry, *Conrad and Imperialism* (London: Macmillan, 1983); and Michael Sprinker, `Fiction and Ideology: *Lord Jim* and the Problem of Literary History', hereafter Sprinker, *FI*, in Phelan, *RN*, pp. 236-249.

[15] Sprinker, *FI*, pp. 244-45.

ethics and politics together in *Lord Jim*.

I want in this article to refuse this dichotomy between ethics and politics in Conrad criticism. I shall offer a reading of *Lord Jim* that shows how these two discourses are so tightly linked in this novel that interpretations of it which focus on either dimension to the exclusion of the other skew the nature of its intervention in turn-of-the-century debates about imperialism, masculinity, and morality. My argument follows two tracks: first, I want to show that Marlow's often contradictory views are not meant to be taken as authoritative and that his hermeneutic activity is eventually subordinated to the text's embrace of perspectivalism; second, I want to argue that the text undermines Marlow's focus on ethics by disclosing how the particular moral code to which he and Jim give their allegiance is inseparable from the politics of imperialism. In what follows, I concentrate initially on Marlow's function as narrator and on his ethical scepticism in order to suggest that analysis needs to go beyond these concerns and to take into account the care with which Conrad connects them to political issues.[16] I then discuss late nineteenth-century imperialism, focusing on the crucial role played by public schools in inculcating its ideology and arguing that their aim of turning boys into `gentlemen' was motivated by political considerations. Having established this, I focus on Jim in order to argue that the novel's emphasis on his status as a `gentleman', as `one of us', and as a young male modelling his behaviour on that of characters from popular adventure stories marks him out as a typical empire boy.[17] I contend that Jim's self-understanding is that of the imperial subject *par*

[16] It is a commonplace that Marlow is not to be taken as Conrad's spokesman, but no critic has to my knowledge argued that the consequence of this with respect to *Lord Jim* is that Marlow's concern with ethics is qualified by the text's deeper understanding of the role ethics played in the political realm.

[17] The phrase is taken from Joseph Bristow's *Empire Boys: Adventures in a Man's World* (London: Harper Collins Academic, 1991), hereafter Bristow, *EB*.

excellence and that such a subject's belief in the myths of the adventure tradition is satirised as a debilitating fantasy (the *Patna*) and shown to have devastating consequences when put into practice (Patusan).[18]

Jim's character and history are mediated through Marlow's narration, a narration that draws attention to its own inadequacy as a reliable discourse. Marlow displaces Jim from the centre of the narrative partly because Jim's story gains its meaning from its relevance to Marlow's own concerns and partly because he foregrounds his active role as its hermeneut. The story becomes, in one sense, *Marlow's* story: `He existed for me, and after all it is only through me that he exists for you. I've led him out by the hand; I have paraded him before you' (*LJ*, p. 224). Marlow's interest in Jim is driven by the latter's ostensible membership of Marlow's own social caste and by the fact that he reminds Marlow of himself as a young man (*LJ*, p. 128). The novel is also about Marlow in that Jim becomes a test-case for Marlow's doubts, doubts that Jim is too obtuse to entertain. The discrepancy between Jim's appearance (as `one of us') and his actions on the *Patna* reveal `depths of horror' (*LJ*, p, 45) to Marlow, since it leads him to consider that his own honourable appearance may be as much a sham as Jim's. Jim's jump from the *Patna* cheats Marlow `of a splendid opportunity to keep up the illusion of [his] beginnings' (*LJ*, p. 131), forcing him to acknowledge that whereas Jim seems to be the `criminal' while he is `the irreproachable man' (*LJ*, p. 153), the truth is more complex: `it seemed to me that the less I understood the more I was bound to him in the name of that doubt which is the inseparable part of our knowledge. I did not know so much more about myself' (*LJ*, p. 221).

---

[18] Andrea White's invaluable *Joseph Conrad and the Adventure Tradition: Constructing and Deconstructing the Imperial Subject* (Cambridge: Cambridge University Press, 1993), hereafter White, *JC*, discusses *Lord Jim* only in passing.

Marlow identifies with Jim on a personal level, but he also sees him as symbolic in a deeper way. The *Patna* incident and Jim's attitude to it get hold of Marlow `as though he had been an individual in the forefront of his kind, as if the obscure truth involved were momentous enough to affect mankind's conception of itself' (*LJ*, p. 93). But what is `momentous' about Jim's case is in my view not that it reaffirms the Fall in secular language but that it exposes the cracks in an ethical system based on `fidelity to a certain standard of conduct' (*LJ*, p. 50). Jim's act of betrayal disturbs Marlow because it opens up the possibility that their code is contingent and arbitrary. Jim can be pronounced `guilty' by a court of law, but for Marlow this is irrelevant since jurisprudence establishes `not the fundamental why, but the superficial how' (*LJ*, p. 56) of the *Patna* affair. Marlow's interest lies deeper. He wants to exorcise his fear that his ethical code has no ontological basis and is therefore only contingently binding: `I see well enough now that I hoped for the impossible — for the laying of what is the most obstinate ghost of man's creation, of the uneasy doubt uprising like a mist, secret and gnawing like a worm, and more chilling than the certitude of death — the doubt of the sovereign power enthroned in a fixed standard of conduct' (*LJ*, p. 50). Marlow confronts two paradoxes throughout the novel: he believes in a rule-governed code of conduct that should guide human action but, at the same time, he accepts the suasiveness of an agent-based ethics which takes motives into account and thus threatens to overturn the code he wants to uphold; he also believes that there are `a few simple notions you must cling to if you want to live decently and would like to die easy!' (*LJ*, p. 43), but at the same time recognises that these have no ontological basis, acknowledging that he has had `to look at the convention that lurks in all truth' (*LJ*, p. 93). Jim's case brings him face to face with both paradoxes. It encourages him to acquiesce in a full-blown conventionalism and to abandon the `few simple notions' of conduct-morality in favour of an extreme version of situation ethics. As Marlow admits, in grappling with Jim's case he risks `being circumvented, blinded, decoyed, bullied, perhaps, into taking a definite part in a dispute impossible of decision if one had to be fair to all the phantoms in possession' (*LJ*, p. 93).

Marlow may find it impossible to judge Jim, but the latter does not escape his narrator's censure altogether. Marlow seems to conclude that Jim cannot be condemned by the moral code that his actions have called into question partly because a contingently established set of rules cannot be finally binding and partly because any such set fails adequately to account for motives. In order to understand Jim, Marlow focuses on his motives rather than on his actions, but in doing so finds himself confronting Jim's exalted aspirations and romantic idealism. Marlow's probing reveals Jim to be driven by a curious kind of self-love. Locked into his high-minded conception of himself, Jim never grasps the implications of his actions on the *Patna*. He focuses in conversation with Marlow not on the people he left to die but on the missed opportunity to make a name for himself, and he views Patusan as a chance to expunge the past because it will allow him to `begin with a clean slate' (*LJ*, p. 185). Marlow understands the link between Jim's moral myopia and the crass values of the adventure tradition and distances himself from both: `I could see in his glance...all his inner being carried on, projected headlong into the fanciful realm of recklessly heroic aspirations.... He was very far away from me who watched him across three feet of space. With every instant he was penetrating deeper into the impossible world of romantic achievements' (*LJ*, p. 83).

Marlow suggests that one way of seeing Jim is as an exalted egoist who aspires to be a romantic hero. But Marlow is not the novel's spokesman. He is, for one thing, a character within the diegesis as well as a (frequently bewildered) narrator. Nor is he a disinterested character, as he himself admits. His interest in Jim is from the outset acutely personal, since Jim belongs to his own social group, reminds him of the now lost illusions of his youth, and represents the collapse of the values he has all his life sought to uphold. Above all, Marlow adopts a perspectival approach to his hermeneutic task, not only foregrounding his own confusion but also canvassing as many opinions on the case as he can. *Lord Jim* is, as a result, a dialogic and recursive text, which refuses to adopt any single viewpoint as authoritative and which returns in different ways to the dilemmas it poses. It also functions by a series of displacements. Its title signals that its principal subject is Jim; it then displaces Jim by highlighting Marlow's hermeneutic function, suggesting that his *interpretation* of Jim's story is more significant than the story as such; it finally displaces Marlow by folding his perspectival account into its embrace of indeterminacy. When the novel is looked at in this way it becomes clear that it is not about ethical doubt alone. *Marlow* is concerned with ethical questions but Marlow, as well as himself being `one of us', is the modernist reverse of the trustworthy omniscient narrator. The text discloses that his understanding is limited and that he, Jim, and their moral code are the products of determinate socio-historical conditions. Jim's perplexing story and Marlow's investigative narrative are component parts of a text that raises profounder questions about the interpenetration of ethics and politics in these conditions than either of these characters is aware. The text shows that their concern with ethics is in fact inseparable from the politics of imperialism.

The history of Victorian imperialism is long and complex. But if I am right that Jim's character and predicament are inseparable from the milieu in which imperialism was hatched and nurtured then this history cannot be ignored when we examine Jim's role in this text. I want to argue that key tenets of late nineteenth-century imperial discourse are relevant to *Lord Jim*, most notably the ethico-political strain that ran through all justifications of empire and that played a defining role in the social construction of the gentleman in Victorian public schools. This strain also found a congenial home in the adventure novels and romances of the period, whose didactic purpose was to inculcate in their male readers the values of imperialism and the worth of a robust masculinity. When *Lord Jim* is seen in the light of Victorian defences of imperialism and the popular literature that gave them imaginative form, it can be seen to collude in imperial ideology less than political critics have hitherto allowed.[19]

Since it was first coined, the word `imperialism' has changed its meaning a number of times.[20] It carried negative connotations in England for many years because it was associated with Napoleon Bonaparte and therefore suggested a despotic Caesarism. It had lost these connotations by the time Gladstone and Disraeli were fighting their battles over the nature of England's foreign policy in the eighteen-seventies. But the debate over what Gladstone in 1878 called `England's mission' was intense. Whereas Disraeli presided over an expansionist policy, Gladstone defended a policy of retrenchment.[21] According to Koebner and Schmidt, the word `imperialism' was `an anti-Disraeli slogan' at this time (Koebner

[19] For those critics who consider Conrad's work to be either ambivalent towards or indeed critical of imperialism, see John A. McClure, *Kipling and Conrad: The Colonial Fiction* (Cambridge, Mass.: Harvard University Press, 1981), hereafter McClure, *KC*; and Stephen Zelnick, `Conrad's *Lord Jim*: Meditations on the Other Hemisphere', *The Minnesota Review*, 11 (1978), pp. 73-89. Neither of these critics discusses Conrad's careful linking of imperialist politics with a justificatory ethical discourse.

[20] For a full discussion of the word's semantic career, see Richard Koebner and Helmut Dan Schmidt, *Imperialism: The Story and Significance of a Political Word, 1840-1960* (Cambridge: Cambridge University Press, 1964), hereafter Koebner and Schmidt, *I*.

[21] Gladstone's views were laid out in `England's Mission', *The Nineteenth Century*, 4 (1878), pp. 560-84, and then robustly defended during the Midlothian campaign of 1880. C.C. Eldridge claims that Disraeli contributed to the imperial idea by providing `a new vision of an expanding, militant empire which was often linked with an undemocratic and illiberal spirit glorifying British achievements and rule overseas'. See his *England's Mission: The Imperial Idea in the Age of Gladstone and Disraeli, 1868-1880* (London: Macmillan, 1973), hereafter Eldridge, *EM*; p. 232. An alternative position is defended by Richard Shannon, who questions whether 1870 can be seen as a watershed in the history of the English empire, and rejects the long-held view that Disraeli was the originator of a new analysis of or approach to imperialism. See his *The Crisis of Imperialism 1865-1915* (London: Hart-Davis, Macgibbon, 1974), p. 41.

and Schmidt, *I*, p. 134). But by the late eighteen-eighties imperialism no longer carried a negative or anti-Disraeli freight and by the eighteen-nineties (at least up to the outbreak of the Boer War) the empire had become a source of national pride.[22] Almost all defences of imperialism in this period combine ethical and political rhetoric in order to stress that its promotion of English interests is inseparable from the benefits it confers on subject peoples. Those who sought to justify imperialism argued again and again that it was motivated not by a grasping after wealth or territory but by a desire to use trade to civilise, Christianise, and introduce good government. The Earl of Carnarvon, speaking of the colonies in 1878, clearly saw the matter in this way: `To them it is our part to give wise laws, good government, and a well ordered finance, which is the foundation of good things in human communities; it is ours to supply them with a system where the humblest may enjoy freedom from oppression and wrong equally with the greatest; where the light of religion and morality can penetrate into the darkest dwelling places. This is the real fulfilment of our duties; this, again, I say, is the true strength and meaning of imperialism'.[23] Twenty years later, J. Lawson Walton described English imperialism in similar terms. He argued that it comprised four elements: the emotion of pride in an imperial heritage seen as a sacred trust; the conviction that imperialism is educationally and morally good both for the colonies and for England; the determination to accept the burden of administering and defending the empire; and belief in the creed that the English race is sufficiently strong and resourceful to bear its imperial tasks. For Lawson Walton, the imperialist holds that `the spread of British rule extends to every race brought within its sphere the incalculable

---

[22] There were, of course, exceptions. The most notable among intellectuals were the Radical John Morley and the New Liberals of the 1890s such as L.T. Hobhouse, C.F.G. Masterman, J.L. Hammond and J.A. Hobson.

[23] Earl of Carnarvon, `Imperial Administration', *Fortnightly Review*, 30 (1878), pp. 751-764, p. 764.

benefits of just law, tolerant trade, and considerate government'.[24] Joseph Chamberlain's imperial policy was based on identical sentiments. Imperialism could only be justified, he argued, if it brought `security and peace and comparative prosperity to countries that never knew these blessings before. In carrying out this work of civilisation we are fulfilling what I believe to be our national mission'.[25]

It is apparent from the kind of language used by nineteenth-century imperialists just how deeply ethical and political considerations connect here. Those who wished to evade the imputation that English political intervention abroad was based solely on the promotion of English interests (the charge Gladstone raised against Disraeli) almost always justified it on ethical grounds. Lawson Walton is even explicit about the inseparability of these two discourses, pointing out that in `the opinion of our day the sphere of "morality touched with feeling" and the sphere of political philosophy overlap and cover common ground' (Lawson Walton, *I*, p. 306). This overlap is evident in the composite picture that emerges from analysis of the numerous defences of empire in the period. Imperial discourse dissociates the empire from the taint of both despotism and economic greed; it portrays the empire as the means by which the benefits of civilisation — peace, prosperity, democratic government, social order, and Christianity — are brought to the benighted of the earth; above all, imperialism is sanctioned by racial superiority and a benevolent Providence that directs the English to pass on their values, through conquest if need be, to the world's less fortunate peoples. The historian W. Locke, writing in 1878, could claim: `God has wonderfully blessed England, though but a speck on this earth; He has made its people known over the whole world for wisdom and just dealing, and has given it sovereign domination in almost every part of the globe, so

---

[24] J. Lawson Walton, `Imperialism', *Contemporary Review*, 75 (1899), pp. 305-310, hereafter Lawson Walton, *I*; p. 306.
[25] Quoted in Eldridge, *EM*, p. 254.

that the sun always shines on some part that belongs to us'.[26] Imperialism is a duty, an honour, and an (at times) onerous burden that must be borne uncomplainingly for the greater good. That the empire is closely bound up with economic gain is nothing to be ashamed of, partly because trade and commerce aid both coloniser and colonised and partly because they are the spearhead of the civilising and christianising mission that follows in their wake.[27] In short, if the empire had become a source of pride to many in the late nineteenth century this is precisely because imperial discourse successfully translated political and economic activity abroad into the language of ethics.[28] In doing so, it sought to detach the empire from any notion of exploitation or mercenary gain, portraying it as a sacred mission that incurred moral obligations, combined economic development with civilising ardour, and tied all this in to an English version of manifest destiny.[29]

A variety of interlocking and mutually reinforcing cultural practices helped to sustain imperial discourse and to educate young men in its central presuppositions. Historians and cultural critics have argued that the role of public schools and didactic popular

[26] W. Locke, *Stories of the Land We Live In* (London, 1878), p. 5.

[27] Patrick Brantlinger points out that for `writers as various as Macaulay, Carlyle, Martineau, and Dickens, free trade was the dawn that would bring the full light of day to the dark places of the world'. See his *Rule of Darkness: British Literature and Imperialism, 1830-1914* (Ithaca: Cornell University Press, 1988), hereafter Brantlinger, *RD*; p. 32.

[28] For a useful discussion of the way that the empire was promoted by professional historians at the turn of the century, see the discussion of the Imperial Studies Movement in J.G. Greenlee, `"A Succession of Seeleys": The "Old School" Reexamined', *The Journal of Imperial and Commonwealth History*, 4.2 (April 1976), pp. 266-282.

[29] Richard Faber argues that imperialism's defenders saw the English as somehow `more moral' than other races, presenting the English as `firmer, less excitable, juster, more humane, more practical and reliable'. See his *The Vision and the Need: Late Victorian Imperialist Aims* (London: Faber and Faber, 1966), p. 122. For more on this point, see Koebner and Schmidt, *I*, pp. 210-211; and Eldridge, *England's Mission*, pp. 241-42.

literature aimed at adolescents was particularly significant in this respect. Public schools fostered the code of the `gentleman' by emphasising such values as honesty, fair play, duty, group solidarity, and chivalry to the opposite sex; encouraged patriotism by teaching Whiggish versions of English history and its recent acquisition of empire; prepared boys for service overseas by instilling in them belief in the virtues of a rigid masculine identity and teaching them that because of this identity they were especially fitted to take up the white man's burden; and inculcated in them a profound faith in the beneficence of the empire.[30] J. Lawson Walton put forward a typical ruling-class view of the matter: `Our public schools, "the playing fields of Eton," can furnish an unstinted supply of youth with the stuff out of which great administrators are made; men who will bear their powers and dignities meekly, who will be ever ready to sacrifice self to duty, and whose one effort will be to govern with a single eye to the good of the population committed to their charge' (Lawson Walton, *I*, p. 308). Bishop Welldon, headmaster of Harrow between 1885 and 1898, claimed that public schools educated the greater part of England's governing class and argued that this education was the cornerstone of English imperialism: `One who has received the education of an English gentleman will not wholly fail, however tight the place may be in which he finds himself.... When he is put down in the face of duty...he will know what to do, and he will do it. It is this reserve power lying hidden in the British race which is, I think, the hope of the Empire'.[31]

For my purposes, something else is equally significant here. It

---

[30] See A.P. Thornton, *The Imperial Idea and its Enemies: A Study in British Power* (London: Macmillan, 1985), pp. 89-94; W.J. Reader, *At Duty's Call: A Study in Obsolete Patriotism* (Manchester: Manchester University Press, 1988), hereafter Reader, *ADC*; pp. 86-99; Mark Girouard, *The Return to Camelot: Chivalry and the English Gentleman* (New Haven: Yale University Press, 1981), hereafter Girouard, *RC*; pp. 164-170.

[31] Bishop Welldon, `The Training of an English Gentleman in the Public Schools', *The Nineteenth Century*, 60 (1906), pp. 396-413, p. 410.

is noticeable that in this period, as Welldon emphasises, the public school is increasingly seen as the means by which boys of relatively humble background may be turned into gentlemen. The boy need not be a gentleman by birth; it is by virtue of the education he receives that he will *become* one. This denotes a shift from an older conception of the gentleman based on heredity and blood to a newer one based on socialization and subsequent proof of merit. The gentleman is now marked out more by his moral character and education than by his birth. W.J. Reader claims that the late nineteenth-century gentleman was `expected to observe exacting standards of personal conduct, particularly in matters of truth, honesty, and the performance of duty', and his role was to `provide leadership, to command and to govern' (Reader, *ADC*, p. 96). Mark Girouard argues that the Victorian gentleman was a deliberate social construct created to `produce a new model for the ruling classes, to train, in fact, an elite'. For Girouard, central to this training process was the chivalric ideal, which was resurrected in public schools because it could establish a code of conduct and also make it compelling through its link to a romantic view of the past. Ethics was wheeled in to serve politics: `The aim of the revival of the chivalric tradition was to produce a ruling class which deserved to rule because it possessed the moral qualities necessary to rulers. Gentlemen were to run the country because they were morally superior' (*RC*, p. 260, p. 261). Upward social mobility was the result, allowing boys from middle-class homes not just to aspire to gentlemanly status but to assert that they had attained it, since they too were helping to run the country and to administer the empire.

The relevance of all this to the character of Jim should be obvious, for no account of him as a moral protagonist can be persuasive if it ignores the clues we are given to his class position and his place in a given social economy. The novel clearly portrays him as a late nineteenth-century imperial subject of the gentlemanly type created in the public schools. Numerous aspects of the novel signal this: his physical appearance — boyish, fair, stocky — which is exactly that of countless adventure story heroes; his characteristic locutions (`Jove!', `bally ass', `You are a brick!', `beastly shame', `Honour bright!'); his conception of duty and his shame at his failure to fulfil it; his preference for the immaculate white clothing favoured by colonial administrators; and his conformity to the model of masculinity provided by Victorian public schools and codified in adventure novels and romances.[32] The clearest pointers, however, are Jim's view of himself as a `gentleman' — which is borne out both by those who identify with him and by those of lower class origin who hold him in contempt — and Marlow's persistent use of the phrase `one of us'.[33]

Jim's class background is respectable but humble; his father is a country parson with a living that `had belonged to the family for generations' (*LJ*, p. 5). His defensive sense of himself as a gentleman strongly suggests that he is a product of the public school system.[34] As he self-consciously remarks to Marlow: `"Of course I wouldn't have talked to you about all this if you had not been a

---

[32] These exclamations occur on pp. 183-184, 233, 269. References to Jim as a `gentleman' abound - see pp. 10, 67, 117, 131 and 190. The phrase `one of us' has a variety of connotations; I discuss it in more detail later.

[33] The chief of the *Patna*, who despises Jim for refusing to help in the escape from the steamer, says of him: `"You're a fine sort! Too much of a bloomin' gentleman to put his hand to it"' (*LJ*, p. 117). Later, when Jim is working for Egström and Blake, the *Patna*'s second engineer turns up, making sly appeals to Jim's largesse: `"Don't you be uneasy, sir," he says. "I know a gentleman when I see one, and I know how a gentleman feels. I hope, though, you will be keeping me on this job"' (*LJ*, p. 190).

[34] The debate about the efficacy and value of public school education was already well under way by the eighteen-nineties. Critics of the schools argued that their post-Arnoldian emphasis on sports and games was dangerously narrow and complained that they were churning out too many `gentlemen' for whom no decent occupations could subsequently be found. One critic pointed out that, before Arnold's tenure at Rugby, gentlemen came from the upper or upper middle classes but now, alas, `the middle class receives a Public School education, and we have a generation of young gentlemen out of all numerical proportion to the general increase of our population'. See S. H. Jeyes, `Our Gentlemanly Failures', *Fortnightly Review*, 61 (1897), pp. 387-398, p. 388.

gentleman.... I am — I am — a gentleman, too...."' (*LJ*, p. 131).
Jim's status as a gentleman sheds light on the meaning of the phrase
`one of us'. This much-discussed phrase has a wide range of
connotations, all amply supported by the text, but I want to focus
on its class and racial resonances.[35] Jim appears to be `one of us'
to characters such as Marlow and Brierly because he is an
Englishman who represents the values of a particular social group,
a group that at all times distances itself not only from the self-
serving behaviour of mercenary whites (the *Patna* skipper, Chester,
Robinson, Cornelius, Brown) but also from all non-Europeans.
Indeed, the plot of *Lord Jim* turns on the commitment Jim has to his
code of honour and on his inability to live down his betrayal of it.
Why should a single act of cowardice, which is understood (if not
condoned) by figures such as Marlow, Brierly, the French
lieutenant, and Stein, so burden Jim? And why should Marlow (as
well as the apparently impeccable Brierly) be so concerned with the
implications of Jim's act and his subsequent fate? It is not simply
because Jim has betrayed a shared code of conduct but because part
of that code's function is to signal white racial superiority and
therefore to justify the imperial presence. Brierly's disgust with Jim
for refusing to run is clearly motivated by racial considerations:
`"This infernal publicity is too shocking: there he sits while all
these confounded natives, serangs, lascars, quartermasters, are
giving evidence that's enough to burn a man to ashes with shame"'
(*LJ*, p. 67). The shame lies not so much in the act of cowardice on
the *Patna* as in the public exposure of a white man's fallibility to

---

[35] For Cedric Watts, the phrase `means variously: "a fellow-gentleman",
"a white gentleman", "a white man", "a good seaman", "an outwardly-honest
Englishman", "an ordinary person" and "a fellow human being"'. See *Lord
Jim* (Harmondsworth: Penguin, 1989), p. 354. For further discussion of this
issue, see also Robert F. Lee, *Conrad's Colonialism* (The Hague: Mouton,
1969) pp. 35-36; D.C.R.A. Goonetilleke, *Joseph Conrad: Beyond Culture
and Background* (London: Macmillan, 1990), pp. 23-24; and Jeremy
Hawthorn, *Joseph Conrad: Language and Fictional Self-Consciousness*
(London: Edward Arnold, 1979), hereafter Hawthorn, *JC*; pp. 41-42.

the potentially critical gaze of those he is meant to rule. It is *appearances* that are important to Brierly. The racial implications of the us/them distinction are clearer still in two other instances. First, when Dain Waris, despite his valour, is said to lack `Jim's racial prestige' because `he was still one of *them*, while Jim was one of *us*' (*LJ*, p. 361). Second, when Marlow's `privileged man' (*LJ*, p. 337) asserts the classic imperial view: `You said...that "giving your life up to them" (*them* meaning all of mankind with skins brown, yellow, or black in colour) "was like selling your soul to a brute." You contended that "that kind of thing" was only endurable and enduring when based on a firm conviction in the truth of ideas racially our own, in whose name are established the order, the morality of an ethical progress' (*LJ*, p. 339). To belong to `us' in the context of this novel is emphatically not to belong to 'them' — it is to have behind you the racial prestige of whiteness, the class status of education, and the political power of imperialism. It is to be, in the nineteenth-century sense of the word, a gentleman.

The chivalric code that was so integral to the Victorian ideology of the gentleman was greatly aided in its promotion of that ideology by its association with the literature and history (however heavily mythologised) of England. Popular literature for boys played a significant role in imperial discourse because it buttressed the educational program that was being carried out more formally in the public schools. Critics have demonstrated a close link between the adventure tradition and the ideology of imperialism, showing that writers such as Frederick Marryatt, Richard Dana, Gordon Stables, G.W. Henty, W.G.H. Kingston, and R.W. Ballantyne contributed to the social construction of a male imperial identity.[36] Such stories

---

[36] See Brantlinger, *RD*; J.S. Bratton, *The Impact of Victorian Children's Fiction* (London: Croom Helm, 1981), and `Of England, Home and Duty: The Image of England in Victorian and Edwardian Juvenile Fiction', hereafter Bratton, *EHD*, in John MacKenzie, (ed.) *Imperialism and Popular Culture*

(continued...)

should be seen as *constitutive* of this identity, as Robert H. Macdonald notes: `The intended readers of the historical romances were boys, who were not just instructed how to behave, but were told, both directly and by example, who they were'.[37] These novels sweeten the didactic pill with romance. They teach by example, inviting their readers to identify with heroic figures, but they portray these figures in a way calculated to appeal to the romantic imagination. The adventurous spirit, which is seen as definitive of English national identity, is central to their combination of exemplary virtue and romance. W.H. Davenport Adams, who wrote numerous popular books extolling the English and their empire, sounds the keynote in his epigraph to *`In Perils Oft': Romantic Biographies Illustrative of the Adventurous Life*: `England was made by Adventurers, not by its Government; and I believe it will only hold its place by Adventurers'.[38] The ideology of adventure is didactic. It promotes clearly defined imperial values such as the inherent superiority of whites to all `natives', class and racial loyalty, the importance of trade to the civilising mission, and the necessity of converting colonised peoples to Christianity.[39] Once again, ethics and politics intersect. The adventure tradition justifies and encourages political acts by recourse to an ethical discourse that portrays them as benevolent, disinterested, and providential. It also

---

[36] (...continued)
(Manchester: Manchester UP, 1986), pp. 74-93; Bristow, *EB*; Patrick A. Dunae, `Boys' Literature and the Idea of Empire, 1870-1914', *Victorian Studies*, 24.1 (Autumn, 1980), pp. 105-121; Reader, *ADC*; and White, *JC*.

[37] Robert H. Macdonald, *The Language of Empire: Myths and Metaphors of Popular Imperialism, 1880-1918* (Manchester: Manchester University Press, 1994), hereafter Macdonald, *LE*; p. 70.

[38] W.H. Davenport Adams, `*In Perils Oft': Romantic Biographies Illustrative of the Adventurous Life* (London: John Hogg, 1885), hereafter Davenport Adams, *IPO*; p. 47. The words of the epigraph are General Gordon's.

[39] Two good examples of this kind of writing are Ballantyne's much-discussed *Coral Island* (1858) and W.G.H. Kingston's less well-known *The Three Midshipmen* (1873).

unites ethics and politics under the emotive banner of national identity — the civilising mission turns out to be a peculiarly English destiny. Hence J.S. Bratton's claim that this literature offers `a powerful and multi-faceted presentation of Englishness, as a moral and ethical baseline, and therefore a starting point for the justification of Empire' (Bratton, *EHD*, p. 78).

Lord Jim's central protagonist has his being in a novel that both belongs to and deconstructs the romance and adventure genres. Critics have discussed in some detail the careful way in which Conrad portrays Jim as a type of the would-be questing hero of countless Victorian romances.[40] Suffice to say that the novel's frame-narrator is explicit about Jim's predilection for story-book fantasies and that his self-understanding clearly derives from the adventure tradition.[41] His exaggerated sense of his own importance, his hunger for crises in which he will show his valour, and his belief that he will prove to be courageous when tested, all disclose his reliance on the model of masculinity articulated in that tradition. Indeed, the novel goes further still. It shows that Jim is not just the passive product of this tradition but that he actively constructs his identity in accordance with its ethos.[42] The novel's emphasis on Jim's boyishness and immaturity is part of its critique of the adventure tradition, which extols boys who are more brawn than brain.[43] Imperial romances value action over reflection and glorify

---

[40] For three useful discussions of this point, see Marianne DeKoven, *Rich and Strange: Gender, History, Modernism* (Princeton: Princeton University Press, 1991), pp. 151-53; Robert Hampson, *Joseph Conrad: Betrayal and Identity* (London: Macmillan, 1992), p. 126, pp. 130-31, hereafter Hampson, *JCBI*; and Hawthorn, *JC*, pp. 37-38.

[41] There are several examples of Jim's tendency to read the life of the merchant navy in terms of the adventure tradition, but see in particular *Lord Jim*, pp. 5-9.

[42] See *LJ*, pp. 5-8, 233-234, 260, 262-264.

[43] In 1857, *The Spectator* described Tom Brown, an exemplar of manly boyhood, as `a thoroughly English boy. Full of kindness, courage, vigour and

(continued...)

physically adroit youngsters who believe so implicitly in their culture's ethos that they hardly need to think at all.[44] J.S. Bratton argues that this kind of character is deliberately portrayed as none too bright; he `can do his bit perfectly well by being a decent average sort of chap, as long as he internalises the values offered to him completely; too much brain is indeed often said to get in the way of action' (Bratton, *EHD*, p. 84). Jim is exactly of this type.[45] His ordinariness and lack of intellectual acumen are fundamental to the novel's portrayal of him as a character out of the adventure tradition, right down to his preference for storming stockades over the more perplexing task of settling domestic disputes and to his obtuseness about Jewel's love for him.[46]

If, as Marlow claims, `Romance had singled Jim for its own' (*LJ*, p. 282), then romance and the delusions it fosters are subjected to a scornful critique in this text. The *Patna* section satirises the adventure tradition by showing how deeply it distorts the reality of life at sea. When Jim actually goes to sea, he enters `the regions so

[43] (...continued)
fun — no great adept at Greek and Latin, but a first rate cricketer, climber and swimmer, fearless and skilful at football, and by no means averse to a good stand-up fight in a good cause'. Quoted in J.A. Mangan, `Social Darwinism and Upper-class Education in Late Victorian and Edwardian England', in J.A. Mangan and James Walvin (eds.), *Manliness and Morality: Middle-class Masculinity in Britain and America, 1800-1940* (Manchester: Manchester University Press, 1987), pp. 135-159, p. 137.

[44] For the close link between constructions of masculinity and imperial ideology in the popular literature of the period, see especially Bristow, *EB*, Macdonald, *LE*, and Mangan and Walvin, *MM*.

[45] The bachelor to whom Marlow first sends Jim writes of him that he `was good-tempered, had not much to say for himself, was not clever by any means, thank goodness' (*LJ*, p. 187).

[46] Thus Jim: `"And the talk! Jove! There didn't seem to be any head or tail to it. Rather storm a twenty-foot-high old stockade any day. Much! Child's play to that other job"' (*LJ*, p. 269). And again: `"And — and — hang it all — she was fond of me, don't you see.... I, too...didn't know, of course...never entered my head...."' (*LJ*, p. 304).

well known to his imagination' only to find them `strangely barren of adventure' (*LJ*, p. 10), and the *Patna* crisis undercuts all schoolboy fantasies of heroism, since it `"happen[s] in such a quiet way and so very suddenly"' (*LJ*, pp. 29-30). But whereas the discrepancy between illusion and reality is made clear to the reader, Jim never bridges the gap. His account of the *Patna* crisis remains couched in the language of the romance genre. It had not been `"like a fight"' (*LJ*, p. 130), and he had not been `"given half a chance — with a gang like that"' (*LJ*, p. 124); thus he remains `confident that, on the square, "on the square, mind!" there was nothing he couldn't meet' (*LJ*, p. 95). The Patusan section, in turn, provides Jim with the scope for acting out his fantasies and thus offers us the possibility of assessing what might be the consequences of a behaviour modelled on romantic myths. It signals the continuity in Jim's character by portraying his Patusan self as a figure out of a schoolboy romance and by hinting that this second adventure will end as disastrously as the first. To Marlow, Jim is `voluble like a youngster on the eve of a long holiday with a prospect of delightful scrapes', and, Marlow warns, `such an attitude of mind in a grown man and in this connection had in it something phenomenal, a little mad, dangerous, unsafe' (*LJ*, p. 234).[47]

Conrad critics have long known that Jim's behaviour in Patusan is in part modelled on the career of Sir James Brooke, the Rajah of Sarawak.[48] What matters here is that *Lord Jim* discloses the way that popular literature translates a life like Brooke's into a mythic idiom and then shows what can happen when a naive reader like

---

[47] The similarity between this description of Jim and the following passage from a particularly egregious example of the adventure tradition is striking: `The crew of the Hankow Lin set to work to prepare for a fresh struggle with all the alacrity and glee of schoolboys going out for an unexpected holiday'. See John C. Hutcheson, *The Penang Pirate* (London: Blackie and Son, 1888).

[48] The link was first established in John D. Gordan's `The Rajah Brooke and Joseph Conrad', *Studies in Philology*, 35, pp. 613-634.

Jim tries to translate myth back into reality.[49] The critique of Jim in Patusan remains in this sense a critique of the adventure tradition. As is well known, Brooke's initial actions in Sarawak were well received in England, but his vigorous reprisals against Malay pirates in 1848 were heavily criticised and led to questions in the House of Commons. Public opinion was divided. Brooke's supporters defended his actions according to imperial principles, arguing that he was a benevolent ruler who had needed to act autocratically in order to introduce the benefits of civilisation — peace, order, trade. Even the naturalist Alfred Russel Wallace, an Owenite socialist who had some scathing things to say about English imperialism, saw Brooke (in his *The Malay Archipelago*) as `a great, a wise, and a good ruler', claiming that he should not to be `sneered at as an enthusiast adventurer, or abused as a hard-hearted despot'.[50] Reasoned defences of Brooke represented one line of defence; another, imaginatively more potent one, was to exalt him as a romantic hero. Brooke quickly passed into the pages of popular literature where he could be eulogised as an exemplar of the adventure tradition. Davenport Adams's `*In Perils Oft*', for example, devotes a chapter to Brooke, portraying him as one of its illustrative heroes. Never, declares the author, `was the ideal of a benevolent despotism more happily realised' than in Sarawak under

[49] Andrea White, in a slightly different context, usefully describes Jim as a `proven consumer and misreader of fiction' (*JC*, p. 171).

[50] Alfred Russel Wallace, *The Malay Archipelago: The Land of the Orang-Utan, and the Bird of Paradise. A Narrative of Travel, With Studies of Man and Nature* (London: Macmillan, 1869), I, p. 147. Wallace elsewhere wrote more fully of Brooke as follows: `It is a unique case in the history of the world for a private English gentleman to rule over two conflicting races — a superior and an inferior — with their own consent, without any means of coercion, but depending solely upon them both for protection and support, while at the same time he introduces some of the best customs of civilization, and checks all crimes and barbarous practices that before prevailed'. See James Marchant (ed.), *A.R. Wallace: Letters and Reminiscences* (London: Cassell and Co., 1916), II, p. 182.

Brooke's rule; Brooke's `marvellous success', he continues, `reads like a chapter from a romance' (Davenport Adams, *IPO*, p. 304, p. 333). Adams's hagiography is significant because it suggests that a gentleman-adventurer like Brooke was a positive role-model for imperialists and because it shows how such figures were transformed into mythic heroes in the pages of romantic literature.[51] Charles Kingsley contributed to the myth of Brooke in a more oblique way.[52] Outraged at the criticism to which Brooke was subjected, he dedicated *Westward Ho!* to him, thereby establishing a link between his fictional gentleman-adventurer, Amyas Leigh, and the real figure of Brooke.[53] Robert H. Macdonald describes *Westward Ho!*, a confident and rousing evocation of English expansionism, as `the most widely read and influential historical romance of the early Victorian period'.[54] It is an archetype of

[51] For an excellent discussion of the construction of such imperial myths in Victorian England, see John M. MacKenzie, `Heroic Myths of Empire', in John MacKenzie (ed.), *Popular Imperialism and the Military, 1850-1950* (Manchester: Manchester University Press, 1992), pp. 109-138.

[52] For a discussion of Kingsley's attitude to the Brooke affair, see Brenda Colloms, *Charles Kingsley: The Lion of Eversley* (London: Constable, 1975), pp. 122-123, pp. 166-167.

[53] The dedication is to Brooke and to Bishop Selwyn of New Zealand. It reads: `This book is dedicated by one who (unknown to them) has no other method of expressing his admiration and reverence for their characters. That type of English virtue, at once manful and Godly, practical and enthusiastic, prudent and self-sacrificing, which he has tried to depict in these pages, they have exhibited in a form even purer and more heroic than that in which he has drest it, and than that in which it was exhibited by the worthies whom Elizabeth, without distinction of rank or age, gathered round her in the ever glorious wars of her great reign'.

[54] Macdonald, *LE*, p. 69. Kingsley's Amyas Leigh is a gentleman-adventurer who represents most of the values Kingsley wants to uphold (chivalry, courage, simplicity, honourableness, love of adventure), except that he needs to be taught a deeper Christian faith, which he acquires, Samson-like, at the end of the novel. For Kingsley, Leigh is `a symbol...of brave young England longing to wing its way out of its island prison, to discover

(continued...)

precisely the kind of fiction *Lord Jim* deconstructs.

In Patusan, Jim is a liberal reformer and modernizer who introduces free trade to the area but can only maintain order among the region's different groups by becoming a benevolent autocrat of the kind lauded by Davenport Adams, Wallace, and Kingsley.[55] But the parallels between Jim and Brooke should not be pushed too far. Jim is in Patusan as the representative of a large trading concern (Stein's), and his actions are at least in part motivated by his desire to fulfil his obligations to Stein by safeguarding his commercial interests. (*LJ*, pp. 285-287). In attempting to do his duty by Stein, he involves himself in local politics more deeply than most traders ever did.[56] His aim is to ensure that trade prospers by establishing

[54] (...continued)
and to traffic, to colonize and to civilize, until no wind can sweep the earth which does not bear the echoes of an English voice' (*Westward Ho!* [London: Macmillan, 1875], p. 9). Jim is a debased version of Amyas, betokening a loss of faith in both the imperial project and the model of masculinity that made it possible. Whereas *Westward Ho!* invokes `the nobleness which lies in every young lad's heart' (*WH*, p. 146) and praises a beneficent providence, *Lord Jim* agonises over the `infernal alloy in [Jim's] metal' (*LJ*, p. 45) and describes a secular world in which no external guidance can be expected.

[55] For a discussion of the novel's indebtedness to the history of Sarawak under Brooke and of Jim's actions as ruler of Patusan, see Michael Valdez Moses, `Conrad: The Flight from Modernity' in his *The Novel and the Globalization of Culture* (Oxford: Oxford University Press, 1995), hereafter Valdez Moses, *NGC*; pp. 67-104.

[56] Robert E. Elson argues that mercantile capitalism in the Malay Archipelago was a `deliberately self-limiting exercise' that `eschewed interference with indigenous politics except to make necessary arrangements for the delivery of desired goods'. See Robert E. Elson, `International Commerce, the State and Society: Economic and Social Change' in Nicholas Tarling (ed.), *The Cambridge History of Southeast Asia: The Nineteenth and Twentieth Centuries* (Cambridge: Cambridge University Press, 1992), pp. 131-195, p. 136. Nicholas Tarling points out that Brooke intervened in Sarawak in an attempt to establish law and order and to safeguard commerce. See Tarling, `The Establishment of the Colonial Regimes' in Tarling, *Cambridge History*, pp. 5-78, p. 23-24.

peace (or at least detente) between Patusan's warring factions. The preservation of trade becomes inseparable from the imposition of a social order founded on nineteenth-century English principles. For Jim, as for most of the period's imperialists, trade and the benefits of civilisation go together. As he says to Marlow: `"And do you know what's the best in it?.... It's the knowledge that had I been wiped out it is this place that would have been the loser"' (*LJ*, p. 245). The model for his actions in Patusan is that of `imperial trusteeship', first elaborated by Dilke in *Greater Britain* and then developed and defended by Gladstone in `England's Mission'.[57] Gladstone maintained that imperialism could never be justified by reference solely to English interests; it had to bring the benefits of civilisation — peace, social order, justice, and good government. Integral to `England's mission' overseas was the duty `to rear up free and congenital communities', to exercise `foreign influence as a member of the great community of Christendom', and to respect `the equal rights of all states and nations' (*EM*, p. 569, 568, 571, 578, 584). Jim's rule in Patusan needs to be seen in these terms, for he behaves in an exemplary Gladstonian manner, perfectly illustrating Koebner and Schmidt's claim that, for the empire's moral spokesmen, imperialism `was a service, was keeping the peace between tribes or settlements that would otherwise fight endless bloody wars...was serving mankind, in fact, by its humanizing effort ' (*I*, p. 154).

But Jim can do this only by autocratic rule. The state he builds up proves to be fragile partly because it is so contingent, depending on the authority and law of one man, and partly because it has not addressed — still less resolved — the underlying hostility between Patusan's different social groups. Patusan's various factions are merely kept in check by their fear of Jim's power. Brown's eruption onto the scene when Jim is absent immediately exposes the superficial nature of the recently established `state': `The social

---

[57] Charles Dilke, *Greater Britain: A Record of Travel in English-Speaking Countries During 1866 and 1867*, 2 vols. (London, 1868).

fabric of orderly, peaceful life, when every man was sure of to-morrow, the edifice raised by Jim's hands, seemed on that evening ready to collapse into a ruin reeking with blood' (*LJ*, p. 373). And collapse it does, despite the fact that Jim's actions, by the lights in which he has been educated, seem to be honourable. He seeks to bring peace to Patusan, he tries to resolve quarrels as impartially as he can, and he clearly believes that commerce and civilisation reinforce each other. Yet the `edifice' he constructs on the basis of these ideals proves to be built on shifting sands and engulfs both him and the Bugis in a cataclysm. It is here that the suspicion of Jim's motives and actions articulated by Doramin and Jewel is most relevant. Doramin and Jewel both question the prudence of placing too much trust in Jim because they fear that his final allegiance will be given to his own people. They understand that Jim's motives and purposes are not theirs and correctly predict that a time will come when the tension between his loyalty to his own race and his commitment to them will be unresolvable. Doramin displays great political acumen in wanting Jim to install Dain Waris as the future ruler of Patusan, since he suspects that neither Jim's presence nor his modernizing efforts will be lasting: `Doramin was anxious about the future of the country, and I was struck by the turn he gave to the argument. The land remains where God had put it; but white men — he said — they come to us and in a little while they go. They go away. Those they leave behind do not know when to look for their return. They go to their own land, to their people, and so this white man, too, would....' (*LJ*, p. 274). There is a sharp reversal here of the `privileged man's' ethnocentric perspective; his confident faith in European benevolence is turned upside down by Doramin's `view from below', which suggests that the civilising mission is a more ambivalent affair than convinced imperialists are ever likely to see. Jewel also refuses to believe that Jim can be entirely trusted. Her knowledge that she was abandoned by her father, just as her mother had been abandoned by her's, leaves her with little faith in the fidelity of European males.[58] Like Doramin, she fears that Jim's loyalty to her will be undermined by the inexorable pull of the `world beyond the forests' (*LJ*, p. 318). When she is proved right, her indictment is devastating: ` "He has left me," she said quietly; "you always leave us — for your own ends.... Ah! you are hard, treacherous, without truth, without compassion. What makes you so wicked? Or is it that you are all mad?" ' (*LJ*, p. 348).[59] These words — like Doramin's analysis of the political situation in Patusan — disclose how differently the us/them distinction looks from `their' perspective.

Marlow's own unreliability is nowhere more exposed than here, for his bluff assurances to Doramin and Jewel as to Jim's faithfulness turn out to be empty promises. The text subverts the ideal of imperial trusteeship by showing how fragile is the new order in Patusan, hinting that the region's inhabitants never entirely trust Jim, and disclosing that Jim's motives are to the very end ambiguous. This last point is crucial because it suggests that Jim never frees himself from the public-school ethos he first betrayed on the *Patna* and that, far from having gone native, his deepest allegiance is to the `home' he will never see again.[60] Two aspects of the text support this reading: the encounter with Brown; and Jim's on-going desire for approbation from the metropolitan centre of empire. It is of course no accident that Brown first sees Jim as `a man in European clothes, in a helmet, all white' (*LJ*, p. 379), and that these signs of Jim's class background enable Brown to

---

[58] See *LJ*, p. 314 and Padmini Mongia, ` "Ghosts of the Gothic": Spectral Women and Colonized Spaces in *Lord Jim*', in Andrew Michael Roberts (ed.), *Conrad and Gender* (Amsterdam: Rodopi, 1993), pp. 1-16.

[59] For a different reading of Jewel's role in the text, see Ruth L. Nadelhaft, *Joseph Conrad* (Hemel Hempstead: Harvester Wheatsheaf, 1991), pp. 50-59.

[60] For a very different reading, see Valdez Moses, who argues that Jim `dies a tragic hero, a willing sacrifice to the traditional customs and exacting ethical demands of a non-European community that he had endeavoured to serve and that he embraces as his own', *NGC*, p. 70.

exploit his presumed morality. Brown not only plays on Jim's guilt by making insidious references to their shared heritage but also questions his racial loyalty by raising that scariest of imperial spectres — the white man who has gone native: `"You have been white once, for all your tall talk of this being your own people and you being one with them. Are you?"' (*LJ*, p. 381).[61] But Jim is not. His role as paternalistic ruler of Patusan and his release of Brown according to the code of `fair play' imply that his actions are still guided by European principles.[62] This view is further supported by the novel's references to Jim's desire for approval from `home' and to the ambiguity of his motives in Patusan. [63] Despite his good reputation in Patusan, Jim seeks recognition from elsewhere, remarking to Marlow: `"Yes. I have got back my confidence in myself — a good name — yet sometimes I wish.... No! I shall hold what I've got. Can't expect anything more." He flung his arm out towards the sea. "Not out there anyhow"' (*LJ*, p. 333). Jim also reveals that his actions in Patusan are partly motivated by a desire to justify himself to an imaginary European audience: `"Yes, I've changed all that...but only try to think what it would be if I went away. Jove! can't you see it? Hell loose. No!.... No. I can't say — enough. Never. I must go on, go on for ever holding up my end, to feel sure that nothing can touch me. I must stick to their belief

[61] For detailed discussions of the Brown episode, see Hampson, *IB*, pp. 132-35.

[62] John W. Griffith also reads this scene in terms of its racial implications. I concur with his claim that `Jim never truly escapes from the bonds of ethnicity'. See his *Joseph Conrad and the Anthropological Dilemma* (Oxford: Clarendon, 1995), p. 186.

[63] Marlow, we should remember, articulates a commonplace of imperial discourse when he avers that those who embark on service overseas must return home to `render an account' to `those whom [they] obey, and those whom [they] love' (*LJ*, pp. 221-222). The nineteenth-century historian J.R. Seeley, for example, writes of colonists that `they go out into the wilderness of mere materialism, into territories where as yet there is nothing consecrated, nothing ideal. Where can their gods be but at home?'. See *The Expansion of England: Two Courses of Lectures* (London: Macmillan, 1885), p. 155.

in me to feel safe and to — to...to keep in touch with...with those whom, perhaps, I shall never see any more"' (*LJ*, pp. 333-334). *Lord Jim* suggests that this doubleness of motive is inescapable in the colonial encounter. Jim embodies imperialism's contradictions because his commitment to the civilising mission is shown to be at least in part driven by metropolitan imperatives that have nothing to do with the `good' of Patusan's inhabitants. A psychological reading of Jim might point out here that the novel shows altruism to be inseparable from egoism, and this reading can certainly be supported by the novel.[64] But its careful delineation of Jim as an imperial subject who belongs to a specific class fraction suggests that such a reading can only be half right because it misses the complex ways in which Jim's personality is also shown to be socially constructed. Jim's doubled motives and his inability fully to understand or to defend his adopted people's interests do not stem from individual selfishness and lack of perspicacity alone but are the results of an ideological formation that *produces* certain kinds of blindness.

Lord Jim exhibits a regressive structure that leads from Jim (via a frame-narrator) to Marlow and then to the text. Jim is displaced by Marlow, who is in turn displaced by the textuality of his narrative. As a result of this modernist form, we are left neither with a clear view of Jim nor with a full understanding of Marlow but are offered a plethora of competing perspectives that remain

---

[64] Marlow, for example, when noting that Jim feels `deeply' and `solemnly' about his work in Patusan, since it `had given him the certitude of rehabilitation', observes that this is `why he seemed to love the land and the people with a sort of fierce egoism, with a contemptuous tenderness' (*LJ*, p. 248). John A. McClure stresses the psychological dimension of Conrad's critique of imperialism when he claims that `Conrad's argument is against the whole venture, and his rhetorical strategy seems to be to show that even the best Europeans are not clear-sighted and unselfish enough to preside over communities so different from their own as those they encounter in the colonial world' (*KC*, p. 5).

mutually incommensurable. However, the text's embrace of indeterminacy points us in a certain direction, since it suggests that a final judgment on Jim's case can never be reached. The text may put forward several interpretations of Jim's life, and may imply that some are more plausible than others, but by the novel's end Jim is still to some extent inscrutable. The text does not so much abandon the quest for moral knowledge as disclose that there is no escape from incertitude. Its refusal of closure supports Marlow's claim that he is involved `in a dispute impossible of decision if one had to be fair to all the phantoms in possession' (*LJ*, p. 93), a claim that fits with the view of art expressed by Conrad in a letter written a year after *Lord Jim* was published: `The only legitimate basis of creative work lies in the courageous recognition of all the irreconcilable antagonisms that make our life so enigmatic, so burdensome, so fascinating, so dangerous — so full of hope' (*CL*II, pp. 348-49).

Lord Jim's perspectival mode is aporetic. The novel stages a series of paradoxes, which are then shown to be unresolvable. It suggests, for example, that an ethical code predicated on rules for conduct and policed juridically may be socially necessary but is at the same time inadequate because it is contingent and because it takes no account of motives. *Lord Jim* is perpetually on the verge of falling into the morass of nihilism, construing ethics as nothing more than an arbitrary set of practices with no ontological warrant.[65] Marlow, for example, may invoke the earth's `severity...saving power...[and] secular right to our fidelity, to our obedience' (*LJ*, p. 222), but he quickly admits that this affirmation is just rhetoric, since it is `some such truth or some such illusion — I don't care how you call it, there is so little difference, and the difference means so little' (*LJ*, p. 222). Epistemology is jettisoned

---

[65] Conrad himself frequently comes close to a full-blown nihilism, as his letters to R.B. Cunninghame Graham attest. See *CL*I, pp. 417-419 and pp. 422-426, *CL*II, pp. 24-25 and pp. 29-31. See also the extraordinary passage in which Conrad writes that he has `come to suspect that the aim of creation cannot be ethical at all' and `that its object is purely spectacular' (*PR*, p. 92).

here in favour of a desperate faith in the ethical naturalism that his own narrative has so devastatingly undermined. But the novel also questions Marlow's moral code in another way. By rejecting any decisive judgment of Jim's actions as right or wrong and urging the reader to see them in terms of complex and overdetermined inner motives, it suggests that a rule-governed code that focuses primarily on the outcome of behaviour provides too `thin' an account of human morality. Above all, what is lost in any such account is the irreducible particularity of the individual. The point is pithily put by Marlow when he laments of situations like Jim's that `in each case all I could see was merely the human being' (*LJ*, p. 94).[66]

Yet to argue in this way about *Lord Jim*'s scepticism is itself misleading, for it is to imply that the novel's ethical implications can be severed from its political concerns. To speak of the tension between a rule-governed moral system and the inner motives of particular individuals is already to fall into the trap of discussing *Lord Jim* in an abstract way. It is to detach ethics from politics in precisely the way that Marlow does and is to ignore the fact that Marlow — nowhere more `one of us' than here — is embedded in a text that not only ironises him but also asks more searching questions about the imperial enterprise than he ever could. It is, we might say, in Marlow's *interest* to focus on the moral dimension of Jim's story, given his own involvement in imperial trade and his endorsement of Jim's rule in Patusan.[67] The distance between Marlow and Conrad becomes apparent when one considers that the latter's similar involvement in the British merchant navy did not blind him to imperialism's sordid and self-serving aspects.[68] My

[66] Marlow's compassion persistently threatens his allegiance to the code. When he puts Brierly's plan of escape before Jim, he admits that `[t]here was no morality in the impulse' (*LJ*, p. 152).

[67] As Marlow tells his auditors, Jim's power `was the power to make peace. It is in this sense alone that might so often *is* right' (*LJ*, p. 261).

[68] For Conrad's positive remarks about the British merchant navy, see the articles `Well Done' (1918), `Tradition' (1918), and `Confidence' (1919) in *Notes on Life and Letters*, pp. 241- 260, pp. 261-270, pp. 271-279.

point is not that ethics needs to be *supplemented* by politics when we read *Lord Jim* but that the novel discloses the inseparability of these two discourses at the historical juncture that it describes. It suggests that the supposedly `ethical' code of conduct over which Marlow agonises is complicit with imperialist politics and shows that this politics depends in turn on the language of morals for its warrant. To read the novel in relation to either one of these discourses without reference to the other is not only to repress the way it shows that ethical and political considerations reinforce each other in Victorian justifications of empire but also to ignore the way it questions such justifications by pointing to the economic motives behind empire and by exploring the consequences of practices based on imperial assumptions. These, for Conrad, were the sombre political realities that lay concealed behind the comforting illusions of altruism, as he declared in a letter to Cunninghame Graham: `You with your ideals of sincerity, courage and truth are strangely out of place in this epoch of material preoccupations. What does it bring? What's the profit? What do we get by it? These questions are at the root of every moral, intellectual or political movement' (*CL*II, p. 25).

The economic side to imperialism is signalled by Jim's membership of the merchant navy, his identity as a gentleman-adventurer, his various jobs for European trading concerns, and his role as Stein's representative in Patusan. And Stein, who is so often held up as a moral authority in this text, is also caught up in imperial ambivalence, as Marlow admits when he observes of him that `he tried in his incorrigible way to season with a pinch of romance the fattening dishes of his commercial kitchen. There were very few places in the Archipelago he had not seen in the original dusk of their being, before light (and even electric light) had been carried into them for the sake of better morality and — and — well — the greater profit, too' (*LJ*, p. 219). The novel makes clear the tragic consequences of acting on imperial assumptions, in turn, through its portrayal of its central protagonist. Jim's subjectivity is shown to be culturally constructed. He is not an isolated monad but an educated middle-class English male whose values are those of a society that in great measure defines itself in terms of the imperial enterprise. The novel identifies Jim's romantic idealism as the product of a specific ideology; his status as a `gentleman', his sense of duty and honour, and his belief in the civilising mission are all pointers to his membership of a gendered class fraction at a given period in history. Conrad questions this ideology by satirising the way Jim models himself on characters in the literature of adventure, which articulated in so potent a way the myths of empire, and by tracing the logic by which a Gladstonian ideal of moral trusteeship leads to Jim's doom and to disaster for the Patusan community. The Patusan cataclysm is the last act in a drama whose origins lie in the fatal conjunction of ethics and politics that defined the imperial stage.

If ethics depends on some kind of belief in the agent's free-will, so that he or she can be regarded as blameworthy or praiseworthy with respect to their acts, then it is easy to see why so much ethical literary criticism focuses on the isolated individual who must make moral choices. *Lord Jim* might be thought to be exemplary in this respect, since it appears to concentrate in great detail on the history of one such individual, exhaustively analysing the motives for his acts and choices in order to ascertain whether or not he is morally culpable. This is why it seems to lend itself so readily to decontextualised ethical readings. But individuals are not, as Iris Murdoch has argued, `isolated free choosers, monarchs of all [they] survey'; they are embedded in social and historical forms of life, which are in a fundamental sense constitutive of their subjectivity and their subsequent conceptions of moral agency.[69] I have tried to show that to foreground the ethical dimension of *Lord Jim* by treating Jim as though he were an unfettered agent is to occlude the novel's careful representation of him as a member of a particular class and gender at a particular historical period. To read Jim in

---

[69] Iris Murdoch, `Against Dryness: A Polemical Sketch', *Encounter*, 16.1 (January 1961), pp. 16-20, p. 20.

purely ethical terms is to repress the text's `other' — politics. Ethical accounts conceived in this way are as misleading as political readings that reject discussion of ethics because they see it as a form of ideological mystification. Both fail to see that nineteenth-century imperial discourse cannot be deciphered if its interweaving of political and ethical considerations remains unacknowledged; they also fail to grasp that *Lord Jim* carefully signals its awareness of this conjunction and subtly undermines it. The novel makes it clear that the moral code whose aporias it explores cannot be separated from the political realm — the code is implicated in the ideology of imperialism because it inculcates in its subjects the values that are required for the successful administration of empire. Patrick Brantlinger acknowledges the intertwining of ethics and politics in imperial thought when he writes: `Empire involved military conquest and rapacious economic exploitation, but it also involved the enactment of often idealistic although nonetheless authoritarian schemes of cultural domination. The goal of imperialist discourse is always to weld these seeming opposites together or to disguise their contradiction' (*RD*, p. 34). *Lord Jim*, I would argue, *exposes* this contradiction by demonstrating how profoundly justifications of imperialism depended on moral idealism and then showing how this seasoning of politics with the romance of ethics could have disastrous consequences in the outposts of `progress.'

ETHICS AND UNREPRESENTABILITY IN *HEART OF DARKNESS*[1]

ANDREW GIBSON

The past two or three decades have seen a decline in confidence in ethical modes of reading fiction. To some extent, at least, it is the rise of theory that has been blamed for this, notably in David Parker's recent book *Ethics, Theory and the Novel*.[2] Parker is surely right to reaffirm the importance of ethical discourses on the novel. But the ethical discourses that are now most significant for the novel are not ones opposed to theory, as Parker would have it, but discourses that have emerged within or engaged with or been produced by theory. To put it differently: it is important that we explore the relevance to fiction of what Zygmunt Bauman has called post-modern ethics[3] — a non-foundational ethics that does not assume knowledge or stable categories prior to praxis, articulation, event — and the implication of that ethics for our reading. The point would be to return to ethics without returning to an ethical tradition, to reflect on how and how far new ways of thinking ethics might also transform the terms of our thought about reading novels.

Of all the unexamined assumptions according to which an older ethical criticism of fiction proceeded, one of the most crucial was the assumption that in fiction, ethics and representation are inseparable. Such an assumption makes it impossible for a novel to

[1] I am most grateful to my co-editor for his help with this essay.

[2] David Parker, *Ethics, Theory and the Novel* (Cambridge: Cambridge University Press, 1994).

[3] Zygmunt Bauman, *Postmodern Ethics* (Oxford: Blackwell, Oxford, 1993).

have an ethical dimension outside what is deemed to be its mimetic project. Ethics cannot subsist in a novel other than in relation to characters understood as clearly defined and represented entities. Hence, for example, the dearth, even now, of ethical readings of Beckett's work, where such entities cannot be imagined to exist, where discourse takes precedence over representation, and where the ethics in question would have to be considered, in the first instance, as a discursive ethics. But the point about ethics and representation is not to be confined to a comparatively extreme example like Beckett. It is an issue that can be — perhaps needs to be — addressed on a variety of different levels, in a variety of different kinds of text. *Heart of Darkness*, for instance, is a predominantly representational text that obstinately insists on the limits to representation and insistently dwells on the significance of those limits.[4] As far as Conrad's text is concerned, the question seems to me to be this: what is the meaning, in a representational text with obviously ethical concerns, of a kind of faltering or failing of its representational project; and does not that faltering or failing recast the ethical import of the text in question far more radically than we have commonly thought?

One of the reasons why *Heart of Darkness* is so absorbing in this context is that the link in criticism of Conrad's text between ethical questions and questions of representation is a long-established one. It goes back as far as Leavis. It is worth recalling the terms of Leavis's argument, not merely because they are germane to my own case, but also because they are helpful as an illustration of an ethical reading of a more classical kind. Leavis, of course, detected two kinds of writing, two modes of discourse in

---

[4] See for example James Guetti, `*Heart of Darkness* and the Failure of the Imagination', *Sewanee Review*, 73.3 (1965), pp. 488-504; Peter Brooks, `An Unreadable Report: Conrad's *Heart of Darkness*', *Reading for the Plot* (Cambridge, Mass: Harvard University Press, 1992), pp. 238-63; and Robert Hampson, `*Heart of Darkness* and "The Speech That Cannot Be Silenced"', *English*, 39.163 (Spring 1990), pp. 15-32.

Heart of Darkness. The first one — for Leavis, the `strong' kind — involves an art of `objective correlatives', evoking `a whole wide context of particularities' which convey `values' and `carry specificities of emotion and suggestion'.[5] This is what Leavis calls Conrad's `art of vivid essential record' (*GT*, p. 176). The phrase is interesting: Conrad's is an art that is at one and the same time both `vivid' and `essential'. On the one hand, it is an intensely particular art. On the other hand, it is an art in which `significance' also resides in the presented particulars, in which the `essential', whilst never `separable from the thing rendered', is nevertheless always implicit within it, as qualities like `ordinary greed, stupidity and moral squalor' are translated to us `in terms of things seen and incidents experienced' (*GT*, id.). This is an art in which characteristics are `embodied' in particulars — to use a term that Leavis employs with reference to *The Shadow-Line* (*GT*, p. 188) — but where the relationship implied in `embodiment' is somehow mysteriously effaced, as though particularity and essence were one and the same thing; as though the vivid record of life and what Leavis calls the `pattern' of `moral significances' in *Heart of Darkness* were somehow identical (*GT*, p. 179). What runs counter to this art, in *Heart of Darkness*, counter to this `strong discourse', is another discourse that effects an `actual deepening' of the novel. According to Leavis, the consequences of this discourse are `little short of disastrous' (id.). This second discourse involves an `adjectival and worse than superogatory insistence on "unspeakable rites", "unspeakable secrets", "monstrous passions", "inconceivable mystery" and so on' (id.). This constitutes what Leavis calls Conrad's `insistence on the presence of what he can't produce', an insistence merely betraying an `absence' or `nullity' (*GT*, p. 180). In other words, for Leavis, what radically flaws *Heart of Darkness* and weakens its ethical force is its insistence on the limits to representation and the power of the unrepresentable.

---

[5] F.R. Leavis, *The Great Tradition* (London: Chatto and Windus, 1948), hereafter Leavis, *GT*; p. 174.

Leavis's essay on Conrad was first published in 1941,[6] yet his conception of what novels are and how they work (or fail to work) is still very much with us today, at least in England, in three respects that are particularly relevant here. Firstly, Leavis assumes that a novel's ethical power is inseparable from a kind of mimetic adequacy (`an art of vivid record'). No ethics is conceivable outside a mimetic project, at least so far as fiction is concerned. Certainty in and of representation is the *sine qua non* of ethics in narrative, the foundation without which that ethics cannot begin to function. Secondly, the moral power of fiction is inseparable from its certainty as to moral knowledge, the clarity of its moral categories. Of course, it would be absurd to suppose that Leavis was not aware of moral ambiguities in the masterworks of the great tradition. The reverse is often the case: he insists on the degree to which, at its best, the art of Conrad and James is a morally deliberative art that both works in terms of fine and careful moral discriminations and requires such discriminations of its readers. Nonetheless, for Leavis, Conrad knows his ethical terms from the start. He is endowed with a firm, secure, confident consciousness of the moral qualities, is sure of them as they are, unalloyed, beyond any modification or transformation by local context, contingency or history. Conrad knows `greed', `stupidity' and `squalor', for example, as they exist in themselves, in self-sameness, for all people, under all skies. In Conrad's `art of essential record', the categories exist prior to their specific embodiments and their articulation in a specific language. Thirdly, for Leavis, the ethical power of a given novel is inseparable from its fusion of clearly defined category and vividly recorded particular (`an art of vivid essential record'). The particular is numinous, pregnant with a significance that both precedes and will outlast it and is not for an instant to be confused merely with the conventions of the language in which it is articulated.

[6] `Revaluations: Joseph Conrad', *Scrutiny*, 10.1 (1941), pp. 22-50; 10.2 (1942), pp. 157-81.

In other words, for Leavis, the ethical power of great fiction is inseparable from ontology on the one hand and cognition on the other: from a knowledge of essences, including the essence of the thing as it is known and rendered through language. But *Heart of Darkness* can be read in the reverse direction. Its ethical force is arguably located precisely in what it does not or cannot say, or breaks off from saying.[7] To read it thus is to assimilate it to a strain in contemporary ethics that derives from Levinas's work and questions any automatic or unreflective valuation of cognitive and ontological assumptions in ethical thought.[8] For Levinas, of course, ethics cannot be constructed on a foundation of essences. Indeed, ethics is not a question of cognition. The ethical relation — for Levinas, the first relation — takes place in an immediate realm where the relation to or encounter with the other is antecedent to all knowledge, and brings with it the burden of responsibility to the other. To proceed towards the other on the basis of what is deemed to be prior knowledge is at once to have neutralized the alterity, the complexity, the freedom of the other; to have reduced the other to the order of the same. `In the word "comprehension"', writes Levinas, `we understand the fact of taking [*prendre*] and of comprehending [*comprendre*], that is, the fact of englobing, of appropriating' (*TI*, p. 70). To comprehend is to produce the other as totality. Certainly, `men can be synthesized', as Levinas says. `Men can easily be treated as objects' (*TI*, p. 170). But to approach

---

[7] Note David Thorburn's response to Leavis in *Conrad's Romanticism* (New Haven: Yale University Press, 1974), hereafter Thorburn; though Thorburn can no more resist the assumption of essences than Leavis: `Marlow's characteristic diction, his persistent reliance on what might be called a vocabulary of uncertainty, is intimately related to [his] confessions of limitation and bafflement...the famous adjectival insistence which has so disturbed Leavis and others is for the most part an essential aspect of the novel's meaning' (pp. 117-118).

[8] My main point of reference, here, will be Levinas's earlier work, chiefly *Totality and Infinity*, tr. Alphonso Lingis (Martinus Nijhoff: The Hague, 1961), hereafter Levinas, *TI*.

the other by way of objective cognition and its totalizations is not to institute but rather to deny all ethical relation to the other. That denial emerges as what — significantly for *Heart of Darkness* — Levinas calls `ontological imperialism' (*TI*, p. 44). In Levinas's terms, this latter is the expression of the naive, arbitrary, spontaneous dogmatism of the self which directs the understanding at its thitherto obscure object as a clarifying `ray of light' (id.), delivers being out of secrecy — out of its heart of darkness — and, in so doing, neutralizes the other as it encompasses him or her. This, says Levinas, is `the very movement of representation and of its evidence'.[9] Representation, totalization, ontology are all manifestations of and exercises in what Levinas calls freedom. Freedom is to be identified with what Spinoza famously called the *conatus essendi*, the `right to existence' which Spinoza defined as the engine of all intellection. Levinas, however, has described his whole work as directed against that principle and what he takes to be its Hellenic endorsement as the latter is still prevalent today. For the principle of freedom or the *conatus essendi* is an egology and a principle of violence. According to the Levinas of the essay `The Ruin of Representation', it is so precisely in representation itself.[10] For representation takes as its premise a correspondence or adequation between thought and being, and thereby endorses the illusion of the sovereign and creative intellect.

Cognition and representation, then, are both an exertion of violence, what Levinas calls negation, a denial of the independence of existents. `The absolutely foreign alone can instruct us', he writes (*TI*, p. 73). Thus a significant ethics can have nothing to do with any transcendental sanction, any abstract principles or rules.

---

[9] By contrast, the process of mapping implicit in Marlow's narrative in *Heart of Darkness* replaces a blank with a darkness. See Christopher L. Miller, *Blank Darkness: Africanist Discourse in French* (Chicago: Chicago University Press, 1985).

[10] See Levinas, `La Ruine de la Représentation', in *En Découvrant l'Existence avec Husserl et Heidegger* (Paris: J. Vrin, 1987), pp. 125-36.

For such principles or rules will always have set terms for the encounter with the other in advance; they will always insist on our thinking and knowing beforehand. For Levinas, ethics is different from thought or knowledge. And not only that. It cuts right across ontology. It is radically and irreducibly other than all thought of essence. The ethical relation is the encounter with the other. Ethics intrudes in this relation precisely in the alterity of the other, an alterity which forever exceeds all knowledge I can have of her or him. An ethical priority emerges, not as my knowledge dominates the other, but as the moral height of the other dominates me and all the terms — being, essence, identity, principle, the same — in which I would seek to encompass her or him. The other overflows all ideas I can have of the other, and the consequence is shame; shame at the sheer contingency, the radical smallness of the ideas in which I would seek to encompass the other; shame at the stark exposure of the *conatus essendi*, the self-will that proposes those ideas as valid and important. What shames me, above all, says Levinas, is infinity as revealed in the other. Levinas understands this infinity, in the Cartesian sense, as always overflowing the thought that thinks it. The ethical relation, then, is a relation to infinity rather than the thought of totality. It is a question of `metaphysics', in the terms particular to Levinas, rather than `ontology'. Because it is infinity that I encounter with and in the other as I cannot encounter it in myself, it is always the other who commands me. I am always responsible to the other. The ethical relation, finally, begins precisely as the other in its infinity exceeds my representation of it. It begins precisely in the faltering or failing or, as Levinas has it, `the ruin of representation'.

Such an account of ethics has large implications for both the ethics of reading and the ethics of fiction.[11] At the very least, it enjoins us to grow more thoughtful about the ways in which novels

---

[11] For an excellent account of some of these implications, see Robert Eaglestone, *Ethical Criticism: Reading After Levinas* (Edinburgh: Edinburgh University Press, 1997).

themselves address questions of representation and the limits of representation. There is arguably more at stake, here, than is commonly recognized in all the various and prolific, post-modern discussions of self-reflexivity, anti-realism, the writerly versus the readerly and so on. In the context of Levinas's thought, the issues in question take on an ethical dimension. This seems to me to be precisely the case with discussions of representation in *Heart of Darkness*. In one of its aspects, the novella is pervaded by two discourses. We might partly think of them, respectively, as Kurtzian and Marlovian discourse. But they are not to be identified with single characters. Indeed, to identify them thus would precisely be to begin to construct the ethics of Conrad's text around two persons understood as essences or homogenous entities. In Levinas's terms, Kurtzian discourse is ontological. Kurtz is persistently associated with the word `all' and the concept of the whole:

> You should have heard him say, 'My ivory.' Oh yes, I heard him. 'My Intended, my ivory, my station, my river, my —' everything belonged to him. It made me hold my breath in expectation of hearing the wilderness burst into a prodigious peal of laughter that would shake the fixed stars in their places. Everything belonged to him.... (*HD*, p. 116)

Kurtz's urge is precisely towards the domination of the whole: `By the simple exercise of our will', he writes, `we can exert a power for good practically unbounded' (*HD*, p. 118). If everything supposedly belongs to Kurtz then, of course, Marlow also informs us that `All Europe contributed' to his `making' (*HD*, p.117). If Kurtz's drive is towards total possession, he also serves as a kind of total summation. In all its various implications and with all their various nuances, the meaning of Kurtz's story cannot be separated from the will to totalize, to think the whole that characterizes him throughout. Whichever aspect of his trajectory one chooses to emphasize, the totalizing impulse is intrinsic to it. Indeed, that impulse underlies all the various ethical inflections to Kurtz's career and is the very crux of the moral predicament that he both endures and embodies. In this respect, like Levinas, Conrad surely suggests that the ethical issues with which he is chiefly concerned are inseparable from the limits of a particular and culturally specific epistemology.

For both Levinas the philosopher and Conrad the novelist, ethical questions are bound up with questions of how one knows, the terms in which one knows and in which one chooses to express one's knowledge. Thus in the phrase `Exterminate all the brutes!' (*HD*, p. 118), we should underline the relatively inconspicuous second word. If it gives the idea of `extermination' full weight and makes its meaning wholly explicit, the word also emphasizes a totalizing habit of thought and perception without which the idea of extermination itself is impossible. What hangs over Kurtz's deadly sentence is partly a question about the very reflexes that lead us to think peoples or races — for instance — as wholes. In fact, the word `all' is sufficiently momentous, here, for it to echo on afterwards in Marlow's subsequent discourse (`he had apparently forgotten all about that valuable postscriptum'; `I had full information about all these things', etc.). Kurtz's last words equally function as the statement of a grim totality: `wide enough to embrace the whole universe', says Marlow, `piercing enough to penetrate all the hearts that beat in the darkness. He had summed up — he had judged' (*HD*, p. 151). The ironic tone to the passage strikes as much at the very fact of summary judgment — that queer native custom — as it does at the nature of the judgment passed. It is of course an irony to which a whole tradition — supremely, perhaps, an English tradition as exemplified in Leavis — is not immune. Once again, too, Marlow insistently and repetitively emphasizes how far the Kurtzian predicament and the sombreness of Kurtz's closing moods are inseparable from the habit of thinking totality:

'The horror!'…. After *all*, this was the expression of some sort of belief; it had candour, it had conviction, it had a vibrating note of revolt in its whisper, it had the appalling face of a glimpsed truth — the strange commingling of desire and hate. And it is not my own extremity I remember best — a vision of grayness without form filled with physical pain, and a careless contempt for the evanescence of *all* things — even of this pain itself. No! It is his extremity that I seem to have lived through. True, he had made that last stride, he had stepped over the edge, while I have been permitted to draw back my hesitating foot. And perhaps in this is the *whole* difference; perhaps *all* the wisdom, and *all* truth, and *all* sincerity, are just compressed into that inappreciable moment of time in which we step over the threshold of the invisible. Perhaps! (*HD*, p. 151, italics mine).

The `wisdom' with whose conviction Marlow ironically toys, here, is of a piece with the `knowledge of unexplored regions' with which Kurtz is also associated (*HD*, p. 153). Its totalizing aspiration — its overbearing grandiosity — finds an appropriate vehicle in grandiloquence. Crucially — perhaps even in the first instance — Kurtz's will to mastery manifests itself as a will to dominate through language, through a totalizing discourse. For Levinas, the corruptions of ontology are precisely and pointedly evident in *rhetoric*. Rhetoric is unscrupulous, calculating, a function of the intelligence that has designs upon and seeks to subdue others. The rhetorician takes `the position of him who approaches his neighbour with ruse':

> Rhetoric, absent from no discourse, and which philosophical discourse seeks to overcome, resists discourse.... It approaches the other not to face him, but obliquely — not, to be sure, as a thing, since rhetoric remains conversation, and across all its artifices goes unto the Other, solicits his yes. But the specific nature of rhetoric (of propaganda, flattery, diplomacy, etc.) consists in corrupting this freedom. It is for this that it is preeminently violence, that is, injustice — not violence exercised on an inertia (which would not be a violence), but on a freedom, which, precisely as freedom, should be incorruptible. (*TI*, p. 70)

Rhetoric closes off all possibility of dialogue with the other in her or his irreducible alterity. Rhetoric is the violence which refuses to listen, refuses exchange, assimilation, hybridization, self-reflexivity.

By contrast, on the one hand, conversation maintains the ethical relation with the other, with the possibility always of unsaying what is said; and, on the other hand, philosophical discourse seeks to avoid violence in turning away from rhetoric as discursive mode. In Levinas's sense, Kurtz is no philosopher. He is rather a discourser:

> I made the strange discovery that I had never imagined him as doing, you know, but as discoursing. I didn't say to myself, 'Now I will never see him,' or 'Now I will never shake him by the hand,' but, 'now I will never hear him.' The man presented himself as a voice.... The point was in his being a gifted creature, and that of all his gifts the one that stood out preeminently, that carried with it a sense of real presence, was his ability to talk, his words.... (*HD*, p. 113)

Kurtz may be the author of `splendid monologues' on `love, justice, conduct of life' (*HD*, p. 132), but his famed `magnificent eloquence' (*HD*, p. 131) is precisely a rhetoric that permits no encounter with the other. `You don't talk with that man — you listen to him', says the Russian harlequin (*HD*, p. 123). Coppola catches this very finely in *Apocalypse Now* in having Brando's head isolated in darkness as he talks to Sheen, as though he were one of Dante's damned. Humanistic at first, Kurtz's rhetoric can speedily reverse into the opposite of humanism. Humanism and nihilism appear as twin sides of the same coin, at least insofar as both are inextricable from a rhetoric that speaks totalities. Indeed, in Kurtz, the totalizing rhetoric is a figure for an egology finally revealing itself as insane catastophe. `"My ivory"', says Marlow, mournfully. `"My Intended, my ivory, my station, my river, my...."' It is thus that `everything belong[s]' to Kurtz (*HD*, p. 116). At the same time, there is a point to be made about the double set of quotation marks as I have just used them. I shall return to it very shortly.

In *Heart of Darkness*, then, the Kurtzian principle is one of grandiose and summary representation which seeks to encompass and articulate the whole. As such, it is by no means confined to

Kurtz. Indeed, there is a sense in which `everything' might be thought of as `belonging' to almost any given (European) character in the tale. For the kind of totalizing discourse most obviously associated with Kurtz is one from which no European character is free: the chief accountant, the brickmaker, the general manager, the Russian harlequin — each of them is disposed to discoursing on the whole. `Transgression — punishment — bang!' says Marlow's papier-mâché Mephistopheles, with reference to the `beaten nigger': `Pitiless, pitiless. That's the only way. This will prevent all conflagrations for the future' (*HD*, p. 80). Kurtz's final call for extermination may redound more ironically than this, but otherwise the distinction between the sentences is only one of degree. In the case of the Russian harlequin, of course, it is actually Kurtz himself who occupies the place of the desired totality: `It was curious to see his mingled eagerness and reluctance to speak of Kurtz', muses Marlow. `The man filled his life, occupied his thoughts, swayed his emotions' (*HD*, p. 128). As Marlow himself notes, the totalizing habit, here, is that of the idolater.[12] Much more pressingly and significantly, however, it is the habit of the emperors of the earth, who `are accustomed to look upon' it in `the shackled form of a conquered monster' (*HD*, p. 96). In a sense, *Heart of Darkness* takes as its principal theme the Heideggerian nightmare, the impending triumph of Western metaphysics as it is ensured by and properly indistinguishable from the triumph of Western power. It is thus appropriate that all the European characters in the story should be representative of or instrumental to the spread of Empire whilst also doggedly articulating or reproducing an ontological discourse that insists on the priority of existence over existents, in Levinas's

---

[12] For a discussion of the significance of idolatry in *Heart of Darkness* - and of the relationship between ideas and idolatry in Conrad's novella - see Patrick Brantlinger, *Rule of Darkness: British Literature and Imperialism 1830-1914* (Ithaca: Cornell University Press, 1988).

terms, of the Idea over embodiment, enactment, materiality.[13] Everywhere, it is ontology that provides the justification imperialism seeks, that serves as the latter's torch and sacred fire. It is evident enough in a conviction as to the principles of justice, for example, which is not only broached by the brickmaker, but runs through the tale like a refrain.

Here Marlow's wonderful, wicked, brief, parodic sketch of the Scottish sailmaker stands as comment on the European enterprise itself:

> I knew once a Scotch sailmaker who was certain, dead sure, there were people in Mars. If you asked him for some idea how they looked and behaved, he would get shy and mutter something about 'walking on all-fours.' If you as much as smiled, he would — though a man of sixty — offer to fight you. (*HD*, pp. 81-82)

The vignette functions as a kind of comic *reductio ad absurdum* of the sort of certitude repeatedly evident in the Europeans in the story, a certitude that, in ethical terms, is profoundly disabling. In *Heart of Darkness*, no-one escapes ontology. Kurtz's `cousin', who calls on Marlow at the end, is an obvious enough example, with his assertion that Kurtz was a `universal genius' (*HD*, p. 154). But ontology is by no means the preserve of the less appealing characters. Indeed, part of the subtlety of Conrad's achievement arguably has to do with his recognition that, if ontology and the thought of totality spread everywhere, they do so at the expense of the more familiar moral distinctions — between liberal enlightenment and benighted reaction, for instance — that some might otherwise seek to sustain. Thus the first narrator, for instance, is a conspicuous example of the ontological principle, awaiting illumination, as he does, the key to Marlow's narrative:

[13] For an important account of the relevance of an emphasis on materiality to an ethics of alterity, see Thomas Docherty, *Alterities: Criticism, History, Representation* (Oxford: Clarendon Press, 1995).

The others might have been asleep, but I was awake. I listened, I listened on the watch for the sentence, for the word, that would give me the clue to the faint uneasiness inspired by this narrative that seemed to shape itself without human lips in the heavy night-air of the river. (*HD*, p. 83)

If there is a `clue' to the `uneasiness' in question, of course, it is perhaps inseparable from the hunger for an answer that so desires such clues.

Above all, Marlow himself is by no means offered to us as having somehow moved beyond ontology. We should bear in mind the fact that, in the first narrator's terms, he is not only a `wanderer' but also a `seaman':

...most seamen lead, if one may so express it, a sedentary life. Their minds are of the stay-at-home order, and their home is always with them — the ship; and so is their country — the sea. One ship is very much like another, and the sea is always the same. In the immutability of their surroundings the foreign shores, the foreign faces, the changing immensity of life, glide past, veiled not by a sense of mystery but by a slightly disdainful ignorance; for there is nothing mysterious to a seaman unless it be the sea itself.... For the rest, after his hours of work, a casual stroll or a casual spree on shore suffices to unfold for him the secret of a whole continent, and generally he finds the secret not worth knowing. (*HD*, p. 48)

The passage from which this quotation comes is usually read in terms of its final assertion of Marlow's distinctive difference.[14] But it is surely the case that what these lines offer us is a crude and extreme version of what are nonetheless features of Marlow himself. Part of his mind does indeed have the `stay-at-home order' of the seaman's — the order of ontology, in which home is always with one and sameness prevails over difference. In particular, the oracular, generalizing Marlow is unable to escape the totalizing

[14] See for example Cedric Watts, *Conrad's `Heart of Darkness': A Critical and Contextual Study* (Milan: Mursia International, 1977), pp. 41-42.

principle, the assumption of the one truth, the conviction of universals and essences. This is strikingly evident, of course, in his view of women:

> It's queer how out of touch with truth women are. They live in a world of their own, and there had never been anything like it, and never can be. It is too beautiful altogether, and if they were to set it up it would go to pieces before the first sunset. Some confounded fact we men have been living contentedly with ever since the day of creation would start up and knock the whole thing over. (*HD*, p. 59)

The voice, here, is surely that of Marlow the seaman and not Marlow the wanderer, a Marlow for whom, indeed, `a casual stroll' on shore `suffices to unfold for him the secret of a whole continent'. Hence the tone of unreflective superiority to feminine self-deception.[15] Marlow's problem is in large measure his implicit faith in a singular knowledge. Its necessary consequence is the assumption that others are excluded from the possession of such knowledge. For this Marlow, essences always proceed singularities. This Marlow enters a lady's room and finds that it looked `just as you would expect a lady's drawing-room to look' (*HD*, p. 59). For him, realities lie deeper than appearances. `Belief' must be opposed to `acquisitions, clothes, pretty rags — rags that would fly off at the first good shake' (*HD*, p. 97). There are `essentials...under the surface' (*HD*, p. 100). This Marlow insistently returns to the conviction that there is a `truth of things', even if he may feel kept away from it (*HD*, p. 61). In bluff, virile terms, he asserts that one must `meet that truth with his own true stuff' (*HD*, p. 97). This Marlow knows about *Geist* in that he knows what an `absolutely pure' spirit might be (*HD*, p. 126). Hence the fact that he can

---

[15] Ruth Nadelhaft has suggested that Marlow disparages women because he finds it difficult to be indebted to them. See *Joseph Conrad* (Hemel Hempstead: Harvester Wheatsheaf, 1991), p. 49. Nadelhaft suggests that, as men `cling to the "idea" in the face of the "facts"' (p. 45), so Marlow substitutes anxious idealization for `the humanity of any woman' (p. 49).

conceive of Kurtz as having `filled' the life of the Russian harlequin (*HD*, p. 128). It is therefore not surprising to find Marlow suggesting that, if the colonial enterprise is to be redeemed, it will be only by the `idea *at the back of it*' (*HD*, p. 51, italics mine). The predicament of this Marlow is partly a matter of the limited — not to say banal — range of his spatial metaphors for knowledge. But then, part at least of the originality of *Heart of Darkness* has to do precisely with the connection it repeatedly establishes between, on the one hand, the mentality that sees truth in terms of what is `within' or `inside', as `hidden' (*HD*, p. 93) or buried, and its discovery as an unearthing or penetration (*HD*, p. 95); and, on the other, the drive `to tear treasure out of the bowels of the land' (*HD*, p. 87).

Marlow, then, is himself much given to thinking the totality. Indeed, it is one of the story's most significant ironies that we cannot be certain how far the totalizing principle as exemplified in Kurtz is not in fact a projection of Marlow's own drive to totalization. It is Marlow, after all, who is responsible for conveying the Kurtzian principle to us, in what is at times a grandiloquent rhetoric that is hardly distinguishable from Kurtz's own. In part, Marlow's rhetoric might actually be imagined as a translation of Kurtz's, revised and improved. Equally, it is Marlow who is the allegorist; Marlow who tells us, for example, that all Europe went into Kurtz's making; Marlow who ultimately suggests that Kurtz's stare `was wide enough to embrace the whole universe, piercing enough to penetrate all the hearts that beat in the darkness' (*HD*, p. 151). Hence my point, earlier, about the double quotation marks. Everything that Kurtz says in the story is in double quotation marks. It is speech incorporated into Marlow's speech. In a sense, Kurtz is absorbed into Marlow's very substance, is even the corruptive principle within that substance; except, of course, that there is an aporia as to the `origin' of the tale. Kurtz is both the pretext for and in that sense the origin of Marlow's story, and yet also its product. It is even possible to read *Heart of Darkness* as psychomachia, with Marlow engaged in a struggle with the Kurtz present both in himself and in his narrative.

Marlow, then, is deeply complicit with Kurtzian discourse, with ontology. As he ruefully admits at one point in his story, `I also was a part of the great cause of these high and just proceedings' (*HD*, p. 65). There is a profound double irony to his respect for the chief accountant (*HD*, p. 68), the `apple-pie order' of whose books is surely bound to remind us of the `stay-at-home order' of the seaman's mind (*HD*, p. 68). It is precisely here that the other discourse in *Heart of Darkness* — the one that Leavis found so `disastrous' — becomes important. Leavis saw this discourse as having the `strained impressiveness' of a rhetoric that seeks to generate a vague sense of `profound and tremendous significance' (*GT*, p. 180). But the stress for example on `implacable force' and `inscrutable intention' (*HD*, p. 93) in the tale is surely part of something larger that runs insistently through Marlow's discourse both as narrator and as character. Indeed, it also runs through the discourse of the first narrator: in that sense, like Kurtzian discourse, it is finally impersonal, not individuated, not to be reduced to a particular subjectivity. What pervades Marlovian discourse is a sense of epistemological dead-end, of determinate limits to knowledge and representation, the irreducibly complex mystery of the world as it is encountered by the cognitive intellect.[16] In this discourse, representation itself is constantly threatened by the `unfathomable enigma' (*HD*, p. 105) whose mention so dismays Leavis. In Levinas's terms, this is a discourse that starts from the principle of infinity, as opposed to totalizing discourse. It is the discourse of a Marlow well-known for his accounts of `inconclusive experiences' (*HD*, p. 51). This Marlow is worried by the `incomprehensible' (*HD*, p. 62). Of course, what most obviously balks understanding, in Marlow's case, is Africa, `the silence of the land...its mystery, its greatness, the amazing reality of its concealed

---

[16] Cf Thorburn: `...as Kurtz's eloquence and Marlow's tormented narrative indicate, art itself and even the grounds of Western epistemology are challenged by the darkness' (p. 124).

life' (*HD*, p. 80). But equally, once recognized for what it is, the fact of ineluctable mystery radiates everywhere. If Africa is irreducible to European terms then, equally, Europe must be imagined as a source of perplexity to Africa, `an insoluble mystery from the sea' (*HD*, p. 64). So, too, Europeans are puzzles to each other. `They can only see the mere show, and never can tell what it really means' (*HD*, p. 85). The Russian harlequin, for instance, is imagined as `improbable, inexplicable, and altogether bewildering', like the jungle (*HD*, p. 126). Indeed, the image of the vast tangle of the jungle might partly be thought of as Conrad's metaphorical reproof to all epistemological assurance:

> The great wall of vegetation, an exuberant and entangled mass of trunks, branches, leaves, boughs, festoons, motionless in the moonlight, was like a rioting invasion of soundless life, a rolling wave of plants, piled up, crested, ready to topple over the creek, to sweep every little man of us out of his little existence. (*HD*, p. 86)

But then, in Marlow's terms, the amazed encounter with alterity — an alterity that will subsequently be subdued — lies at the very root of the European experience. His imaginary commander of a Roman legion in Britain, for example, is pictured as tormented by living `in the midst of the incomprehensible' (*HD*, p. 50). It is precisely the recognition of the encounter with alterity that baffles all representation, making it `impossible', for instance, `to convey the life-sensation of any given epoch of one's existence':

> It seems to me I am trying to tell you a dream — making a vain attempt, because no relation of a dream can convey the dream-sensation, that commingling of absurdity, surprise, and bewilderment in a tremor of struggling revolt, that notion of being captured by the incredible which is of the very essence of dreams.... (*HD*, p. 82)

Indeed, the encounter with alterity seems to ask for full expression in terms that go beyond anthropomorphism, into the further reaches of time and space: `prehistoric earth' on the one hand; on the other, the `unknown planet' (*HD*, p. 95). The Marlow who finds those terms, of course, is most certainly one of the `wanderers' (id.), not at all the man who positions himself as the sane onlooker `secretly appalled...before an enthusiastic outbreak in a madhouse' (*HD*, p. 96).

Yet, as we have seen, there is an ample measure of the seaman's as there is of the wanderer's disposition in Marlow, and this mixture is also there in *Heart of Darkness* itself. My point is not that what I have called Marlovian discourse somehow `overcomes' or `resists' or neutralizes the ontological discourse in Conrad's tale. Rather, it gnaws away at it, like an unease that cannot be stilled. It provides an insistent reminder that ontology itself has a history, that ontology is itself a discursive construction. In this respect, Marlovian discourse *deconstructs* Kurtzian discourse, in what I take to be the better sense of deconstruction: it does not destroy ontology; it leaves ontology standing, but as a hollow shell. It indicates the finitude of ontological discourse, its lack of purchase on the real. This is partly the consequence of the modes of ironic play which Marlow adopts during the course of his narration. In *Heart of Darkness*, Marlovian discourse might be said to open up an ethical space in which alterity is registered precisely as it persistently and forever exceeds cognition and indicates the limits of ontology. But this is by no means simply a question of a Conradian ethics of discourse. On another level, that ethics is also `dramatized', not least in the conclusion of the novel, the encounter with the Intended.

It is interesting to note what happens to Marlow before that encounter takes place. Under Kurtz's spell, in Levinasian terms, he comes close to rejecting infinity for totality. The `totalizing vision' in question, of course, is Kurtz's at the end of his life. It is the vision of Kurtz the despairer, not the colonialist or bringer of enlightenment. But it is none the less imposing for that. Marlow believes, after all, that he has seen `the appalling face of a glimpsed truth' (*HD*, p. 151), and the proleptic significance of the metaphor will shortly be apparent. The `truth' in question, of course, is that of the `impalpable grayness, with nothing underfoot, with nothing around' (*HD*, p. 150.). Part of Marlow's problem is his aptitude for double voicing as indicated by those double quotation marks. For if the advantage conferred by such an aptitude is a disposition to irony, the disadvantage is a propensity for being submerged or absorbed:

> ...it is not my own extremity I remember best — a vision of grayness without form filled with physical pain, and a careless contempt for the evanescence of all things — even of this pain itself. No! It is his extremity that I seem to have lived through. (*HD*, p. 151)

Hence his conviction that all wisdom `and all truth, and all sincerity' may after all have been `compressed' into Kurtz's summary judgment (id.). Indeed, Marlow's more nightmarish version of this is his image of Kurtz on his stretcher, `opening his mouth voraciously, as if to devour *all* the earth with *all* its mankind' (*HD*, p. 155, italics mine). This Marlow — now back in Europe — is no longer a baffled intelligence on the threshold of the wilderness. He is rather caught up once more in a European agonistics of knowledge, in a conflict with all those `intruders whose knowledge of life was to me an irritating pretence, because I felt so sure they could not possibly know the things I knew' (*HD*, p. 152).

For Levinas, of course, the ethical relation is not abstract but personal. It is first and foremost an encounter with a face. The `situation where totality breaks up', writes Levinas, is precisely `the gleam of exteriority or of transcendence in the face of the Other' (*TI*, p. 24). The face is `a living presence', expression (*TI*, p. 66). As such, in its mobility and multiplicity, it escapes any `form' to which I might seek to reduce it or its possessor. It cannot be `contained...comprehended, that is, encompassed' (*TI*, p. 194):

The face of the Other at each moment destroys and overflows the plastic image it leaves me, the idea existing to my own measure and to the measure of its *ideatum* — the adequate idea. (*TI*, pp. 50-51)

Thus the principle of irreducibility — of infinity itself — is experienced in the face of the Other and its unmasterable `foreignness' (*TI*, p. 194). The `epiphany of the face' involves an experience of its `nakedness' or destitution as supplication or demand (*TI*, p. 75). The face asks for a response of me. It engages me in responsibility, because it requires that I give. It commands me from an absolute height, in Levinas's phrase, and its `mastery' of me (id.) is inseparable from the fact that, in principle, I cannot master it. Thus

...the presence before a face, my orientation toward the Other, can lose the avidity proper to the gaze only by turning into generosity, incapable of approaching the other with empty hands. (*TI*, p. 50)

The `generosity' in question manifests itself in the first instance as communication: in Levinas's terms, in language. As an `exchange of ideas about the world', language actually presupposes `the originality of the face' (*TI*, p. 202). Language breaks out of us in response to the other and his or her destitution. As Blanchot describes it, the Levinasian imperative insists that `I will not speak of the other or about the other but I will speak...*to* the other'.[17] For the primary feature of language is `the interpellation, the vocative':

The other is maintained and confirmed in his heterogeneity as soon as one calls upon him, be it only to say to him that one cannot speak to him, to classify him as sick, to announce to him his death sentence; at the same time as grasped, wounded, outraged, he is 'respected.' The invoked is not what I comprehend: *he is not under a category*. (*TI*, p. 69)

[17] Maurice Blanchot, `Our Clandestine Companion', in Richard A. Cohen (ed.), *Face to Face with Levinas* (Albany: State University of New York Press, 1986), pp. 41-50, p. 45.

Thus the encounter with the face and through language has an absolute ethical priority over cognition and representation, over any impulse to know the other. For to speak in response to the other is always, in the first instance, to refuse to reduce him to terms, to greet him or her in his or her alterity.

The crucial point about Marlow's final encounter with the Intended seems to me to be that, in what Levinas calls the face to face, Marlow turns aside from the notional priority of `the things I knew'. He abandons his own conclusive truth, the truth he has represented and produced in his own narrative, the truth to which his narrative has led. He does this in the service of a higher claim: the immediate demand of the other. Throughout the tale, Marlow has repeatedly been aware of the demand or supplication of the face, notably in the case of the `moribund shape' beneath the tree:

> ...I saw a face near my hand. The black bones reclined at full length with one shoulder against the tree, and slowly the eyelids rose and the sunken eyes looked up at me, enormous and vacant, a kind of blind, white flicker in the depths of the orbs, which died out slowly. (*HD*, p. 66)

But he also repeatedly withdraws from the face into thinking what Levinas calls the category. (`The man seemed young — almost a boy — but you know with them it's hard to tell', *HD*, p.67). If, from the start, for Marlow, the Intended appears as an unreal figure or `Shade' (*HD*, p. 160), it is precisely because she comes to him as a face of whose appeal he is immediately and agonizingly aware:

> She came forward, all in black, with a pale head, floating towards me in the dusk.... This fair hair, this pale visage, this pure brow, seemed surrounded by an ashy halo from which the dark eyes looked out at me. (*HD*, p. 157)

The destitution or `awful desolation' (id.) of the face of the Intended is something of which Marlow is at once aware, and to which he cannot but respond. (`I saw her and him in the same instant of time — his death and her sorrow — I saw her sorrow in the very moment of his death', id.). Equally, `the appealing fixity of her gaze, that seemed to watch for more words on my lips' (*HD*, p. 158) repeatedly summons Marlow into speech. But, more remarkably, it compels him into an acknowledgment of the absolute priority of the other. For he now not only repeatedly responds to the need of the face, but surrenders his own knowledge and truth to it. As the ethical demand persists, so the clarities of enlightenment begin to fade:

> 'You knew him best,' I repeated. And perhaps she did. But with every word spoken the room was growing darker, and only her forehead, smooth and white, remained illumined by the unextinguishable light of belief and love. (*HD*, p. 158)

The significance of the final lie thus becomes evident: it is in no respect a defeat for Marlow, but a triumph. For it involves a final abandonment of truth and the category in the service of the ethical demand. It gives priority to the face and the need to respond to the face. Marlow gives up his knowledge in favour of the other's need. In doing so, he resorts to a very different conception of justice to the patriarchal one that has hitherto dominated the novel and is exemplified in the brickmaker:

> It seemed to me that the house would collapse before I could escape, that the heavens would fall upon my head. But nothing happened. The heavens do not fall for such a trifle. Would they have fallen, I wonder, if I had rendered Kurtz that justice which was his due? Hadn't he said he wanted only justice? But I couldn't. (*HD*, p. 162)

Various editors point out that Marlow is here recalling the Latin maxim, `*Fiat justitia, ruat coelum*'.[18] The implication of the end of the story is something like the reverse of that maxim: it is when such a conception of justice is abandoned that ethics — like

---

[18] See, for example, Joseph Conrad, *Heart of Darkness*, ed. Robert Hampson (Penguin, 1995), p. 139.

Marlow's `infinite pity' (*HD*, p. 161) — is made possible.

But finally, how adequate a response is *Heart of Darkness* in such a reading to the questions — of race, gender and the colonial enterprise — that it raises today? Achebe has insisted that what should be the `real question' in Conrad's story — `the dehumanization of Africa and Africans' as the result of an `age-long' European attitude — never really gets mooted at all.[19] Is an account of *Heart of Darkness* which reads its self-deconstructive impetus in ethical terms an adequate rejoinder to Achebe's argument? Undoubtedly not. But perhaps Achebe's case should not exactly be `answered'. There is conceivably a certain implausibility, an element of wishful thinking, to attempts to turn Conrad into a post-modern liberal — or any kind of contemporary liberal — *avant la lettre*, at least, in *Heart of Darkness*. But, however compelling Achebe's account of Conrad's complicities in certain respects, it has at least one feature in common with liberal and equally with conservative accounts of *Heart of Darkness*: it assumes that, in principle, the story speaks of and addresses a whole, claims the attention of a whole readership. Yet Conrad himself puts such totalizing discourse radically into question. Even if it is indeed the case that the story had nothing much of positive value to say to blacks (or women) — even if its significance is a matter of particular historical and cultural proportions — that significance is not negligible. Contemporary thought has repeatedly suggested that the cruelties and injustices of imperialism and patriarchy, and the miseries that have been their consequence, may finally be inseparable from Western ontology, from a habit of thought that deems it possible and necessary to speak of and therefore master the other as whole, to reduce the other to the terms of the same. In *Heart of Darkness,* in playing Kurtzian discourse off against Marlovian discourse, Conrad plays totality off against infinity, the thought of being and the representation of being against the thought

---

[19] Chinua Achebe, `An Image of Africa: Racism in Conrad's *Heart of Darkness*', pp. 251-62, p. 257.

of an alterity that overflows all ideas and representations of being. In that respect, he begins to deconstruct a discourse upon which imperialism depends for its conviction and survival, the `idea at the back' of the `conquest of the earth' (*HD*, pp. 50-51). It is precisely in that practice that I would want to locate the more significant ethics in *Heart of Darkness*. It may be that thus, like others more or less contemporary with him (Nietzsche and Freud, for example) and with similar resistances and complicities, Conrad begins the long job of winding white, European, masculine culture towards the end of its power, in a manner from which modern, white European males have chiefly to learn.

NO REFUGE: THE DUPLICITY OF DOMESTIC SAFETY IN CONRAD'S FICTION

CAROLA M. KAPLAN

Throughout Conrad's fiction, there is a fundamental connection between the public and private spheres in which the domestic world reflects in miniature the larger world outside it. The nature of this connection emerges in a common narrative pattern wherein the apparent safety of the domestic sphere proves to be illusory. Not only do the dangers of the larger world intrude upon the private world, but the narrative discloses that they already exist within it.

I will begin by listing the common elements of this recurrent narrative pattern: in it, a character — usually, but not always, a woman — seeks refuge in the domestic sphere from the dangers of the outside world. The character is promised such protection, but this promise is not fulfilled because the domestic world turns out to be as dangerous as the larger one. Over time, the domestic drama reveals with terrifying clarity just what the dangers of the larger world are — and how impossible it is to elude or escape them. Finally, the character seeking refuge is either betrayed within the domestic sphere itself or is destroyed in the outside world when attempting to protect both self and would-be rescuer.

This is the basic pattern of the domestic narrative in *Lord Jim*, `Amy Foster', *The Secret Agent* and *Victory*. In *Lord Jim,* Jim and Jewel's partnership is threatened from without by the intrusion of the world Jim left behind and from within by Jim's egotism and sense of cultural superiority. On the one hand, Jim offers Jewel protection from domestic violence, which she refuses, stating that she feels quite capable of killing her oppressor herself, but chooses not to. On the other hand, Jim fails to provide Jewel with the security and emotional commitment she seeks. In the end, Jewel loses Jim, as she feared, to his own culture, which seeks him out in the figure of Gentleman Brown, whose claims he acknowledges, as he has never acceded to Jewel's.

In `Amy Foster', the Polish castaway, Yanko, turns to the English servant girl, Amy, to protect him from the cruel treatment he has suffered at the hands of her countrymen. Since she alone has shown him kindness, he hopes in marrying her to escape the hatred of the larger society. In time, however, Amy too succumbs to the distrust of outsiders that is her cultural inheritance, and she abandons Yanko to die alone. Thus, the xenophobia of the larger world resurfaces in the heart of Yanko's family to undo him. In *Victory,* Lena and Heyst's alliance is threatened from without by the greed, lust and rapacity of others, but also from within by Heyst's misanthropy and paranoia. Their relationship is doomed as much by Axel Heyst's conviction that `he who forms a tie is lost' (*V*, pp. 199-200) as by the overt threat of the desperadoes who invade their island retreat. In the end, the plot reverses the cliche with which it began — the rescue of a girl in danger by a courageous older man — in Lena's heroic self-sacrifice in attempting to deliver her ambivalent saviour.

Of all Conrad's fictions, *The Secret Agent* shows the most extreme failure of the domestic sphere to provide refuge from the larger world. Unlike the other three works, it presents an unrelievedly grim picture of domestic life in a marriage in which there is no love, no mutual promises, no idealism, only subterfuge and delusion. When the social contract of marriage fails Winnie and her domestic sanctuary is betrayed from within, she becomes the novel's most radical anarchist and only successful terrorist. Unlike Verloc, who fails in his plan to blow up Greenwich Observatory, Winnie does manage to stop time — Verloc's, Ossipon's and her own.

Yet what makes the vision of *The Secret Agent* truly terrible is not its cynicism about marriage but its depiction of a world so fundamentally dangerous that personal betrayal is almost beside the point. In a surrealistic vision that prefigures Kafka, *The Secret Agent* reveals that the greatest danger comes from beyond home and society. The real threat is the threat of the Real, as Jacques Lacan terms it — a surplus beyond the Imaginary and the Symbolic realms, from beyond human life itself. It emerges as an entropic force, without human form or shape, as a potential for the obliteration or evacuation of the subject. The Real, the third term in Lacan's system, is an element that exists beyond the opposition of the Imaginary and the Symbolic that constitutes the experience of the subject. Although it radically transcends the symbolic order that defines and circumscribes the subject, the Real intrudes upon this order, making its presence felt in the anomalous, the chaotic, and the fragmentary. Most disconcertingly, the Real resides within the subject itself, as an abyss, a void that swallows meaning and threatens implosion.[1]

Conrad recognizes the existence of what Lacan terms the Real and describes it most powerfully in his image of the cosmic knitting machine:

> There is a — let us say — a machine. It evolved...itself out of a chaos of scraps of iron and behold! — it knits. I am horrified at the horrible work and stand appalled. I feel it ought to embroider — but it goes on knitting. You come and say: 'this is all right; it's only a question of the right kind of oil. Let us use this — for instance — celestial oil and the machine shall embroider a most beautiful design in purple and gold'. Will it? Alas no. You cannot by any special lubrication make embroidery with a knitting machine. And the most withering thought is that the infamous thing has made itself; made itself without thought, without conscience, without foresight, without eyes, without heart. It is a tragic accident — and it has happened. You can't interfere with it. The last drop of bitterness is in the suspicion that you can't even smash it.... [I]t is indestructible!

[1] Jacques Lacan, *Écrits, A Selection*, tr. Alan Sheridan (New York: W.W. Norton, 1977), pp. 168-169, p. 196.

It knits us in and it knits us out. It has knitted time space, pain, death, corruption, despair and all the illusions — and nothing matters. (*CLI*, p. 425)

This image of the universe as a monstrous machine in which humans are trapped, a machine whose workings are oblivious to human need and desire, is the key to understanding the pervasive dissatisfaction, malevolence, and destructiveness that characterize human behaviour in *The Secret Agent*. It is this essential nonadaptation of the universe to human desire rather than any specific and remediable social injustice that engenders the inextinguishable *ressentiment* that governs the daily actions of most of the characters as well as the futile talk and gestures of the novel's so-called revolutionaries. The Professor exemplifies this pattern: having been thwarted in his youthful desire for `undisputed success' (*SA*, p. 80), he obtains `the appearances of power and personal prestige' (p. 81) by making bombs. As the narrator comments, `the way of even the most justifiable revolutions is prepared by personal impulses disguised into creeds' (p. 81). Throughout, the novel points repeatedly to the humanly unsatisfactory nature of the symbolic order. It continually points out elements that, try as they may, humans cannot control. In *The Secret Agent*, death continually threatens to extinguish human life; and violence may erupt at any moment to destroy human ramparts erected against catastrophe. In this way, Winnie Verloc's efforts to call Stevie to her husband's attention for her brother's benefit only lead to Stevie's destruction. In describing the Verlocs' marriage, the narrator seems to comment as well on the relation of humans to the symbolic order: `Their accord was perfect, but it was not precise' (p. 245).

The imprecision of this accord results from the disastrous intrusion of the Real. As Joan Copjec describes the relation of the symbolic order to the Real, the Symbolic protects itself from `the terrifying real' by declaring `its impossibility'. The Symbolic, in other words, must include the negation of what it is not. This declaration leads to the paradox that `the symbolic will not be filled only with itself, since it will contain this element of its own negation'.[2] The question then is, since the Real is that which cannot be represented within the Symbolic, that which has no signifier, how does it make its presence known? The answer is, through anomalous effects within the symbolic order. For such an intrusion of the traumatic Real into the symbolic order, Lacan coined a term: *extimité* or `extimacy', which he described as `the intimate exteriority...that is the Thing'.[3] Interestingly, in explicating Lacan's idea, Jacques-Alain Miller gives as an example of an `extimacy' a bomb: Miller explains that an extimacy is `an object incompatible with the presence of the subject: it implies a physical disappearance of bodies that...represent the subject. If you can sit down opposite a painting and chat with people next to you, it is not so with the bomb; when you speak about this type of object, the subject disappears'.[4] Slavoj Zizek further explains that the extimacy or `extimate kernel' is at the very heart of the subject and, although it cannot be symbolized, it produces `a residue, remnant, a leftover...that is more than the subject, yet simultaneously constitutive of the subject'.[5] In addition, the extimacy `has a series of properties — it exercises a certain structural causality, it can produce a series of effects in the symbolic reality of subjects' (Zizek, *SOI*, p. 163).

In *The Secret Agent,* Conrad depicts the effects of the intrusion of the Real into the symbolic order in a number of ways: through reversals of logic; through gaps or holes in space and time (the most important of these is, of course, the explosion, the

[2] Joan Copjec, *Read My Desire: Lacan Against the Historicists* (Cambridge, Mass.: MIT Press, 1994), p. 120.

[3] Jacques Alain-Miller (ed.), *The Seminar of Jacques Lacan, Book VIII: The Ethics of Psychoanalysis, 1959-60* (Routledge, 1992), p. 139.

[4] Jacques-Alain Miller, `Extimité', *Prose Studies*, 11.3 (December 1988), pp. 121-31, p. 127.

[5] Slavoj Zizek, *The Sublime Object of Ideology* (New York: Verso, 1991), hereafter Zizek, *SOI*; p. 180.

unrepresented event whose absence is at the center of the novel);[6] through repetition (such as Stevie's drawings of circles within circles, suggesting `a rendering of cosmic chaos', Hillis Miller, *PR*, p. 52); through anomalous elements that portend death; through inexplicable symbolism and strange language effects.[7] For the purpose of this paper, I will deal briefly with four ways in which Conrad suggests the radically disruptive effects of the Real on the symbolic order: in three areas of human endeavour — the organization of human relationships, the regulation of time, and the mapping of space — and in a series of anomalous effects that portend disintegration and death.

That entropy prevails in the symbolic order is demonstrated in the perverse nature of human relationships in the novel. All ostensibly intimate relationships fail — marriage in particular. All married couples in the novel act at cross purposes: the Verlocs; the Commissioner and his wife; Mrs. Neale and her `debauched' husband; Winnie's mother and father. Also, all marriage relationships are in fact triangles. For each pair, there is a crucial third party: Stevie, `the salt of passion' in Winnie's otherwise `tasteless life' (*SA*, p. 174); Toodles, the private secretary (unpaid) to Sir Ethelred; and the society hostess whom Annie, the Assistant Commissioner's wife, dotes on. On the other hand, apparently adversarial relationships have a kind of intimacy in that both parties understand each other, communicate clearly, and operate to common purposes. Thus Verloc, comprehending nothing of Winnie, understands Vladimir, `whom in virtue of subtle moral affinities he was capable of judging correctly' (*SA*, p. 53); and Heat finds he can

---

[6] See J. Hillis Miller, *Poets of Reality: Six Twentieth-Century Writers* (Cambridge, Mass.: Harvard University Press, 1965), hereafter Hillis Miller, *PR*; p. 51.

[7] See Michael Mageean, `*The Secret Agent*'s (T)extimacies: A Traumatic Reading Beyond Rhetoric', in Carola M. Kaplan and Anne B. Simpson (eds.), *Seeing Double: Revisioning Edwardian and Modernist Literature* (New York: St. Martin's Press, forthcoming).

`understand the mind of a burglar, because, as a matter of fact, the mind and the instincts of a burglar are of the same kind as the mind and the instincts of a police officer' (*SA*, p. 92).

Not only personal relationships but time is out of joint for human beings — and none of the characters in *The Secret Agent* can set it right. Chief Inspector Heat boasts that he has all potential criminals under twenty-four hour surveillance, yet in due course even Heat is forced to acknowledge that

> in the close-woven stuff of relations between conspirator and police there occur...*sudden holes in space and time.* A given anarchist may be watched inch by inch and minute by minute, but a moment always comes when somehow all sight and touch of him are lost for a few hours, during which something (generally an explosion) more or less deplorable does happen. (*SA*, p. 85, emphasis mine).

Similarly, just before his murder, Verloc acknowledges the extimacy that spoiled his plan and led to Stevie's death:

> The position was gone through no one's fault really. A small, tiny fact had done it. It was like slipping on a bit of orange peel in the dark and breaking your leg. (*SA*, p. 236)

If time proves ungovernable by the human characters in *The Secret Agent*, space turns out to be chaotic as well. As Verloc walks through London streets en route to his meeting with Vladimir, house numbers and street names change for no apparent reason. Even more disconcertingly, throughout the novel the distinction between interior and exterior space disappears. The contents of interiors spill out into the streets, while the public life of the streets makes its way within. In this way, Verloc wears his outdoor clothing — his coat and hat — at table. Just as incongruously, the dangerous encounter between Chief Inspector Heat and the Professor with his bomb takes place in a street where parlor furniture has been set outside. Among these items is a couch, generally a symbol of comfort and domestic repose, which in this scene serves as a prop for the Professor as he threatens to blow himself and Heat to pieces. By association, this `unhappy, homeless couch' (*SA*, p. 82) calls to mind `the horsehair sofa on which Mr. Verloc loved to take his ease' (*SA*, p. 153), and on which he will later be murdered. Thus the `outcast couch' (*SA*, p. 83) becomes one of many objects that prefigure the deaths of the principal characters.

Throughout the novel, death lies in wait. Two recurrent sets of images — one suggestive of drowning and the other of explosion — prefigure the deaths of Stevie and Winnie. Whenever characters descend into the London streets, they seem to be on the verge of drowning. The London air is described as unable to support life, containing water rather than oxygen. The street is compared to `a slimy aquarium' (*SA*, p. 147). When Winnie goes outside after murdering her husband, `the open air had a foretaste of drowning; a slimy dampness enveloped her, entered her nostrils, clung to her hair' (*SA*, p. 269). Even Winnie's mother, Michaelis, and the cabdriver are all described as bloated: they resemble waterlogged corpses and thus uncannily foreshadow Winnie's drowning.

Furthermore, the ever-present possibility of the disintegration of the subject is figured throughout the novel in the constant descriptions of characters as fragments or assemblages of body parts. Thus, Privy Councillor Wurmt is reduced to `the bald top of a head, and a drooping dark grey whisker on each side of a pair of wrinkled hands' (*SA*, p. 16) and Karl Yundt, to `a narrow, snow-white wisp of a goatee hanging limply from his chin' (*SA*, p. 42). These images call to mind Stevie's fragmented remains. Often people are described as objects or in conjunction with objects, so much so that the distinction between human life and inanimate matter dissolves. A police constable is designated `part of inorganic nature, surging apparently out of a lamp-post' (*SA*, p. 14). When the Professor walks away, a mechanical player-piano goes on playing (*SA*, p. 79), as if it has taken his place. Finally, Winnie just before her death resembles a corpse: her face is described variously as `a mask' (*SA*, p. 212), as `frozen' (*SA*, p.

241), and as `stony' (*SA*, p. 260). These descriptions suggest how quickly the animate can become inanimate, how easily death can extinguish the subject.

By the end, all the principal characters have been evacuated from the symbolic order of the novel and all human levels, distinctions, and relationships have disappeared. Early in the novel, the public sphere collapses into the private sphere, which the Assistant Commissioner acknowledges when he calls the bombing `a domestic drama' (*SA*, p. 222). In the private sphere, the family has already imploded, past and future generations compressed into Winnie's emotionally incestuous relationship with her brother. Finally, the domestic sphere disappears altogether: Stevie dies; Winnie kills Verloc; Winnie commits suicide. All spheres of human action and relationship having collapsed, the final scene narrows to a single image, that of the Professor, bomb in pocket, pursuing his solitary course through dark London streets, like a black hole that has absorbed all light.

In the eradication of human constructs and in the obliteration of human subjects in *The Secret Agent,* Conrad shows the reader the terrible workings of the knitting machine. More than any human actions in either the public or domestic sphere, these traumatic intrusions of the Real make of the world a place that can never be domesticated, a place in which the human subject is permanently homeless. Thus, neither Conrad's characters nor his readers can ever feel `at home' in his fictions.

READING SHADOWS INTO LINES: CONRAD WITH LACAN

JOSIANE PACCAUD-HUGUET

Has there ever been anything like a magic signifier on which one might pin one's faith, or a unified subject in full command of human destiny? Such are the questions which *The Shadow-Line* answers negatively. `Nothing should ever be taken for granted.... "I feel it's all my fault"' (*SL*, p. 95) concludes Conrad's captain narrator, after discovering his predecessor's treachery over the quinine in the medicine chest — the panacea kept in the `miraculous shrine' (*SL*, p. 79) that was supposed to save the ship from deadly peril. But why should such questions be raised so crucially in a text written during the first act of the tragedy of modernity, in 1914-1915, when `the heavy thud of a collapsing structure'[1] delivered the Western world into the jaws of a war that was commonly figured as a man-eating monster calling from the abyss for some collective sacrifice? Conrad provides a literary clue in the epigraph he chose from `La Musique' for his `Calm-piece':[2] in Baudelaire's poem, the sea, `calme plat, grand miroir/ De mon désespoir', offers a reflecting screen. So, too, *The Shadow-Line* uses the sea to stage the drama of man's longing for what Jacques Lacan, in his study of

---

[1] Jacques Lacan, *Écrits: A Selection*, tr. Alan Sheridan (London: Tavistock Publications, 1977), hereafter Lacan, *E*; p. 115.

[2] In the Author's Note to *'Twixt Land and Sea*, Conrad observes that `if there is to be any classification by subjects, I have done two Storm-pieces in "The Nigger of the *Narcissus*" and in "Typhoon"; and two Calm-pieces: this one and "The Shadow Line," a book which belongs to a later period' (*TLS*, p. ix).

Antigone, calls the state of being `Entre-Deux-Morts'. The argument here will be that, like *Antigone*, but also like Virginia Woolf's *Jacob's Room* and D.H. Lawrence's `The Fox' — two nearly contemporary pieces — *The Shadow-Line* reads like an oblique exploration of the death-drive and its related motifs: guilt, fear and the unavowable truth of man's ob-scene *jouissance*. All three of these war-pieces present worlds poised on the edge of an abyss — a gulf — whose deadly silence maddeningly undermines any hope of command or mastery, casting shadows between the lines of generation, whether historical or artistic.

It is here that psychoanalysis will be needed as a mode of thinking the constitution of subjectivity in the face of the Real after the fall of what Lacan calls the wall of semblance, in one of those periods of crisis when the vein of liberal humanism[3] with its pretty fictions reaches a point of exhaustion. The concepts of symbolic castration, of the paternal metaphor and *jouissance*[4] will help to

---

[3] In `The Freudian Thing', Lacan speaks of psychoanalysis as a revolution in knowledge `worthy of Copernicus...if it can be said that as a result of that discovery the very centre of the human being was no longer to be found at the place assigned to it by a whole humanist tradition' (*E*, p. 114).

[4] I will frequently refer to Nestor Braunstein's most helpful book *La Jouissance: un Concept Lacanien* (Paris: Point Hors Ligne, 1992), hereafter Braunstein, *JCL*, which clearly establishes the distinctions and relations between, on the one hand, *la jouissance de la Chose*, inaccessible to human culture, and, on the other, the types of *jouissance* available through language. Lacan defines the concept of the Thing in terms of `ce qui du Réel pâtit du signifiant' (*L'Éthique de la Psychanalyse* [Paris: Seuil, 1986], hereafter Lacan, *EP*; p. 142), i.e. that part of the Real which never comes into existence because of the presence of the signifier. It is through the effect of the semiotic bar that the Thing forever remains outside the pale of language. As such, it holds the place of the absolute, forever lost object which sets desire in motion because of its inaccessibility, as `la Chose réelle et en même temps mythique, effet rétroactif de la symbolisation primordiale, objet absolu et à jamais perdu du désir' (Braunstein, *JCL*, p. 98). As such, it is often associated in symbolic representations with maternal figures (the mother being the first love object) and with death (the ultimate loss).

awaken many textual resonances dormant in Conrad's text which, in its turn, illuminates the structure of human desire in relation to death and language.

The Shadow-Line, like *The Secret Sharer*, is a title with many reverberations. Are we to take the text at its word and believe that the title simply refers to a young man's crossing the boundary between youth and age?

> One closes behind one the little gate of mere boyishness — and enters an enchanted garden. Its very shades glow with promise. Every turn of the path has its seduction. And it isn't because it is an undiscovered country. One knows well enough that all mankind had streamed that way. (*SL*, p. 3)

What are we to make then of the uncanny prose, of the curious reference to the `undiscovered country' — the phrase which, in Hamlet's soliloquy, designates death — suggesting, as it does, that the truth might be a little more elusive indeed than it first seemed? As Conrad himself wrote in a letter of 1917 to Sidney Colvin, the nightmare of history made it impossible to write pleasing stories at this particular time:

> To sit down and invent fairy tales was impossible then. It isn't very possible even now. I was writing that thing in Dec., 1914, and Jan. to March, 1915.... Here I'll only say that experience is transposed into spiritual terms — in art a perfectly legitimate thing to do, as long as one preserves the exact truth enshrined therein.[5]

The idea of transposition — i.e. of a metaphorical process — seems crucial to a reading of this `fairly complex piece of work' (Author's Note, *SL*, p. v), which stages obliquely man's unavowable desire to reach beyond the pleasure principle, once the bar of the paternal

---

[5] Letter to Sir Sidney Colvin, 27 February [1917], in G. Jean-Aubry (ed.), *Joseph Conrad: Life and Letters* (London: William Heinemann, 1927), II, pp. 182-183.

metaphor has broken open. The imaginary grapple with the primitive *jouissance de la Chose* in the stillness of the womb/tomb: such is the pattern underlying the dramaturgy of the young captain, Mr Burns and Ransome on the becalmed ship, which is no doubt an emblem of what Henry James called the tragic `plunge of civilisation' into an `abyss of blood and darkness'. Conrad's appreciation of James invokes the image of the artistic individual confronting `a dying earth' and `courageous enough to interpret the ultimate experience of mankind in terms of his temperament', while the last surviving humans `clustered on his threshold to watch the last flicker of light on a black sky, to hear the last word uttered in the stilled workshop of the earth'.[6]

The Shadow-Line also makes us hear and see some `Thing' from the `stilled workshop of the earth'. It brings its `additional turn of the racking screw' (*SL*, p. 114); not, however, by telling some hair-raising ghost-story, but by bringing `the effect of a mental shock ... on a common mind' (p. vi) to bear on the very lines of a narrative contaminated by a disease of negativity, in which we can recognize the mark of Conrad's own style. It would be a mistake, obviously, to believe that the undertones of the `valley of the shadow of death' are specifically modernist, although they are surely dominant in modern writing. Conrad's novella is inscribed in the line of a literary tradition that goes back to David's *Psalms*[7] or, closer to us,

---

[6] Joseph Conrad, `Henry James: An Appreciation', *Notes on Life and Letters*, pp. 11-19; pp. 13-14.

[7] An interesting passage significantly deleted from the published version of *The Shadow-Line* refers to the young captain's dream of the bull of Bashan, a direct reference to *Psalms* 22.12: `Many bulls have compassed me: strong bulls of Bashan have beset me round'. The deleted passage is worth quoting: `...the unpeopled stillness of that gulf weighed on my shaken confidence...I resisted it.... I welcomed a great wave of fatigue that all at once overwhelmed me from head to foot...I dreamt of the Bull of Bashan. He was roaring beyond all reason on his side of a very high fence striking it with his forehoof and also rattling his horns against it from time to time. On my

(continued...)

`The Rime of the Ancient Mariner', one of the most explicit
literary fictions about the imagined space between mental and
biological death. In the Argument that precedes the poem,
Coleridge summarises the narrative as `How a Ship having passed
the Line was driven by Storms to the cold Country towards the
South Pole'.[8] The poem itself presents this voyage as involving an
encounter with the `Nightmare LIFE-IN-DEATH' (1.193). The
mariner who murdered the albatross, the bird of life, confesses:

> Since then, at an uncertain hour,
> That agony returns:
> And till my ghastly tale is told,
> This heart within me burns.　　　　(582 ff.)

The telling of the tale, then, is a necessity related to some desire
called up by the conventional image of the `burning heart'. In *The
Shadow-Line*, this becomes a full character, Mr Burns — a
projection space for the temptation of the gulf, `l'immense gouffre',
whose strain speaks to the desire of Baudelaire's splenetic *damné* in
the poem partly quoted in Conrad's epigraph:

> Je sens vibrer en moi toutes les passions
> 　　D'un vaisseau qui souffre;
> Le bon vent, la tempête et ses convulsions
> 　　Sur l'immense gouffre
> Me bercent. D'autres fois, calme plat, grand miroir
> 　　De mon désespoir.

---

[7] (...continued)
side of the fence my purpose was (in my dream) to lead a contemplative
existence. I despised the brute, but gradually a fear woke up in me — that he
would end by breaking through — not through the fence — through my
purpose. A horrible fear'. *The Shadow-Line*, ed. Jeremy Hawthorn (Oxford:
Oxford University Press, 1985), hereafter Hawthorn; p. 140.

[8] `The Rime of the Ancient Mariner' in Samuel Taylor Coleridge, *Poetical
Works*, ed. Ernest Hartley Coleridge (Oxford: Oxford University Press,
1969), pp.186-209, p.186.

Conrad omitted the reference to the gulf, but it returns as a central metaphor in his war-tale. We know since Freud that metaphor, a form of condensation, is one of the processes through which unconscious desires may formulate themselves.

The polysemy of the word `gulf' is indeed productive in Conrad's fiction: there are analogies to be drawn between Decoud's last moments on the Golfo Placido, a mortal plunge into the primitive womb of the Great Mother, and the young captain's experience on the Gulf of Siam after Captain Giles's parting words: `Don't let anything tempt you over' (*SL*, p. 45)

Crossing the Bar

Here we need to return to *The Secret Sharer* and take a detour via the signifier `Koh-ring'. Both *The Shadow-Line* and *The Secret Sharer* have been called tales of hubris, whose purpose is to shatter the `unconscious arrogance of their protagonists'.[9] In each of them, `Koh-ring' sounds like a foreign name in which, it has been noted, the first syllable of Korzeniowski can be heard. Thus it is likely that the symbolism of the `towering shadow' (*TLS*, p. 141) is loaded with connotations related to the structure of the Name-of-the-Father as that first signifier (Lacan's S1) which takes the place of the unspeakable Thing (the Freudian *Ding*) and as such marks the beginning of the signifying chain which Lacan symbolizes as `S2...Sn'.[10]

In *The Secret Sharer*, the shadowy island ultimately erects a bar between the young captain and the temptation of imaginary

[9] Douglas Brown, *Three Tales from Conrad* (London: Hutchinson, 1960), p. 31.
[10] `Signifiant 1 qui prend la place de la Chose, de ce trognon du Réel qui pâtissait à cause du phallus, signifiant zéro, inarticulable, et se place à la limite de la batterie signifiante, en dehors de l'Autre' (Braunstein, *JCL*, p. 98).

identification with the destructive bent he recognizes in Leggatt, his `own reflection in the depths of a sombre and immense mirror' (*TLS*, p. 101). With Leggatt, in imaginative sympathy, at least, he has penetrated into those '*uncharted* regions' beyond Koh-ring (*TLS*, p. 134, emphasis mine) — in other words, into the pre-symbolic void of the Real. The ending of the tale formulates the necessary return, however, as the young captain surrenders Leggatt to an embryonic version of civilisation:

> `There,' I said. `It's *got to be* Koh-ring.... It *must* be inhabited. And on the coast opposite there is what looks like the mouth of a biggish river — with *some town*, no doubt, not far up....' The black southern hill of Koh-ring seemed to hang right over the ship like a towering fragment of the everlasting night. On that enormous mass of blackness there was not a gleam to be seen, not a sound to be heard (*TLS*, p. 134, p. 139, emphasis mine)

The `towering fragment of the everlasting night' is the limit beyond which the young captain is in danger of dissolution in a sombre mirror. Yet, as such, it provides the first land*mark*, a cultural symbol signalling — like Virginia Woolf's lighthouse — the necessity (what `must' be, has `got to be') of lack, and, thus, the constitutive moment of the paternal *metaphor*.

We needn't go very far from Koh-ring to find the mark of separation from the temptation of dissolution in the uncharted regions, a point when some signifier functions as that `marque du manque', the mediating symbol which bars the gates of the primitive *jouissance* of fusion in sameness, in the womb/tomb or the maternal waters.[11] This signifier is the Lacanian phallus, the mark of the negativity of language, the zero signifier anterior to the

---

[11] It is `en premier lieu le signifiant qui s'imprime sur le Réel, le nom du manque chez l'Autre, la barre sur le désir de la mère...signifiant impair, degré zéro, indicateur de l'impossibilité radicale de l'accès à la Chose, symbole qui installe la division des sexes et des jouissances...qui s'imaginarise comme manque dans l'image désirée' (Braunstein, *JCL*, p. 98).

advent of the paternal metaphor. Far from being an object — sexual or other — it is in fact

> a signifier [incarnating] the very function of the semiotic *bar* — the very principle of imposition of a limit, the principle of censorship and of repression which forever *bars* all access to the signified as such.... It can only play its role under a veil.... It then becomes that which...bars the signified.[12]

The white floppy hat — a synecdoche for Leggatt's body — floating on the water after the painful parting clearly fulfils the function of the phallic veil as that *mark* — a symbol in the absence of the thing desired — *saving* the captain from wreckage:

> ...a white object floating within a yard of the ship's side. White on the black water. A phosphorescent flash passed under it. What was that thing?...I recognised my own floppy hat...the saving mark for my eyes. (*TLS*, p. 142).

The ambiguity of the phrase `that thing' is surely not accidental: we may read it anaphorically in reference to the phosphorescent flash — a sign from the underworld where Leggatt's desired body disappears — or cataphorically in reference to the hat, the remains of the lost object of desire after the temptation of fusion with the secret sharer has been dispelled. Thus the very *language* of Conrad's text is a recognition that the phallus is Janus-faced, with one side looking toward the unnameable Real and the other toward the beginning of a signifying chain. We should also note here the peculiar `delayed decoding' effect, today acknowledged as an authentic marker of Conrad's narrative style. The semantic delay stems from a pause in the reader's progress on the page, whereby `that thing' appears briefly to give us a glimpse of the captain's

---

[12] Lacan, quoted in Soshana Felman, `Turning the Screw of Interpretation', in *Literature and Psychoanalysis* (Baltimore: The Johns Hopkins University Press, 1982) pp. 94-207, hereafter Felman, *TSI*; p. 172.

private fantasy world, only immediately to deny the possibility of such a reading by the reference to a trivial object, the floppy hat. We will see that the same sort of effect of recognition/denial returns, amplified as it were, in *The Shadow-Line*.

The very topography of Conrad's war novella suggests that the voyage functions like some sort of imaginary regression, a crossing of the bar in the opposite direction back to a moment anterior to the function of the phallus. In his introduction to the World's Classics edition, Jeremy Hawthorn suggests that the phrase `we crossed the bar' can also `be used to refer to the act of dying, and perhaps chimes with the earlier reference to Hades', pinpointing the vein on which Conrad has struck here.[13] On the glassy mirror of the sea, after crossing the bar where the old captain lies buried `right in the ship's way...out of the Gulf' (*SL*, p. 83), the ship moves closer to the abyss, *back* to the uncharted regions past Koh-ring:

> The Island of Koh-ring, a great, black, upheaved ridge amongst a lot of tiny islets, lying upon the glassy water...seemed to be the centre of the fatal circle. It seemed impossible to get away from it...the black relief of Koh-ring, looking more barren, inhospitable, and grim than ever. (*SL*, p. 84)

Daphna Erdinast-Vulcan has argued that the quest pattern in *Heart of Darkness*, *Under Western Eyes* and *The Shadow-Line* is a projection of the protagonists' `need to be authored and given identity by a sovereign Word'. The quest, however, ends in the 'eventual exposure of a glaring vacuum where the metaphysical object was believed to be found', resulting in `the loss of the Absolute, the authorial and authorizing Word'.[14] I would suggest

---

[13] Hawthorn, p. 137, n. 47. In another note about the captain's reference to Hades, Hawthorn observes that `the association between signing on or off for a voyage and being ferried across the river Styx to Hades is effectively used by Conrad at the start of *Heart of Darkness*' (p. 136, n.7).

[14] Daphna Erdinast-Vulcan, *Joseph Conrad and the Modern Temper* (Oxford: Clarendon Press, 1991), p. 89; hereafter, Erdinast-Vulcan, *JCMT*.

that what is more precisely at stake in *The Shadow-Line* is an unconscious, destructive desire to *deny* the paternal metaphor in order to follow the demonic potentiality inherent in the fairy-tale pattern.

Shadowy Figures

The shadowy effect of the paternal metaphor in relation to the written word is suggested by the devious path of the purloined letter of notification in the Sailors' Home. At the outset, the young seaman knocks at a door `labelled in black letters' and enters a room smelling of `decaying coral', filled with the mournful groans of the steward, who looks at the captain from behind a *barrier* of cardboard boxes (*SL*, pp. 9-10). The Sailor's Home itself sounds like a place of waiting between two worlds; it is reminiscent of the Casa Viola in *Nostromo* where Decoud writes to his sister before embarking on the Golfo Placido.[15] Later on, once he has gained his command, a second letter, the doctor's letter, that `half-sheet of notepaper' that was supposed to guarantee the authenticity of the quinine, produces a disquieting, eerie effect on the new captain, leaving him `with a queer sense of dealing with the uncanny' (*SL*, p. 80).

The passage on land is actually a confrontation with shadowy figures of authority, whose words seem to have a cutting edge diminishing his own stature. Captain Kent agrees to pay him off with a `soft, cryptic utterance which seemed to reach deeper than any *diamond-hard tool* could have done' (*SL*, p. 6). Captain Giles, an outsider in the harbour, equally bears the attributes of the

---

[15] `By the time this pocket-book reaches your hands much will have happened. But now it is a pause under the hovering wing of death in that silent house buried in the black night, with this dying woman, the two children...and that old man.... And I, the only other with them, don't really know whether to count myself with the living or with the dead' (*N*, p. 249).

symbolic father marked by the shadow of otherness: he is credited with `some mysterious tragedy in his life' (*SL*, p. 14) and, despite his Master's certificate, works only casually as an attendant to shipmasters. Last but not least, the presence of Captain Ellis, `redoubtable ... because of his unwarrantable assumptions' (*SL*, p. 30), makes him feel

> in common with the other seamen of the port, merely a subject for official writing, filling up of forms with all the artificial superiority of a man of pen and ink to the men who grapple with realities outside the consecrated walls of official buildings. What ghosts we must have been to him! Mere symbols to juggle with in books and heavy registers... (*SL*, p. 34)

It is that condition of ghost and symbol subjected to the letter in the hand of the Other — the effect of the paternal metaphor — that the fiction of magic command at sea is meant to deny. The young captain constructs a fairy tale in which he views himself as like `a king in his country...I mean an hereditary king, not a mere elected head of a state' (*SL*, p.62): in other words, a self-authorized subject, not someone appointed by the shadowy, *castrating* power of the pen — `mightier than the sword' (*SL*, p. 31) — which Captain Ellis drops at the end of the interview.[16]

Why should the fantasy of magic command be construed as a

---

[16] We find similar moments in Conrad's fiction when the dropping of a pen heralds a subject's progress toward the ultimate denial, i.e. death by suicide, a kind of self-inflicted castration, the last gesture of mastery: the most significant are probably to be found in *Lord Jim* and *Nostromo*, when a character attempts to write letters — Jim to Jewel, Decoud to his sister — before moving on to his death. Jim writes in his last `attempt to deliver himself': `[L]ook at the ink blot resembling the head of an arrow under these words'. Marlow adds: `The pen had spluttered, and that time he gave it up.... he had seen a broad gulf that neither eye nor voice could span' (*LJ*, pp. 340-341). In *Nostromo*, we are told that `[w]ith the writing of the last line there came upon Decoud a moment of sudden and complete oblivion. He swayed over the table as if struck by a bullet. The next moment he sat up, confused, with the idea that he had heard his pencil roll on the floor' (*N*, p. 249).

form of denial? Clearly because it implies an instrumental view of language in terms of direct power not only over a body of men but also over the body of the ship perceived as the domesticated feminine Other uncontaminated by any shadow, having `preserved the stamp of her origin' (*SL*, p. 49):

> She was mine, more absolutely mine for possession and care than anything in the world; an object of responsibility and devotion. She was there, waiting for me, spellbound, unable to move, to live, to get out into the world (till I came), like an enchanted princess. (*SL*, p. 40)

The fairy-tale component, therefore, is an attempt to screen the shadows of the paternal metaphor with an imaginary sense of continuity secured by the word 'command', designating by metonymic contiguity the speech act, a subject position and the affected object — the ship: `My rapid glance ran over her, enveloped, appropriated the form concreting the abstract sentiment of my command' (*SL*, p. 50). Unlike the father-figures who got him appointed, the new captain sees himself as the member of a continuous line, a `succession of men...a dynasty' (*SL*, pp. 52-53), finding its origin in the divine order without a shadow or gap. It is the destructive fallacy of this fantasy of origin that the voyage past Koh-ring is meant to reveal.

We might pause here and wonder about the connection with the war anxiety which Conrad experienced at a time when he found it impossible `to write fairy tales'. First it should be noted that like *Lord Jim*, *The Shadow-Line* is a split work with two distinct stages. In the first part — the Western world `outside' Patusan for Jim, the Sailor's Home on land for *The Shadow-Line* — the protagonist is confronted with the shadows of language and subjectivity, while the second part — Patusan, the voyage on the Gulf of Siam — explores the fantasy of denial in the form of a self-authorized world underpinned by the fallacy of magic language. When we come to reflect on it, there is an analogy to be drawn with the rhetoric of war founded on the fantasy that one can control Otherness by being the master of death, the ultimate Other. It seems to me that Conrad's symbolic gesture as a writer was to warn `Borys and all the others', to whom the tale is dedicated, *against* the dangers of believing blindly in the fantasy of origin urging masses of young men to sacrifice their lives for the Mother-Land at the request of autocratic political fathers. Like Joyce in another context, Conrad also warns about the dangers of imaginary identifications which project the issue of Otherness from its real locus — language and subjectivity — onto other people in the belief that once these have been mastered, the problem of difference has been dealt with for good.

What is really at stake therefore in Conrad's war piece is human subjectivity in the face of castration rendered by figures of the fragmented body.[17] In *The Secret Sharer*, Leggatt first appears like a `headless corpse' glimpsed from above, i.e. from a position of mastery (*SS*, p. 97); similarly, the first thing which the new captain looks down at, when stepping on board in *The Shadow-Line*, is not a complete body but `the upper part of a man's body projecting backwards, as it were, from one of the doors at the foot of the stairs' (*SL*, p. 52). Yet the first command in no way confirms the fantasy of unity and power: instead it takes the form of a confrontation with the primal void after the opening of a gaping hole in the *line* of dynasty — which we must certainly read as a metaphor of the collapse of the old order in the collective hysteria of wartime.

---

[17] The castration complex with its correlate, guilt, emerges symptomatically at moments when the shadow-line is crossed, as when the young captain discovers the quinine is missing — `No confessed criminal had ever been so oppressed by his sense of guilt.... I would have held them justified in tearing me limb from limb' (*SL*, p. 96) — or the moment of Burns's fading when the captain again has `the sense of guilt which clung to all my thoughts secretly.... What I felt I wanted were new limbs' (*SL*, p. 121).

The Enigma of the Other

One of the merits of Lacan's theories for the purpose of literary studies is that they have exposed the relation between disorders in human subjectivity — the object of fictional representation — and disfunctions in the symbolic order of culture and language: if the Hamlet who is `subject to his birth' burns, it is with the weight of the father's sins as they are carried by the ghost in the myth.[18] This is a point which sheds light on *The Shadow-Line*, where fragments of Shakespeare's play are frequently overheard; more precisely, it sheds light on the relation between the young captain who `chucked his berth' and his predecessor.

We are told that, for `inscrutable reasons' (*SL*, p. 58), this `uncommunicative' master had opted out of the order of culture, `made up his mind to cut adrift' (*SL*, p. 62): his last days were spent playing madly on his violin, i.e. denying the communal function of speech, instead of attending to his duties, as if responding to a mysterious siren song from the gulf. In the same way, his successor left his berth `as though all unknowing I had heard a whisper or seen something' (*SL*, p. 5). The old man's taste for music — a semiotic system of pure signifiers without signifieds — chimed with his immoderate taste for a `flesh-pot' in Haiphong, a phrase which evokes orality and thus betrays the oral fantasy of the rapacious, threatening (M)other common in fairy tales. The young captain sees a photograph of him in Haiphong:

> and by his side towered an awful, mature, white female with rapacious nostrils and a cheaply ill-omened stare in her enormous eyes. (*SL*, p. 59)

---

[18] `De quoi brûle Hamlet, si ce n'est du poids des péchés du père, que porte le fantôme dans le mythe d'Hamlet...l'héritage du père, c'est celui que nous désigne Kierkegaard, c'est son péché...c'est d'une profonde mise en doute de ce père idéal qu'il s'agit à tout instant'. Lacan, *Les Quatre Concepts Fondamentaux de la Psychanalyse*, (Paris: Seuil, 1973), p. 35.

That she was a musician, and that the old master should have been both an artist and a lover (*SL*, p. 58), recalls the epigraph from `La Musique', in which the poet overhears the call of a *jouissance* alien to language. Thus it is a most disquieting vision of femininity and of language — of sexuality and textuality — that gives free rein to the death-urge to which the mad captain has given himself up in words that sounded `atrocious' to Mr. Burns: `If I had my wish, neither the ship nor any of you would ever reach a port' (*SL*, p. 61). It is usually in fairy tales that one `has one's wish', that the demonic sides with the magic in consequence of the belief in the direct effect of the word: fairy tales are peopled both with enchanted princesses and with ghouls, two *interdependent* visions of femininity in cultural models, whose purpose is to deny the very locus of otherness, which is language.

In other words, the ship and its crew were delivered into the hands of a cruel, tyrannical Other, while the voyage was `like fighting desperately towards destruction for the ship and the men' (*SL*, p. 60). What is foremost is that, buried `a hundred fathom under' with all his sins, this destructive father keeps tormenting Burns, who thinks that the lack of winds delaying the ship is `the *fault* of the "old man"... ambushed down there under the sea with some evil intention' (*SL*, p. 74, emphasis mine). The sins in question are those of Kronos eating his own children, or of the God of the Old Testament demanding from Abraham an impossible sacrifice resolved by the metaphorical substitution of the goat in the place of Isaac. By transposition, these are the sins of the political fathers wishing death for all humanity, as if in a `sort of plot...or else a fiendish joke' (*SL*, p. 93).

Such fathers have betrayed the inheritance in all senses of the phrase: `When it is autumn in the world, the autumn of a human epoch', D.H. Lawrence wrote in 1917, `then the desire for death becomes single and dominant'.[19] The figure of the mad captain

---

[19] `The Reality of Peace', *Phoenix II* (London: Heinemann, 1968), p. 682.

surely symbolizes the loss of the old values in terms of historical contingencies; yet the need for Conrad to write a piece of *fiction* suggests that some deep-rooted truth is also at stake here — the very horror of the truth of human desire in its relation to the Freudian Thing,[20] the one truth `complex in essence...alien to reality...akin to death, and, all in all, rather inhuman', as Lacan notes in `The Freudian Thing' (*E*, p. 145). We might recall Captain Giles's warning, `Do not let yourself be tempted over', which we can surely read as `do not give way to the desire for destructiveness which you recognize as your own' — very much as in *The Secret Sharer*. The `tightness of the chest' (*SL*, p.76) which the new captain experiences foreshadows the awful discoveries both in the medicine *chest* and in Ransome's *chest*, which harbours `our common enemy' (*SL*, p.133). It is surely no accident that Conrad uses the very same word to designate the anxiety of war, thoughts of which `sit on one's chest like a nightmare' (*CL* V, p. 427).

In terms of narrative resolution, the purpose of the eerie voyage is to expose the demonic underpinnings of the magic view of language. It is first the *absence* of winds that breaks the progress of the ship so that the new captain's command cannot take effect. He is compelled to experience difference in the form of a delay that undercuts the metonymic illusion:

> The word `Delay' entered the secret chamber of my brain, resounded there like a tolling bell which maddens the ear, affected all my senses, took on a black colouring, a bitter taste, a deadly meaning. (*SL*, p. 66)

[20] Daphna Erdinast-Vulcan, reflecting on the motivation for the young captain's heavy sense of `guilt and shame', observes that `The "sins" which have "found him out"...are those of his dead predecessor...who had literally and explicitly wished for the destruction of both the ship and her crew' (Erdinast-Vulcan, *JCMT*, p. 137). I would suggest that what he is ashamed of is less `having been passed over by the fever' (*SL*, p. 117) than the recognition of his own desire confessed in the diary: `I feel as if all my sins had found me out' (*SL*, p. 106).

The metafictional implications of this passage are suggested by the concept of `delayed decoding'. What is also at stake, here, is the position of authority for the man of pen and ink when confronted with the ghostly effect of the word.

The confrontation is further dramatised through the episode of the quinine, the difference being that now the element of demonic otherness comes from within language. The text first offers a portrait of quinine, which, in the captain's fantasy, holds the position of some sort of master signifier without a shadow between signifier and signified — Lacan's *imaginary* phallus:

> However, there was the quinine against the fever. I went into the spare cabin where the medicine chest was kept to prepare two doses. I opened it full of faith as a man opens a miraculous shrine.... I believed in it. I pinned my faith to it. It would...like a magic powder working against mysterious malefices, secure the first passage of my first command against the evil powers of calms and pestilence. (*SL*, p. 79, p. 88)

The word `passage' suggests the metonymic linkage which seems to secure the power of the word — as it were without mediation — and therefore the captain's *wish* for a stable identity and authority. And yet the `truth enshrined' in there is other: the magic powder turns out to be a dead letter. The bottles contain no panacea but some mixed white powder, which cannot function as the *saving mark* of lack like the white floppy hat, because, this time, it is the sign of complete betrayal by a father-figure, who has sold the quinine at the request of the Other, the rapacious female companion. Not only does the episode therefore call up the shadows which the magic command has so far attempted to deny. It also lays bare the fact that there is no word without responsibility, i.e. without somebody *answering for* the signified, which is *no object* in itself, as is clear from the deadly hollow sound of the word `quinine'. The purpose of a tale dedicated to Conrad's son and all the young men `who have crossed the shadow-line of their generation' in war time is thus to warn against any form of fetishization of the signifier, whether in the form of magic command or the old captain's demonic music. In the absence of any symbolic limit, of any shadow-line between signifier and signified, the gulf of Otherness now yawns over something beyond the pale of culture, something not `recorded in books' (*SL*, p. 87). The phantom ship has become a `death-haunted command' (*SL*, p. 98) both literally and figuratively, an emblem of lost humanity, of the subject expelled from the Symbolic. The femininity of the `enchanted princess' has been delivered into the hands of the rapacious Other. It is therefore the whole question of generation and authority, both in parentage and in literary creation, that demands a textual resolution. But, before this, the depths of the gulf of Otherness — the `sombre and immense mirror' — must be sounded.

The Temptation of the Gulf

It is now time to turn to a most emblematic character, Mr. Burns, whose satanic features are reminiscent of other Conradian demons like Kurtz, but in a different mode.[21] Conrad was anxious to underscore the significance of Burns's craziness in the structure of the tale:

> Strangely enough, you know, I never either meant or `felt' the supernatural aspect of the story while writing it...What did worry me...was not the `supernatural' character, but the *fact* of Mr Burns's craziness. For only think: my first command, a sinister, slowly developing situation from which one couldn't see any issue that one could *try* for.[22]

[21] Jeremy Hawthorn points out that `Mr. Burns...is frequently associated with satanic references and his value might well be taken to suggest hell-fire.... But Burns...is not a satanic figure in the mould of Kurtz in *Heart of Darkness*' (Hawthorn, p. xv).

[22] Letter to Mrs Sanderson, [1917], in G. Jean-Aubry, *Joseph Conrad: Life and Letters*, II, p. 195.

I would suggest that Burns enacts that pre-cultural moment of subjectivity situated as it were *before* the constitutive stage of the paternal metaphor, after the crossing of the shadow-line. He is the mythical son offered in sacrifice to fill the Other's gap as if such a terrifying thing were possible — just like Abraham's son *before* the substitution of the goat. His value is that of the mediator teetering on the edge, the `predestined victim' prey to an `invisible monster ambushed in the air' (*SL*, p. 67). His hallucinations are flashes of the returning Real,[23] flickering on the screen of subjectivity: on the edge of the abyss, he burns with the desire and terror of the sacrificial victim `radiating heat on someone like a small furnace' (*SL*, p. 67), in alienation and anguish at being delivered to the Other's ob-scene *jouissance* out there in the gulf, off the human stage. Hence the rambling, `unearthly' quality of his speech (*SL*, p. 74) and his superior's sense that the `whole thing took on a somewhat tragic complexion' (*SL*, p. 64).

What is it that terrifies Burns down there? `I seemed to make out it was the *fault* of the old man', the captain notes (*SL*, p. 74). More precisely, Burns fears that after — and because of — the widening of the fault beyond the bar, the old captain's threat might become *literally* true, as if the madman really meant every word of what he said (*SL*, p. 61) and were about to devour the `children of the sea', as if therefore the oral fantasy were to be fulfilled. His desire is locked beneath a master signifier, `fever-devil' (*SL*, p. 103), in a way not unrelated to the young captain's own fetishistic view of the word `quinine'. Just as his superior means to pin his faith on the magic powder, Burns is convinced that the dead captain wasn't mad, but `just downright wicked…a thief and a murderer at heart' (*SL*, p. 118).

Burns is a projection space for his superior's own unavowable

---

[23] In the case of hallucination, from a psychoanalytical perspective, a splinter of the Real threatens subjectivity with dissolution: `éclat du réel pur, dissolvant de la subjectivité…. Le Réel c'est ce qui est perdu. Quand il revient, on l'appelle hallucination' (Braunstein, *JCL*; p. 190).

desire: a potentiality actually foreshadowed by the complex mirror-scene in which their glances converge on the reflecting surface in the captain's saloon (*SL*, pp. 53-54). When the captain later stumbles on his chief mate with a pair of scissors in his hand, he also falls prey to hallucinations, fancying that the latter is about to perform some ghastly ritual of sacrifice:

> He flourished...on the end of a fore-arm no thicker than a stout walking-stick, a shining pair of scissors which he tried before my very eyes to jab at his throat. I was to a certain extent horrified; but it was rather a secondary sort of effect, not really strong enough to make me yell at him in some such manner as: `Stop!'.... In reality he was simply overtaxing his returning strength in a shaky attempt to clip off the thick growth of his red beard.... He turned to me his face grotesque beyond the fantasies of mad dreams, one cheek all bushy as if with a swollen flame.... And while he stared thunderstruck, with the gaping scissors on his fingers, I shouted my discovery at him fiendishly, in six words, without comment. (*SL*, p. 90)

The cheek `bushy as if with a swollen flame' might well be reminiscent of the burning bush in the ritual of sacrifice, as if Burns is the fire that consumes the Real. In Lacan's words, `we do not see what is burning, for the flame blinds us to the fact that the fire catches on the Real' (Felman, *TSI*, p. 148). Actually there is *nothing* to see but the flame itself, hence the withdrawal back into trivial human reality after that flickering return of the Real — the other side of the cheek, `denuded and sunken' (*SL*, p. 90). I would like to draw attention here to the way in which this other example of Conradian `delayed decoding' enacts a pattern of return-withdrawal: one possible reading is projected on to the fictional stage — the unconscious sacrificial fantasy, which carries its own intense *jouissance* through the `secondary sort of effect' — and is then immediately denied by a rational explanation (Burns was shaving). The captain's subsequent comment suggests that the scene works as a phantasmatic enactment of the unavowable desire contained in Giles's warning against the temptation of the gulf: `I heard the clatter of the scissors escaping from his hand, noted the perilous heave of his whole person over the edge of the bunk after them' (*SL*, p. 91).

Burns, who is *literally* devoured by the fever-devil, is thus Hamlet's traveller in the undiscovered country from whose `bourn' no-one returns: a go-between, between the narrator and his unconscious desire to overstep the bounds, to break through the fence at the call of the Bull of Bashan mentioned in the deleted dream passage. The movement of heaving over the edge of the bunk recalls his superior's own regressive desire to `chuck his berth', in which we can overhear the signifier of the primordial threshold — or shadow-line. `To chuck one's birth' might be another phrase for dying, crossing the bourn beyond which the subject dissolves in the encounter with the Real. Hence the importance of Captain Giles's question, `Why did you throw up your berth?' (*SL*, p. 14), itself the echo of an earlier confession (`For no reason on which a sensible person could put a finger I threw up my job — chucked my berth', *SL*, p. 4). This came just before the official handed him his papers, as if they were `passports for Hades' (*SL*, p. 7).

Captain Kent had hoped that the narrator would find what he was `so anxious to go and look for' (*SL*, p. 7).[24] He finds what he was looking for in Burns, whose narrative leaves him `profoundly shocked by [his] immediate predecessor' (*SL*, p. 62). After the trick of the quinine, he finds himself muttering, `I feel as if I were going mad myself'. It gave him a `mental shock' (*SL*, p. 93). He is surprised to find himself speaking like Burns, possessed by that Other whose ghost begins to haunt his own utterances. On mentioning the `fever-devil who has got on board this ship', he is

---

[24] The death-drive is one of the virtualities dormant in the early pages of the tale, where we learn that the young seaman was subject to attacks of spleen that drove him to chuck his berth, as if responding to the call of Otherness: `And suddenly I left all this.... It was as though all unknowing I had heard a whisper or seen something' (*SL*, p. 5).

annoyed to find that he has been talking `somewhat in Mr Burns' manner' (*SL*, pp. 103-104). What does talking like Mr Burns mean if not using the figure of speech `fever-devil' literally, and therefore being oblivious of the semiotic bar, effectively captured by the fantasy?

The moment of ultimate temptation is also the moment of alienation and anxiety before total possession by the Other. Just as Burns is `ravaged by a passion of fear' (*SL*, p. 70), exhausted in `helplessness, and anguish' (*SL*, p. 72), the captain senses the grip of `invincible anguish...a sort of infernal stimulant exciting and *consuming* at the same time' (*SL*, p. 105, emphasis mine). Freud and Lacan after him insist that anxiety arises when the object of *desire* manifests itself, in the recognition that one is about to be en*gulf*ed as the flame of desire catches on the Real. This moment of *fading* leads to the imaginary encounter with `That Thing':

> It was something big and alive. Not a dog — more like a sheep, rather. But there were no animals in the ship. How could an animal.... It was an added and fantastic horror which I could not resist. The hair of my head stirred even as I picked myself up, awfully scared; not as a man is scared while his judgement, his reason still try to resist, but completely, boundlessly, and, as it were, innocently scared — like a little child.
>
> I could see It — that Thing! (*SL*, p. 115)

There is ample textual evidence that Burns offers a projection space for awakening the demonic fantasy left dormant in *Heart of Darkness* after Kurtz's cry of horror. Now, if the purpose of fiction is to provide an imaginary screen for fantasy, which, more than documentary evidence, tells the truth about the human heart, how does it achieve the necessary crossing (out) of the fantasy *back* into the symbolic area of language and narrative? How does the text resist the temptation of dissolution and achieve the return on the safe side of the shadow-line? The beginnings of an answer can be found, if we read carefully the climactic scene when the captain fancies that there, in front of him, the desired object lies:

> I could see It — that Thing! The darkness, of which so much had just
> turned into water, had thinned down a little. There It was! But I did not
> hit upon the notion of Mr Burns issuing out of the companion on all fours
> till he attempted to stand up, and even then the idea of a bear crossed my
> mind first. (*SL*, p. 115)

Something takes place here by `an additional turn of the racking
screw' (*SL*, p. 114) in the very substance of narrative. As in the
example of delayed decoding considered earlier, an interpretation
is foregrounded, as if in unconscious realization of the fantasy, and
then *negated*. The flicker from the Real recedes like a wave into the
background, behind the bar raised by trivial description: the
`Thing' is nothing but Burns in a fur coat. Thus we begin to see
that the `delayed decoding' effect undercuts the Barthesian reality
effect and welds the forces of negativity into the lines of narrative.
What is foremost is that the effect relies on a linguistic feature, a
form of disavowal (`But I did not hit upon the notion of Mr
Burns'), which is particularly prominent in *The Shadow-Line* and
which needs to be accounted for.

From Denial to Disavowal: Shadowy Lines

I have argued elsewhere[25] that the off-stage confrontation with
the `formidable Work of the Seven Days' (*SL*, p. 97) — a reference
to the pre-cultural time of *Genesis* — is the moment of stillness, a
literalization of a process in which desire comes to a halt in the

[25] In a paper delivered at the Joseph Conrad / Henry James International
Conference at the University of Kent in July 1995. This will appear as
`"Another Turn of the Racking Screw": Conrad's *The Shadow-Line*' in Keith
Carabine, Owen Knowles and W. Krajka (eds.), *Conrad, James and Other
Relations* (Boulder: East European Monographs, forthcoming).

primitive *jouissance* of being which is the unspeakable realm of the Thing.[26] This is a sort of zero degree of subjectivity in the maddening illusion of plenitude on another scene where the `eye lost itself in inconceivable depths' (*SL*, p. 110). But there is a threat of dissolution in `an immensity that receives no impress, preserves no memories, and keeps no reckoning of lives' (*SL*, p. 53). How then do we pass from `no reckoning' to ac*coun*ting for human lives? Or from no-Thing to the possibility of a signifying chain — therefore of writing narrative *accounts* that weave metonymies into metaphors? Earlier, Lacan's concept of the paternal metaphor as the first signifier making the chain possible was useful in understanding the function of Koh-ring in *The Secret Sharer*. In *The Shadow-Line*, the ship's and the story's metonymic movement forward become possible after the recognition of a fault-line in language itself whereby the fever-devil who tempted Burns's and the captain's desire becomes a figure of speech, i.e. *no longer* the thing itself:

`This is the sort of thing we've been having for seventeen days, Mr Burns,' I said with intense bitterness. `A puff, then a calm, and in a moment, you'll see, she'll be swinging on her heel with her head away from her course to the devil somewhere.'

He caught at the word. `The old dodging Devil,' he screamed piercingly, and burst into such a loud laugh as I had never heard before. (*SL*, p. 119)

A moment of splitting takes place in the *gap* between the figural phrase `to the devil' and Burns's literal reference to `the old dodging Devil', yielding an effect of intersubjectivity when both the captain and Burns grow aware of the metaphoricity of language: the fever devil is *and is not* the old captain. A shade of Otherness slips into the master's word, producing that moment of what Braunstein

---

[26] We might think of this as `l'aire de la Chose, de la jouissance innommée où domine le silence des pulsions...espaces vides...lieux d'attraction énigmatiques' (Braunstein, *JCL*, p. 98).

calls the `parolisation du manque' in human enunciation which defeats the mechanics of the magic view of command.[27] Thus, as Braunstein explains, it is *symbolic* castration that screens the subject against the Other's *jouissance* and prepares us for the other types of *jouissance* available in language.[28]

Now that the ghost of the old captain has been shaded by the very ghostly effect of metaphor, making it impossible to grasp the Thing beyond the word itself, the `infernal stimulant' of fantasy loses ground. The malevolent father can no longer demand a sacrifice from the bottom of the gulf because it has been *named* and, therefore, symbolically murdered in a process that makes Oneness with the womb/tomb impossible. Now `la Chose' no longer threatens the human stage. It recedes back into the Real outside the pale of the signifier. The metonymy of desire is set in motion, and the ship can now sail on through the *conjunction* of command — the effect of the letter of *noti*fication — with the music of the winds, the `sounding *note*' in the riggings (*SL*, p. 117). The rest of the Other's *jouissance* is now lost in the gulf. Freed from the devouring Other, the young captain joyfully returns to *nourritures terrestres*:

> Presently Ransome appeared before me with a tray. The sight of food made me ravenous all at once. He took the wheel while I sat on the after grating to eat my breakfast. (*SL*, p. 123)

Far from killing anybody through the shadowy effect of the word, the paternal metaphor now turns out to be a gain, because it frees human desire from a destructive oral fantasy, which is always

---

[27] `La loi du langage "déjouifie" le corps. Le désir parolisant maintient la jouissance dans son horizon d'impossibilité'.

[28] `...une fonction d'habilitation pour la jouissance, celle qui porte l'immunité relative et précaire contre cette jouissance maligne de l'Autre qui rejette le sujet hors du symbolique' (*JCL*, p. 109).

dominant in wartime — as, indeed, it is quite common in international politics, where there is always a question of who will devour whom. (Thus, for decades, the Western press represented the USSR as an ogre threatening poor little Europe).

In this fictional narrative, Burns and Ransome represent two subject positions. One must either *consume* oneself in the return to Oneness, which is a moment requiring the sacrifice of the subject to fill the Other's lack; or one must pay the *ransom* of Otherness by going through the work of mourning, by accepting one's own share of mortality and thus paying one's debt to the Other. The fact that both the body and language have to be the locus of Otherness is suggested by the return of the word *chest* to locate a failure in connection with Ransome's body and with the word `quinine'. It is significant that the young captain should pass from blind faith in command — Lacan's `lettre de commandement' — to the act of writing a letter of re*commend*ation for Ransome, who, however invaluable, might yet collapse at any time in the exercise of his duty. The ship's captain here pays the symbolic debt by taking the risk of writing a letter to an unknown addressee, a letter whose meaning is by no means guaranteed, thus making up for that `uneasy feeling that such luck as this has got perhaps to be paid for in some way' (*SL*, p. 83).

As a modern writer, Conrad clearly opts for the second solution: rather than realize the potential for fairy tale in giving up the ghost of his protagonist, he stages a process of dis-possession and distancing on another scene which is the scene of fiction. Standing on the shore, the young captain has a last distant vision of Burns on the deck, looking `like a frightful and elaborate scarecrow set up on the poop of a death-stricken ship, to keep the seabirds from the corpses' (*SL*, p. 130). Similarly, the post-diegetic narrator sees the diary written at the time — `a few detached lines, now looking very ghostly to my own eyes' — from afar, as it were (*SL*, p. 106). How then does the text in its turn keep the seabirds from the corpses, achieve the necessary distancing from the truth about human desire enshrined in the story? How does it erect a bar — like Koh-ring — against the dangers of literalization? Lastly, is there anything in the text that makes room for the `other types of *jouissance*' allowed by language while still bearing the imprint of the lost *jouissance de la chose* glimpsed out there?

Lacan actually suggests the possibility of a relationship between syntax and the unconscious underpinnings of subjectivity:

> La syntaxe, bien sûr, est préconsciente. Mais ce qui échappe au sujet, c'est que sa syntaxe est en rapport avec la réserve inconsciente. Quand le sujet raconte son histoire, agit latent, ce qui commande à cette syntaxe, et la fait de plus en plus serrée. Serrée par rapport à quoi ? — à ce que Freud dès le début de sa description de la résistance...appelle un noyau. (*EP*, p. 66)

Under the pressure of unconscious energy, syntax might then work like a turning screw, `de plus en plus serré', around some empty kernel. For `the meaning of an episode was not inside like a kernel, but outside' (*HD*, p. 48). Might not some *turn of speech* in Conrad's prose be a trace of the attempt to circumscribe the empty kernel?

Even the first-time reader of *The Shadow-Line* will perceive one prominent textual symptom[29] — a metaphor — speaking through the disquieting array of negations and disavowals that dis-possess the reader of any sense of progress or command in a story to which Conrad would himself refer as `that thing' (*LL*. II, p. 182). It is likely that this linguistic feature is the trace of what he called `the shadowy impulses that make the unearthly nature of fiction writing', in words strangely recalling the drama unfolding in *The Shadow-*

---

[29] `Le parlant devient muet et, à sa place, apparaît le symptôme qui est la réversion du discours à la jouissance, une jouissance ignorée et déniée...non sentie, *non sense*, désarticulée. Le mot non-dit, maudit, il est symptôme et jouissance insensée, jouis-sens' (Braunstein, *JCL*, p. 107).

Line: `One's will becomes the slave of hallucinations, responds only to shadowy impulses' (*CLII*, p. 205). Something indeed remains of the temptation toward the mystical marriage with death, of the impulse toward negativity: something *unheard* which manifests itself in the hollows produced by the dis-torsions of articulate speech itself,[30] and thus remains captured in the shadows of the text's lines, evoking a suppressed *jouissance* by its insistence on calling up the ghost of nonsense. Let us recall the very first lines of the tale :

> Only the young have such moments. *I don't mean* the very young. *No.* The very young have, properly speaking, *no* moments. It is the privilege of early youth to live in advance of its days in all the beautiful continuity of hope which knows *no pauses* and *no introspection*.
>
> One closes behind one the little gate of mere boyishness — and enters an enchanted garden. Its very shades glow with promise. Every turn of the path has its seduction. *And it isn't because* it is an undiscovered country. (*SL*, p. 3; my emphases)

It is hardly questionable that we have here a case of linguistic foregrounding in Halliday's sense,[31] motivated by the `shadowy impulses': the linguistic prominence of negations and disavowals casts shadows into the lines semantically, pragmatically and textually, producing a disquieting effect enhanced by the strategic position of the introduction. Here again, one thing is affirmed and then denied so that the text simultaneously releases *and* withdraws repressed material: we have already identified this return/withdrawal pattern in occurrences of delayed decoding,

---

[30] `Quelque chose d'inédit qui baigne la parole et qui se manifeste comme re-torsions de l'articulation langagière elle-même' (Braunstein, *JCL*, p. 165).

[31] See in particular M.A.K. Halliday, `Linguistic Function and Literary Style: An Inquiry into the Language of William Golding's *The Inheritors*', in Seymour Chatman (ed.), *Literary Style: A Symposium* (Oxford: Oxford University Press, 1971), pp. 330-368.

which is the semantic effect of the linguistic bent toward negativity.

Lacan identified a particular distortion of sense in disavowal — both as meaning and direction — which is a manifestation of the death-drive in language.[32] It is no surprise to find that the repressed material is related to the motif of loss, first of all the loss of the quinine, which produces the very hole in the signifier on which the story is built :

> You have guessed the truth already. There was the wrapper, the bottle, and the white powder inside, some sort of powder! But it wasn't quinine. (*SL*, p. 89)

Thus it is not what the word `quinine' designates that gets the story started, but its very failure which prohibits (`inter-dit') the possibility of reference in the very act of indicating it. Similarly, the ghost of the old captain who, `being dead, had no authority, was not in anybody's way, and was much easier to deal with' (*SL*, p. 57), is marked by the very sign of negation; its negative quantity actually becomes the negativity of language, the dark spot of resistance threatening the successor's command.

What, then, is the effect of disavowal in terms of narrative economy? How does it threaten the lines of classic realism? Jakob Lothe observes that `the narrative trick of making the narrator a firmly outspoken opponent to any sort of supernatural explanation'[33] allows the supernatural to come off better. My own view would be that there must be more than a conscious device in a pattern which repeats itself so insistently, like the trace of a deep-rooted conflict between the temptation of negation and the *sense* of writing: what emerges, rather, is the *tension* between these forces, producing the

---

[32] Anthony Wilden, *Speech and Language in Psychoanalysis: Jacques Lacan* (Baltimore: The Johns Hopkins University Press, 1991), p. 84.

[33] Jakob Lothe, *Conrad's Narrative Method* (Oxford: Clarendon Press, 1989), p. 128.

distortions so characteristic of this text — as if it let go of the helm that was supposed to give the story meaning and direction, privileging moments of stillness in its pauses and introspections. The very question of narrative authority is raised in a remarkable passage that again evokes the shadowy impulses:

> It's the only period of my life in which I attempted to keep a diary. *No, not the only one*. Years later...I did put down on paper the thoughts and events of a score of days...*I don't remember* how it came about or how the pocket book and the pencil came into my hands. *It's inconceivable* that I should have looked for them on purpose.... *Neither* could I expect the record to outlast me. (*SL*, pp. 105-6, italics mine)

It may be useful to recall, here, that the problem of beginnings is what poisons the young captain's existence on shore when, as a ghost to the men of pen and ink in offices whose business is the written word, he feels that `there [is] nothing original, nothing new, startling, informing to expect from the world' (*SL*, p. 23), a negation on which the fantasy of magic command was certainly meant to `put a gloss' (*SL*, p. 4), as if an original word could finally be asserted.

Thus the text moves back and forth, denying its own sense, differing and deferring the moment of meaning, toying with the negativity of language in a distinctly modernist gesture whereby real mastery turns out to be dis-possession and `meaning indicates only the direction, points out only the sense toward which it fails' (Lacan, in Felman, *TSI*, p. 133), producing those moments of *jouis-sens/jouissance* — `I overhear meaning/I enjoy overhearing it' — in the nonsense, in the music of language, in the composition of forms that makes up Bloom's `other joy' in *Ulysses*. Similarly Conrad's text bears in its letter the imprint of something that escapes determination and command, a *petit-plus-de-jouir* threatening the lines of the well-made novel. Thus it is not the fullness of meaning but the gaps created by the oblique significance of `gulf' or `berth', the metaphoricity of language splitting up the subject's enunciation, the distortions in the sense of both story and language that have us listening out for the unspeakable. Conrad's text invites us to take up a distanced perspective, erecting a barrier against the fantasy of mastery over words and bodies which has led this century into too many holocausts. *The Shadow-Line* makes us see into the darkest impulses of humanity, into the dangers of giving oneself up to the destructive instinct aroused by the desire for Oneness: a crucial symbolic gesture in a century marked by totalitarian temptations whose ghosts it is certainly one of the tasks of psychoanalysis to exorcise. Lacan saw in psychoanalysis the discipline which has `re-established the bridge linking modern man to ancient myths' (*E*, p. 115), a point which we can also make in relation to those works in modern literature that have given up what Conrad calls `fairy tales, realistic or even epic'.

CONRAD, THEORY AND VALUE

ANDREW MICHAEL ROBERTS

Barbara Herrnstein Smith has argued that `the entire problematic of value and evaluation has been evaded and explicitly exiled' in contemporary literary theory, a tendency which she attributes to the dominance of linguistic rather than sociological or economic models in literary studies.[1] The scientific ambitions of early structuralism, which involved the study of how meaning was produced to the exclusion of aesthetic or moral judgments about that meaning, clearly played a role in the explicit exiling of value and evaluation: indeed, I remember tutoring, as recently as the late eighties, a French student who had been taught on these principles, and who, while producing impressive Propp-style analyses of Shakespearean comedy, positively declined to proceed to any unscientific judgments of value. Another factor, stronger in Anglo-American literary studies, was a reaction against Leavisite and New Critical methods which stressed the ethical and social value of the learned ability to make aesthetic judgments. The result of such an emphasis, in the view of those who came to espouse theory, had been the setting up of a limited canon and the inculcation of a certain set of values which, in Francis Mulhern's words, were `class-restrictive,

---

[1] Barbara Herrnstein Smith, *Contingencies of Value: Alternative Perspectives for Critical Theory* (Cambridge, Mass. and London: Harvard University Press, 1988), pp. 17-18.

(hetero)sexist and ethnocentric'.[2]

Steven Connor, in his 1992 book *Theory and Cultural Value*, considers this `exile of evaluation', which he attributes to `the increasing professionalization and institutionalization of the disciplines of the humanities', in the context of government pressure towards `a positivist and instrumentalist model of education as training': a training in `facts, knowledge and interpretation' rather than in evaluation.[3] This stress on institutional pressures has, I think, interesting implications for an institution such as the Conrad Society (and other author-based scholarly and critical groups), to which I shall return. At present I want to remain with Connor's argument, for he goes on to point out the deeply paradoxical nature of the relationship between theory and value during the seventies and eighties. The `swing away from a concern with judgment and towards a concern with meaning and interpretation' (*TCV*, p. 11) was combined with a predominance of issues which are strongly ethical and evaluative: `the concern with the politics of interpretation and representation, the prejudiced representation of minority groups in literature and art, the violent effects of discourse and the question of the social effects and functions of cultural practices of all kinds' (p. 13). Connor suggests that what took place was not a rejection of value itself so much as a rejection of `unacceptably narrow and implausible views of the value of literary and cultural works' (id.); especially the modernist idea of aesthetic value as autonomous and intrinsic. Nevertheless, he sees a failure to `theorize the question of value itself' (p. 14), suggesting that value and evaluation have been `driven into the critical unconscious'.

As an instance of this which may clarify the process, I would

[2] Francis Mulhern, `English Reading', in Homi Bhabha (ed.), *Nation and Narration* (London: Routledge, 1990), p. 259.
[3] Steven Connor, *Theory and Cultural Value* (Oxford and Cambridge, Mass.: Blackwell, 1992), hereafter Connor, *TCV*; p. 12.

suggest the long-running debates over `essentialism' and the way in which `essentializing' (of identity, or gender, or race etc.) came at times to be used in literary theoretical discourse as an accusation, carrying implications of a politically reprehensible stance on the part of the alleged essentializer. Ethical and political judgments of value were being made under the guise of a philosophical critique of the validity of a concept. This is not to imply that the philosophical questions were not valid and important in themselves, but rather that they functioned to enable a debate about values, theorized as a debate about meaning and interpretation.

Conrad would seem to be a specially interesting case in considering the role of value in literary theory. His work has proved equally appealing to the explicitly evaluative Leavis (who placed it in the `Great Tradition' of the English novel) and to structuralist and post-structuralist critics who have found fertile ground in its complex narrative structures and its thematizing of the problems of perception, understanding, knowledge and truth. Conrad's work seems amenable to both a criticism based on judgment and evaluation and a criticism based on interpretation and meaning. Discussions of Conrad seem inexorably drawn towards his own tempting but ultimately unsatisfying formulation of himself as a `Homo duplex' or `double man' (CLIII, p. 89): Conrad as traditionalist and radical, as Pole and British, as servant and critic of empire, and so on.[4] The present discussion seems to have reached one of those moments when the both/and binary is tempting: Conrad's fiction both asserts and subverts absolute values (such as `duty', `fidelity', `work', `honour'); it is both laden with values and endlessly open to different interpretations. In the next section of this article I want to explore how Connor's formulation of the relations of relative and absolute value, and of value and evaluation, might provide a productive reworking of the idea of a

[4] For such an account of Conrad, see Cedric Watts, *Joseph Conrad: Nostromo* (London: Penguin, 1990), pp. 3-4.

paradoxical Conrad, by seeing the paradox, not as a function of Conrad's nature, upbringing or `vision', but as a condition of value. This is not a manoeuvre intended to detract from Conrad's achievement, since it implies a remarkable registering in his work of the inescapable and paradoxical nature of value, a registering which also has an historical dimension, taking on a specific significance in relation to Conrad's age. In the third section of this article I want to argue for the unsatisfying and limiting nature of any such binary formulations, even when informed by the post-structuralist deconstruction of binaries which pervades Connor's approach to value. I shall do so by considering the relations between three forms of value: ethical, aesthetic and political.

There are two main points which I want to pick up from Connor's book and develop in relation to Conrad: (i) his proposal that we should attempt to think absolutism and relativism together; (ii) the opposition between what he calls the imperative to continue evaluating and the operation of particular values (*TCV*, p. 6). The first of these points involves the deconstruction of a familiar binary opposition between absolute and relative value, while the second sets up a perhaps surprising opposition between the process of evaluation and particular values. Some general comments on these points will be needed before I discuss their relevance to Conrad's fiction.

Firstly, then, we have the proposal to think absolutism and relativism together. Here Connor begins with the observation that most discussions of value revolve around, or at least encounter, the conflict between absolute and relative value. Connor's challenging basic thesis is that there is in fact no authentic possibility of choice between absolutism and relativism, since the two are mutually implicated: each side of the binary opposition not only contradicts but `also requires, confirms and regenerates the other' (*TCV*, p. 1). Essentially, and in somewhat simplified form, his argument is that relativism, with its critique of claims of absolute value, must always make implicit appeal to its own standard of value: as he puts it `scepticism about metanarratives is impossible except as instructed by the hypothesis of some more just, more inclusive metanarrative, in terms of which the suspected metanarrative falls short' (*TCV*, p. 17). On the other hand, `the assertion of absolute value always brings with it a vulnerability to critique in terms of the value proposed' (id.), or, to put it another way, `the assertion of a metanarrative must always leave open, in the name of its very claim to total inclusiveness, the possibility of its discrediting, its failure justly to narrate the totality' (id.).

Secondly, an opposition is asserted between the imperative to continue evaluating and the operation of particular values. The imperative to continue evaluating arises from the inescapability of evaluation in human life: given that evaluation includes `every actual or conceivable action or condition of estimation, comparison, praising or relative preference' (p. 8) then, claims Connor, `the necessity of value is...more like the necessity of breathing than, say, the necessity of earning one's living'. It is not just that we have motives for continuing to evaluate; we know of no way to *stop* evaluating. To take just two examples from Connor, the attempt to create a value-free `objective' discipline involves the attribution of value to objectivity (p. 9); the most negative or despairing attempt to deny all value in life implies a valuing of negativity. The opposition between the imperative to value and particular values arises because `the imperative dimension commands that we continue evaluating in the face of every apparently stable and encompassing value in particular' (pp. 2-3). The process of evaluation always implies the possibility of questioning and revising any particular value. The structure of value itself is therefore inherently paradoxical and conflictual: the establishment of values must always be threatened by the process of evaluation and vice versa.

I want to develop these ideas in relation to two inter-related levels of value: values within the text and value within the processes of reading and literary criticism. I am aware here of a possible objection: that the values `within' the text are only actualised in the process of reading. My point, however, is that, whatever one's model of literary meaning and interpretation there is a double presence of value. One the one hand there are the values of the text (whether one believes that these are the author's values, that they exist autonomously in the text, or that they are a function of the reading process). On the other hand there is the value that we place *on* the text. For example, we might agree that personal integrity is a value evoked in *Under Western Eyes*, but disagree as to whether it is an interesting treatment of this theme, whether it is one of Conrad's best works, whether it is politically naive or sophisticated, and so on. We might think that a particular work is of little aesthetic interest but very valuable as a source of historical information. Without a distinction between these two levels there would be no possibility of dissent in reading: no possibility, for example, of recognizing that a text espoused, embodied or contained values which we wished to condemn.

For the sake of brevity I will refer to these two levels as value *in* the text and the value *of* the text. It might seem tempting to map these two onto the distinction between value and evaluation: to see value as that which is embodied in the text and evaluation as the process to which reader and critic submit the text. This, however, would be a mistake, because it would ignore the inevitable interaction of value and evaluation at all levels: in particular I am going to suggest the importance of evaluation as a process *within* Conrad's texts.

My first point concerning the relation of these ideas to Conrad's fiction is that there may be a play of absolute and relative value both within each of these levels and across the two levels, and that this supports Connor's claim that we need to think absolute and relative value together. I will now focus on *Lord Jim*, which will serve as an instance both for some general points about literary value and for some specific points about value in Conrad. *Lord Jim* seems an obvious and exciting choice here because, I would argue, it shows Conrad himself thinking absolute and relative value together. One of the key phrases of the novel is `the sovereign power enthroned in a fixed standard of conduct' (*LJ*, p. 50), as clear a description of an absolute value as one could ask for. Yet the full sentence in which this phrase occurs places this in the context of hope and doubt:

> I see well enough now that I hoped for the impossible — for the laying of what is the most obstinate ghost of man's creation, of the uneasy doubt uprising like a mist, secret and gnawing like a worm, and more chilling than the certitude of death — the doubt of the sovereign power enthroned in a fixed standard of conduct. (*LJ*, p. 50)

This is not in a direct sense absolute value attacked by relativism: Marlow is not, for example, questioning the `sovereign power' on the grounds it is a value which might not be shared by the Muslim pilgrims on the *Patna*. If he were, that would be more akin to a typical post-modern dilemma about value — the awareness of the existence of seemingly incompatible claims of absolute value by different cultures. Rather what we see here is an example of the second point from Connor's book: the opposition between particular values and the imperative to continue evaluating. For a process of evaluation is precisely what Marlow is engaged in here: both evaluating Jim and evaluating the `sovereign power' itself. And indeed, that process of evaluation both of an individual and of a value is the governing aim and structure of the novel. While Marlow is not directly confronting absolute value with relativism, his testing of the working out of that absolute value does illustrate the way in which, in Connor's terms, `the assertion of absolute value always brings with it a vulnerability to critique in terms of the value proposed'. Hillis Miller implies this when he writes that Marlow `does not doubt the existence of the standard' but `comes to question the power installed behind this standard'.[5] We see here how the imperative of evaluation deconstructs the opposition of absolute and relative value: the `fixed standard of conduct' is an absolute value, but precisely because it is a value, it implies the possibility of evaluation, a testing of its consequences and implications. And this testing may reveal a failure which opens the door to relativism: again, in Hillis Miller's words, `if there is no sovereign power enthroned in the fixed standard of conduct then the standard is without validity' (*FR*, p. 28). (This is a very absolute judgment in itself, allowing no room for the possibility that the standard is valid, but not always possible to live up to.) The absolute standard according to which Marlow seeks to judge behaviour is, in its turn, judged *by* behaviour.

These observations on *Lord Jim* have so far been on the level of value *in* the text, and I hope I have demonstrated a play of absolute and relative value which deconstructs their opposition. I now turn to the play across the two levels: value *in* the text and the value *of* the text. The crux of *Lord Jim*, or at least one such crux, is of course the ending, and one way of putting the question of the ending is: does Jim redeem the `fixed standard of conduct'? As Miller writes:

Marlow's aim (or Conrad's) seems clear: to find some explanation for Jim's action which will make it possible to believe in the sovereign power. Many critics think that in the end Marlow (or Conrad) is satisfied, that even Jim is satisfied.... Jim's end re-enthrones the regal power justifying the fixed standard of conduct by which he condemns himself to death. (*FR*, p. 28)

Murray Krieger explicitly claims that Jim's final action (choosing to accept death) `is a victory over relativism' and expresses

---

[5] J. Hillis Miller, *Fiction and Repetition: Seven English Novels* (Oxford: Blackwell, 1982), hereafter Miller, *FR*; p. 27.

faithfulness to a (probably Christian) `shadowy ideal of conduct'.[6] Let us take a hypothetical reader who does think that Jim redeems the fixed standard, that absolute values of behaviour are ultimately reaffirmed in this novel. Such a reader, we suspect, is quite likely to belong to the proponents of absolute values in general — to value *Lord Jim* precisely *because* it endorses such a value. But not necessarily. Such a reader might turn out to be a relativist themselves, but might also think that Conrad was not (bracketing for the moment the much discussed question of the relationship between Marlow and Conrad). This might lead such a reader to a lower valuation of the text — to see it as an endorsement of a false universalism of value. On the other hand, such a reader might value it very highly for any number of reasons: as historical or biographical evidence, on aesthetic grounds as a work of art, or indeed on ethical grounds if the reader believed that it was just as rewarding to study the work of those whose ethical position one does not share (a very logical belief for a relativist). In other words, it is quite possible to locate an idea of absolute value in a text but to value that text and its representation of absolute value in relative terms. The other reading of *Lord Jim* is as a text which undermines the `fixed standard' and thus undermines absolute value. It might seem more difficult for the interplay of value in and of the text to be the other way round: for a reader to believe *Lord Jim* undermines absolute value yet to ascribe absolute value to it. But this could easily be done if, say, one believed in absolute aesthetic value: that the achievement of the novel as a work of art transcended issues of conduct. Miller's attitude is related to this, though somewhat more complex. As a deconstructive critic, he

[6] Murray Krieger, `The Varieties of Extremity: *Lord Jim*', in his *The Tragic Vision: Variations on a Theme in Literary Interpretation* (New York: Holt, Rinehart and Winston, 1960), pp. 165-79, rpt. in *Lord Jim*, ed. Thomas C. Moser (New York and London: W.W. Norton and Co., 1968), p. 444, p. 446. However, Krieger also claims that as a solution to the moral dilemma Jim's choice is an illusion.

values indeterminacy. He believes that *Lord Jim* undermines fixity of meaning; that it provides a `multiplicity of possible incompatible explanations' and a `lack of evidence justifying a choice of one over the other' (Miller, p. 40). If we cannot determine whether the fixed standard is redeemed, then in one sense it is clearly not redeemed: it is unfixed. Miller's account, in its detailed and subtle attention to the means by which the novel resists definitive interpretation, implicitly ascribes aesthetic value to this very effect. This exemplifies Connor's point that relativism tends to make implicit appeal to its own standard of value. It also illustrates the way in which value has been pushed into `the critical unconscious' by literary theory, through a focus on interpretation which serves as a `constraint on value' (*TCV*, p. 16).

I hope to have shown, so far, the existence of an undecidable play of absolute and relative value both within the text and across the line between the text and our valuing of it. I now want to develop further the idea of the imperative to evaluation in *Lord Jim*. I suggested earlier that the whole narrative of *Lord Jim* revolves around a process of evaluation of a value, and therefore of value itself. This is foreshadowed in the novel's epigraph from Novalis: `It is certain my conviction gains infinitely, the moment another soul will believe in it'. Conviction would express an appropriate attitude towards absolute value and should imply a plenitude of value, yet here it is suggested that a conviction is still subject to increase, to an `infinite' gain in value, if confirmation is available through the evaluative processes of another. The phrase `It is certain' acquires an ironic force when one looks closely at this remark. The play of absolute and relative value and the tension of value and evaluation are both thematised from the novel's opening page on. The gulf between Jim's sense of his own potential value and his sense of his value in the eyes of others is signalled in the opening sketch of his life as a water-clerk:

A water-clerk need not pass an examination in anything under the sun, but he must have Ability in the abstract and demonstrate it practically. (*LJ*, p. 3)

Jim, however, has become a water-clerk as a result of a series of examinations: he has been examined by the sea, which, the narrator tells us, can `show in the light of day the inner worth of a man' (*LJ*, p. 10) and by the Court of Inquiry. The process of evaluation in the novel includes, of course, not only the testing by the sea and the examination by the Court of Inquiry but also Marlow's ruminations, his discussions with the French Lieutenant, Stein's experiment in sending Jim to Patusan, and so on. As Miller observes, the novel is `made up of episodes similar in design. In each a man confronts a crisis testing his own courage, the strength of his faith in the sovereign power enthroned in a fixed standard of conduct' (*FR*, p. 33).

The evaluation process also includes the narrative act: Marlow's act of narrating, but also the overall narration of the text including, for example, the structuring by which the opening chapters lead up to the *Patna* accident and then jump forward to the Inquiry, so that Jim's jump from the *Patna* becomes not one event in a chronological sequence but a problematic act around which an investigative narrative revolves. A value which is determined or assessed as part of a process cannot, in one sense, be a `fixed' value, and in this sense the whole procedure of the book undermines the possibility of the `fixed standard of conduct'. This offers a new way of describing a familiar idea of Conrad's work as pulled two ways by belief and scepticism, affirmation and uncertainty. This tension in Conrad's work is usually described in terms of conflicting sets of values, such as traditionalist and modernist. For example, Daphna Erdinast-Vulcan, in one of the clearest expositions of this conception of Conrad, describes him as `an incurable moralist, infected with the ethical relativism of his age', as a `man of the post-Nietzschean age' but `deeply hostile to the spirit of modernity'.[7] She sees the Nietzschean spirit as leading to nihilism and `the end of all eternal truths and values', a spirit in opposition to which `Conrad set out on a foredoomed quest for "the sovereign power enthroned in a fixed standard of conduct"'. Chris Bongie also sees Conrad's career in terms of foredoomed resistance to a modernity characterised by `a *definitive* loss of value(s)'.[8] Yet one implication of Connor's argument is that such a loss is impossible, that the end of values cannot be reached because, at the end of values, one finds only evaluation and so more values.

In place of the divided Conrad offered by Erdinast-Vulcan and Bongie one might see his work in terms of value and evaluation: Conrad's work does indeed manifest a desire for a fixity within values such as fidelity, truth, duty, community, yet calls those values into question by recognizing the force of the imperative to evaluation. If we accept Connor's plea for a thinking of absolute and relative value together, we then have a model of Conrad, not as pulled between two alternatives (nor do we need to identify him with one or the other), but as enacting in his work what Connor calls the very `structure of value' itself:

> The structure of value is paradoxical, involving the simultaneous desire and necessity to affirm unconditional values and the desire and necessity to subject such values to continuous, corrosive scrutiny. (*TCV*, p. 17)

The remarkable openness of Conrad's work to interpretation and the continuing richness of reading which it generates is, I would suggest, a result of the extent to which it enacts this structure of value. Conrad's fiction is always profoundly concerned with the values of its characters, and often with their attempts to hold on to

---

[7] Daphna Erdinast-Vulcan, *Joseph Conrad and the Modern Temper* (Oxford: Clarendon, 1991), p. 3.

[8] Chris Bongie, *Exotic Memories: Literature, Colonialism and the Fin de Siècle* (Stanford, CA.: Stanford University Press 1991), p. 6.

some certainty of unconditional value. But his narratives always subject this desire to relentless evaluation. The investigative structure of *Lord Jim* is one example of this process, but the fiction generally is full of journeys which test values (as in *Heart of Darkness*, `Typhoon' or *The Shadow-Line*), of investigations (as in *The Secret Agent*), of narrative structures which establish and then call into question systems of value (as in *Nostromo*).

As well as deconstructing the binary of absolute and relative value, and establishing a binary opposition between value and evaluation, Connor also addresses a third pair of terms: the aesthetic and the ethical. In a move which does not quite amount to a deconstruction of a binary, but implies a somewhat vaguer sense of mutual interdependence between forms of value which are often opposed, he advocates an `active engagement with the ways in which the ethical and the aesthetic endlessly transact with and against each other, endlessly produce and enlarge each other's form through their very antagonism' (*TCV*, p. 6). Connor is pointing out and resisting the tendency for these two categories to try to subordinate each other: either the aestheticizing of ethics, as with Nietzsche's aesthetic transvaluation of the fixated values of ethics, or ethical critiques of the aesthetic, as with left-wing analysis of the ideological nature of the aesthetic (*TCV*, p. 5). He points out that, while the ethical is traditionally associated with stable or absolute value and the aesthetic with shifting relativity, it can be the other way round. Seeing the `shifting and unstable forms of ethical and aesthetic value' as an effect of the 'historically dynamic process which works out the stability and flux of value itself' (p. 5), Connor, as with absolute and relative value, wants to avoid privileging one term, arguing that attention to the play between the two terms is the best means of understanding.

Here, despite Connor's sophisticated post-structuralist suspicion of binaries, his thinking seems in some danger of remaining too much within a binary structure. In particular, his formulation of his programme as an endless transaction between the ethical and the aesthetic squeezes out the vexed relationship of a third term, the political. When he refers to left-wing critiques of the aesthetic as subordinating aesthetic to ethical value, he himself subsumes political values within the ethical. While political values and programmes (including Marxist ones) clearly imply an element of ethical judgment (for example a condemnation of oppression, or inequality), ethical values need not include the political since they can focus on the individual (and it is precisely on these grounds that left-wing thinkers tend to criticize ethical approaches to literature). Connor is of course aware of these issues concerning the ethical and the political, and examines some of their ramifications in his chapter on Terry Eagleton, Fredric Jameson and David Harvey. However, the conclusions he draws in that chapter — principally that contemporary Marxist thinkers need to abandon `wishing themselves beyond the problem of value' in favour of `critically and transformatively inhabiting that problem' (*TCV*, p. 157) — do not make clear how such inhabiting would deal with the tension of ethics and politics.

I want to explore this question in relation to Fredric Jameson's discussion of *Lord Jim* and *Nostromo* in *The Political Unconscious* (though concentrating my own discussion on *Lord Jim*), since this is a highly theorised reading of Conrad which also theorises the question of value, and since Connor's chapter on `Exchanging Utopia: Marxism, Aesthetics and Value' includes comments on Jameson's discussion of Conrad.[9] Jameson's piece certainly exemplifies Connor's point concerning the inescapability of value and the attendant problems for Marxist thinking, `in which the critique of false totalizations and absolutisms must find a way to stop short of dissolving its own claims to provide a total or encompassing narrative of oppression and emancipation' (*TCV*, p.

---

[9] Fredric Jameson, *The Political Unconscious: Narrative as a Socially Symbolic Act* (London: Methuen, 1981), hereafter Jameson, *PU*.

14). Jameson's fluent theoretical rhetoric, his ability to generate elaborate and compelling sentences which frequently turn back upon themselves, shift direction, ascend from one level of debate to a meta-level, represents at once the most impressive feature of his writing and a cause for justified suspicion that he manages many slippery sleights of hand. Connor notes one such in Jameson's analysis of value itself (*PU*, pp. 248ff), in that Jameson modulates from describing a Weberian mode of analysis to conducting one. But another and more rapid slippage at the start of this section tends the other way, privileging the `untranscendable horizon' (p. 10) of Marxism over the alternative offered by Nietzsche and Weber in a manner which is very vulnerable to Connor's general observations about the inescapability of value. Jameson alludes to Nietzsche's `transvaluation of all values' and to Weber's `value-free science' as `attempts to project an intellectual space' from which to study the operation of `inner-worldly value' in a secular society. Against this he poses the Marxian position: that `the vocation to study value cannot simply embody one more inner-worldly value (the passion for knowledge? the pursuit of sheer disinterested science?) without at once itself becoming ideological'. `Framed in these terms…the problem…is insoluble' (pp. 248-49), Jameson remarks, confronting momentarily the aporia which is produced by the reflexive attempt to evaluate the ways of studying value. However, he extricates himself by a manoeuvre which, while on the one hand fully in accordance with his declared methodological basis (`always historicize'), is on the other hand blatantly a rhetorical trick: `but what is interesting about it [the problem] for us are its preconditions, namely, the objective historical developments without which such a "problem" could never have been articulated in the first place' (p. 249). If `interesting' in that sentence is anything more than a dummy marker of subjective value, then it can only refer to Marxism's claim to subsume all other forms of knowledge (its own equivalent of `the passion for knowledge' or `the pursuit of sheer disinterested science'). It is at moments such as this that Jameson's analysis seems to me most vulnerable to Jacques

Berthoud's criticism that `by identifying consciousness with ideology, Jameson renders himself completely incapable of acknowledging Conrad's text as offering, like his own, a responsible interpretation of the world'.[10] At times the ambition of Jameson's Marxism to colonise and subdue all other modes of thought produces an arrogance of expression which I imagine prompted some of Berthoud's irritation, as when Jameson refers to `those unavoidable false problems which are named character, event, plot, narrative meaning, and the like' (*PU*, p. 242) and declares (in a sentence which oddly combines hauteur with a certain sulkiness at its conclusion) that:

> to dissolve the verisimilitude of the character of Jim into the mere effect or pole of some larger system would at once discredit and dispatch into critical dilettantism the whole thematics of heroism and individual guilt and expiation about which we have already complained. (p. 243)

What rescues Jameson's discussion for me (apart from the sheer brilliance and profusion of critical, theoretical and historical insights that his method throws off) is a gradual process in which it seems to be seduced by the aesthetic values which it initially seems inclined to dismiss as ideology or displacement. This seduction might be seen, borrowing some of his own terms, as the unconscious of his text, since it is not wholly recognized within that text, yet reflects a certain desire not to abandon the category of the aesthetic. Early in his chapter, in a stunningly suggestive reading of the description of the *Patna* at night, Jameson seems to imply that Conrad's impressionism is an instance of modernist aestheticization which pushes economic and social reality into the `political

---

[10] Jacques Berthoud, `Narrative and Ideology: a Critique of Fredric Jameson's *The Political Unconscious*', in Jeremy Hawthorn (ed.), *Narrative: From Malory to Motion Pictures* (London: Edward Arnold, 1985), p. 113.

unconscious' of the text:

> Ideology, production, style: on the one hand the manifest level of the
> content of *Lord Jim* — the moral problem of the `sleepers' — which give
> us to believe that the `subject' of this book is courage and cowardice, and
> which we are meant to interpret in ethical and existentialising terms; on
> the other, the final consumable verbal commodity — the vision of the ship
> — the transformation of all these realities into style and the work of what
> we will call the impressionistic strategy of modernism whose function is
> to derealize the content and make it available for consumption on some
> purely aesthetic level; while in between these two, the brief clang from
> the boiler room that drives the ship marking the presence beneath
> ideology and appearance of that labour which produces and reproduces the
> world itself, and...sustains the whole fabric of reality continuously in
> being. (p. 214)

Here both the ethical and the aesthetic are strategies by which the literary text obscures material reality, to be understood in political terms. Earlier Jameson has described the aesthetic as a `level of ideological production' (p. 211). Yet sixteen pages later he is reassuring us that his characterisation of Conrad's style as an `aestheticizing strategy...is not meant as moral or political castigation' (p. 230). This leads on to perhaps the most romantic and idealistic passage in Jameson's chapter, in which passages of pure stylistic intensity which he finds in `Typhoon' are used to reread the function of impressionism, not as ideological repression, but as Utopian remaking. At such moments of extreme purity and intensity Conrad's style, rather than perpetuating an ideology, creates `a new representational space':

> This reversal then draws ideology inside out like a glove, awakening an
> alien space beyond it, founding a new and strange heaven and earth upon
> its inverted lining. (p. 231)

Jameson proposes a dialectic of the `ideological' and the `Utopian' within modernism (p. 235): modernism is both an ideological expression of capitalism and capitalism's `reification of daily life' and yet `can at one and the same time be read as a Utopian compensation for everything reification brings with it' (p. 236).

For all the immense sophistication and brilliance of Jameson's thinking, and despite the appeal of this dialectical reading of the political meaning of Conrad's work (which allows one to combine the intellectual satisfactions of critique and enthusiasm), this account seems to me suspiciously similar to the readings of Conrad as `Homo duplex', while extending the valuing of doubleness onto modernism in general (a move familiar from New Critical valuations of ambiguity). Why is the passage which he quotes from `Typhoon' (a description of the approaching storm) Utopian rather than ideological? Jameson essentially offers three arguments. One is a Leavis-like gesture at the text and the experience of reading: `Anyone who doubts the Utopian vocation of Conrad's style at these extreme moments of intensity has only to reread passages such as the following....' (p. 230). The second is a suggestion that here Conrad's impressionism is less akin to Western impressionist painting than to `certain of its Slavic equivalents' (especially Kuindzhi), a suggestion which is intriguing but prompts the (perhaps unfair) suspicion that Jameson feels it is somehow less ideological to resemble a Slavic painter than a Western one. The third is that `the conventional relationship between narrative and ideology is here reversed' (p. 231): rather than the text perpetuating an ideology, an ideology is cited to authorize the alleged 'new representational space' (p. 231). Apart from the oddness of a Utopia authorized by the ideology which it transcends, it is hard to imagine how this statement could be proved or disproved, or even debated in other than highly intuitive terms.

It is Conrad's impressionistic style that is the main focus of Jameson's dialectic analysis in terms of ideology and Utopia. Furthermore, he claims that impressionism, though only one strategy by which modernism responds to `rationalization and reification in late nineteenth-century capitalism' (p. 225), is the dominant one. Therefore impressionism will provide the best starting point for some discussion of aesthetic value in *Lord Jim*. I have pointed out elsewhere that, as an idea, impressionism:

> points two ways: on the one hand towards close attention to physical detail as perceived by the senses — the meaning according to which delayed decoding is impressionist — and on the other hand towards a distancing of events by layers of subjective interpretation and memory. This is not so much a contradiction in the term as a paradox of human experience: the more self-consciously we seek to attend to an external physical world, the more we become aware that perception is always already interpretation.[11]

One might add that perception is also always already evaluation, at least in Conrad. The layers of subjective interpretation and memory surrounding Jim's jump from the *Patna* are explored as part of a hermeneutic structure in which the quest for meaning and the quest for value are inseparable. Hence Ian Watt's use of the phrase `subjective moral impressionism' in his influential discussion of Conrad's impressionism, a phrase which brings together the aesthetic and the ethical.[12]

The section of *Lord Jim* leading up to the *Patna* accident uses the conflicting tendencies within impressionism in a very particular way. The description of the sleeping pilgrims is a set piece of sensory impressionism, with aesthetic qualities of style joined to a focus on what the eye sees: `in the blurred circles of light thrown down and trembling slightly to the unceasing vibration of the ship appeared a chin upturned, two closed eyelids, a dark hand with silver rings, a meagre limb draped in a torn covering....' (*LJ*, p.

---

[11] Andrew Michael Roberts, review, *The Conradian*, 14.1/14.2, (Dec. 1989), pp. 111-112.
[12] Ian Watt, *Conrad in the Nineteenth Century* (London: Chatto and Windus, 1980), hereafter Watt, *CNC*; pp. 169-80, p. 174.

18). The juxtaposition of the rich (silver), the humble (torn covering) and the exotic (a dark hand) is indebted to *fin-de-siècle* aestheticism even while it aspires to fidelity to the visual impression of the moment. The description of the accident itself uses delayed decoding: [the engineer] `suddenly pitched down head-first as though he had been clubbed from behind.... Had the earth been checked in her course?' (*LJ*, p. 26). And when the narrative, following the accident, jumps forward to the enquiry a month or so later, the reader is forcibly presented with Watt's `subjective moral impressionism': `the bounded and ambiguous nature of individual understanding', with which Jim, Marlow and others wrestle in trying to understand and evaluate what has happened. Watt argues that subjective moral impressionism shows reality as essentially private and individual. He does not seem to notice the extent to which this conflicts with the implications of delayed decoding with its `gap between impression and understanding'. Watt argues that delayed decoding shows us the `precarious nature of the process of interpretation in general' (*CNC*, p. 179). However, while delayed decoding is briefly disconcerting, its effect tends to be to reassure us of the existence of a shared (non-private) reality, since it presents us with a false reading of the situation followed by a correct one. Delayed decoding is a sort of ambush for the reader, in which a momentary puzzle is followed by a discovery of reality. But in the episode of the *Patna* accident delayed decoding is itself ambushed by the more radical destabilising of subjective moral impressionism: in the process of finding out what really happened, it is suggested that what really happened is not fully accessible as shared reality. Conrad's narrative and stylistic technique here serves an ethical purpose but is not subsumed in that purpose. The aestheticization of the scene both represents Jim being lulled into a dangerous sense of false security, and symbolises his own idealisation of his work as a merchant officer, but neither of these moral `meanings' of the style exhausts its significance as an aesthetic experience for the reader. Conrad is here using style in a way which can only be understood if we do not seek to resolve the aesthetic into the ethical or vice versa, but read them together. More than that, impressionism as a literary technique as used by Conrad raises questions of interpretation which are also questions of value, and involves a close inter-relation of aesthetic and ethical conceptions of value. The impressionistic style of description, with its aestheticizing qualities, is on one level a representation of aesthetic values operating on Jim and other characters. His self-image, which first leads him into dangerous fantasies of heroism (dangerous because they blind him to the demands of courage in practice) and then drives him in his search for some sort of redemption, is in many ways a form of aesthetic value. Originating in `light holiday literature' (*LJ*, p. 5), it becomes an image which though dangerous is also beautiful, not only to Jim himself, but to others such as Marlow and Stein. When Marlow comments `I liked his appearance; I knew his appearance; he came from the right place; he was one of us' (*LJ*, p. 43), or when he describes Jim as a `white figure in the stillness of coast and sea...a tiny white speck, that seemed to catch all the light left in a darkened world' (*LJ*, p. 336), he is in part responding to the sense of self-worth projected by Jim. Thus Marlow's problematic ethical and political assessments are inextricable from aesthetic responses. On the level of critical assessments, the much-discussed disparity between the two halves of *Lord Jim* has been seen in both aesthetic terms (the second part as exhibiting `a sense of reduced complexity and rapid confluence of the narrative elements') and in ethical terms (that part as marred by `a curiously simple moral polarity').[13] Jameson argues that Conrad parodies romance and then goes on to write one (*PU*, p. 213), while Padmini Mongia finds a gendered motive in this shift: `the end of the novel allows Jim a place in the romantic world of adventure ironized at the beginning of the text' as a way of rescuing his masculinity from the threat of engulfment by the `feminine

---

[13] Watt, *CNC*, p. 308; John Batchelor, *The Edwardian Novelists* (London: Duckworth and Co., 1982), p. 46.

East'.[14] Furthermore, this is a femininity with which Jim himself has been associated by his aestheticization as one who was 'blooming gently — blooming modestly — like a violet' (*LJ*, p. 187, quoted Mongia, *GG*, p. 12). The ironical *mise-en-abyme* of the `light holiday literature' which launches Jim's career (and offers a degraded image of the novel itself) enmeshes questions of aesthetics within the text and its critical reception. As with value and evaluation, there is a play between aesthetic and ethical value both within the text and across the line between value in the text and the reader's valuation of it.

It would be tempting to see Jameson's seduction by the aesthetic in terms of the interplay of the ethical and aesthetic which Connor advocates, were it not for the skewed relationship of Connor's formulation to Jameson's view of ethics and politics. Not only does Jameson refer several times to the misleading projection in *Lord Jim* of the idea that it is a book about ethical issues (e.g. *PU*, p. 214). He also defines the dialectic (a crucial aspect of his methodology) as proposing a stance `outside the subject in the transindividual...from which to transcend the double bind of the merely ethical' (p. 235). Here `double bind' seems to refer to Nietzsche's account of good and evil as based on the assumption that `what is good is what belongs to me, what is bad is what belongs to the Other' (p. 234). Jameson's own position on the function of the work of art proposes an interaction analogous in form to Connor's, though on a different level. Arguing that the work of art `cannot itself be asked to change the world or to transform itself into political praxis', Jameson suggests the need for

[14] Padmini Mongia, `"Ghosts of the Gothic": Spectral Women and Colonized Spaces in *Lord Jim*, hereafter Mongia, *GG*, in Andrew Michael Roberts (ed.), *Conrad and Gender*, (Amsterdam/Atlanta: Rodopi, 1993), p. 14.

a keener sense of the complexity and ambiguity of that process loosely termed reflection or expression. To think dialectically about such a process means to invent a thought which goes `beyond good and evil' not by abolishing these qualifications or judgments but by understanding their interrelationship' (p. 234).

Ultimately the aesthetic value of Conrad's style is redeemed for Jameson because, as reader and critic, he finds a way — however romantic — of transforming it into political value. He does the same with the ethical values explicitly evoked in the text, by the surprising means of passing them through the medium of philosophical existentialism. Arguing that the ethical questions raised by Jim's `apparent quest for self-knowledge' are only a pretext for the examination of philosophical questions about action (pp. 261-262), he then goes on to claim that the results of this examination — the `problematic of the empty act' — are really meaningful only at the collective level, so that Jim's experience becomes `the precondition for the revelation of the texture of ideology' (p. 265). Here we might usefully evoke Connor's observation that both Eagleton and Jameson are at times led by their desire for `the authentic wholeness of that which lies beyond exchange-value' into `wishing themselves beyond the problem of value' (*TCV*, p. 157). For one thing which the evolution of Jameson's reading of Conrad (and indeed that of Connor's reading of Jameson) seems to illustrate powerfully is the endless exchange between different forms of value: the ability of interpretative methods to effect transactions between aesthetic, ethical and political value. The other conclusion which we might draw is that a discourse (even so self-conscious a discourse as that of literary theory) can never fully articulate its own values because the attempt to articulate them always presupposes certain values. This is partly a matter of the inescapability of value, so that in the moment of attempted self-definition or self-critique, more values are coming into play. This is evident in Jameson's discussion of value itself. Like Bongie and Erdinast-Vulcan (though for somewhat different reasons) he associates modernity with an absolute loss of value. Connor notes a certain sleight of hand here, as `the notion of a movement from precapitalist structures of value to capitalist instrumentalization of value becomes the myth of a Fall' (*TCV*, p.152) — the loss of value `as such'. In the very course of this part of his argument, Jameson makes one of his more sweeping value judgments about literature, arguing that in a period of rationalization, instrumentalization and the commodification of labour, when all value is virtually obliterated, `the most interesting artists and thinkers...are those who cling to the experience of meaninglessness itself as to some ultimate reality', a group with whom he plausibly associates Conrad. Again the whole weight of this claim rests on that tenuous value-word, `interesting', and value is asserted in the course of an analysis of its disappearance.

On the basis of this brief consideration of ideas of ethical, aesthetic and political value in *Lord Jim*, and in the theory of Jameson and Connor, I would suggest the usefulness of Connor's proposal for an active engagement with the endless transactions of different forms of value. However, this transaction needs to be seen, not in binary terms (the ethical and the aesthetic), but rather in terms of multiple forms of value. Given the inescapability of value at all levels of discourse, the most appropriate way to conclude this discussion, which has only begun to address some of the questions arising from its topic, may be to make some reflexive comments on the present context. As institutions, both a society devoted to an author (such as the Conrad society) and a volume devoted to an author's work (such as the present one), presuppose certain forms of literary value. They tend towards an assumption of aesthetic value residing in the literary achievement of an individual, although they have proved accommodating to a whole range of political, philosophical and ethical forms of criticism and theory. While single-author based criticism tended to be slower in taking up the challenges of literary theory, it also, arguably, put up some resistance to the `positivist and instrumentalist model of education' which, Connor suggests, pushed the issue of value into the critical unconscious. The study of a particular author is not inclined to neglect either the values presented *in* the works or the question of the value *of* those works. Since Conrad criticism has, by now, been long amenable to all sorts of literary theory, and since (as the existence of Connor's book suggests) we have reached a point when the explicit debate over value has returned to literary theory with some force, then Conrad criticism may have an opportunity to take part in the reconnection of theory and value.[15] Critical discourses presuppose values but they also produce, reproduce and exchange them. The question must remain how we distinguish between the corruption of exchange value, which `subordinates all forms of exchange to the force of one form alone — the economic' (*TCV*, p. 4), and the `multiplication not only of values, but also of the standards or registers of value', which is the utopia towards which Connor's theory of value is orientated.

---

[15] Questions of cultural difference, prominent in much recent Conrad criticism, are likely to be crucial in such a reconnection. These are by and large notably absent from Jameson's account, which takes a Eurocentric view of the history of value.

Notes on Contributors

Sandra Dodson is currently completing a D.Phil. on Conrad at the University of Oxford.

Anthony Fothergill is Lecturer in English at the University of Exeter. He is the author of *Heart of Darkness* in the Open Guides to Literature series (Milton Keynes: Open University Press, 1989) and has recently edited Oscar Wilde, *Plays, Prose Writings and Poems* (London: J.M. Dent, 1996) and Joseph Conrad, *Tales of Unrest* (London: J.M. Dent, 1998).

Gail Fincham is Senior Lecturer in English at the University of Cape Town. She has published on E. M. Forster, Joseph Conrad, Henry James and African literature. She is co-editor (with Myrtle Hooper) of *Under Postcolonial Eyes: Joseph Conrad After Empire* (Rondebosch: University of Cape Town Press, 1996).

Andrzej Gąsiorek is Lecturer in English at the University of Birmingham. He is the author of *Postwar British Fiction: Realism and After* (London: Edward Arnold, 1995).

Andrew Gibson is Reader in English Literature at Royal Holloway, University of London. He is the author of *Reading Narrative Discourse: Studies in the Novel from Cervantes to Beckett* (London: Macmillan, 1990), *Towards a Postmodern Theory of Narrative* (Edinburgh: Edinburgh University Press, 1996) and *Redemptions: Postmodernity, Ethics and the Novel* (Edinburgh: Edinburgh University Press, forthcoming). He is editor of *Pound in Multiple Perspective* (London: Macmillan, 1993), *Reading Joyce's `Circe'* (European Joyce Studies 3, 1994) and *Joyce's `Ithaca'* (European Joyce Studies 6, 1996). He is also co-editor of *Beyond the Book: Theory, Culture and the Politics of Cyberspace* (Oxford, 1996).

Robert Hampson is Reader in English Literature at Royal Holloway, University of London. He is the author of *Joseph Conrad: Identity and Betrayal* (London: Macmillan, 1992), former editor of *The Conradian*, and a Contributing Editor of the Cambridge edition of Conrad's works. He has edited the Penguin editions of *Victory* (1989), *Heart of Darkness* (1996), Kipling's *Something of Myself* (1987) and *Soldiers Three / In Black & White* (1993). He is currently editing *The Arrow of Gold* for Everyman and completing a monograph on Conrad's Malay fiction for Macmillan.

Carola M. Kaplan is Professor of English at California State University, Pomona, and has written on E.M. Forster, Joseph Conrad, Henry James, and T.E. Lawrence. Her most recent publication is a collection of essays, *Seeing Double: Revisioning Edwardian and Modernist Literature*, co-edited with Anne B. Simpson (New York: St. Martin's Press; Basingstoke: Macmillan, 1997). She is currently writing *Cultural Crossdressing: Englishness and Otherness in Joseph Conrad, E.M. Forster, T.E. Lawrence and Christopher Isherwood.*

Josiane Paccaud-Huguet has published extensively on Conrad in *Conradiana, L'Époque Conradienne, Études Anglaises, Language and Style* and in the journal of the Centre d'Études et de Recherches Victoriennes et Edouardiennes.

Andrew Michael Roberts teaches English at the University of Dundee and is former General Editor of *The Conradian*. His publications include various articles on Conrad's work, *Conrad and Masculinity* (Basingstoke: Macmillan, forthcoming), *The Longman Critical Reader on Joseph Conrad* (London: Longman, forthcoming), and the edited collection, *Conrad and Gender* (Amsterdam / Atlanta: Rodopi, 1993). He has also published articles on Romanticism, W.B. Yeats, Mina Loy and Geoffrey Hill.